Indian Banking Sector

M.S. Shetty

ATLANTIC
PUBLISHERS & DISTRIBUTORS (P) LTD

Published by
ATLANTIC
PUBLISHERS & DISTRIBUTORS (P) LTD
7/22, Ansari Road, Darya Ganj, New Delhi-110002
Phones : +91-11-40775252, 23273880, 23275880, 23280451
Fax : +91-11-23285873
Web : www.atlanticbooks.com
E-mail : orders@atlanticbooks.com

Branch Office
5, Nallathambi Street, Wallajah Road, Chennai-600002
Phones : +91-44-64611085, 32413319
E-mail : chennai@atlanticbooks.com

Printed in India at Nice Printing Press, A-33/3A, Site-IV,
Industrial Area, Sahibabad, Ghaziabad, U.P.

Preface

Banking is an interesting subject. Today, almost everyone educated and living in urban area has a bank account. Even many of the uneducated and people from rural and semi-urban areas also have bank accounts. The person dealing with a bank is aware of what banks are and to some extent also aware of the banking business, like deposits and advances. One gains knowledge about banks through one's exposure to the banking services one is availing. One may know that banks are important and that there are many banks owned by the Government. But still one may feel at times, that one may learn a little more about banks, i.e. what are they, how they work, and what is their importance in the financial world. One may be curious to know about banks and how banks function.

Banking business is a very old activity existing in all human societies of the world. Banking business has evolved over a period and in today's world, banks are the custodians of money for the nation.

Banking is the backbone of the financial system of a country. In modern economy, bank accounts have replaced the money as financial transactions are now taking place through the medium of bank payment systems without requiring the actual money. Deposits with banks now form a component of money supply in the economy besides the actual cash held by individuals. As financial transactions are routed through bank accounts, banks are at the centre of all financial activities.

In view of the prominent place the banks occupy in the economy, banking regulations have come up and a central banking authority has been created to oversee the banking business in the country.

Banks are mostly private organisations, and in some countries like ours, some banks are state owned. There were many bank failures in the past and such failures were creating small ripples in the economy since the depositors of that bank lost their money. But now banks have grown in size. In the modern world, a major bank failure can cause havoc to the economy of the country. Governments the world over are now concerned about this problem and more and more controls on banks' working are now being exercised.

Indian banking was in private hands till 18th century and thereafter a few state-owned banks came into the picture mainly for undertaking Government business. Three presidency banks were started and they were later merged to form Imperial Bank of India. Then State Bank of India (SBI) was created in 1955 which took over the business of Imperial Bank of India. There were also eight other banks functioning as banks for the princely states earlier and these banks were converted as subsidiaries of SBI in the year 1959.

In the year 1969, Indian Government nationalised 14 large banks of the country and again in the year 1980 it nationalised 6 more banks.

In the 1950s, the Government also promoted co-operative banks for rural development. Starting from the year 1975, the Government promoted a new category of banks—regional rural banks for rural development.

In the year 1990-91, the country faced balance of payment crisis in its foreign trade. The crisis was averted by borrowing from International Monetary Fund (IMF). After this development, the Government decided to globalise the economy and started liberalisation measures. Financial sector reforms, particularly the banking sector reforms, were introduced. Under these reforms, entry of new private sector banks was allowed and foreign banks were allowed to expand. These changes brought some improvements in the banking sector with resultant higher growth of the economy. Many things have changed since then and the reforms agenda is still not over. Some more changes in the banking sector are in the pipeline and some more may come in future.

The book is an attempt to give useful information on Indian banks. The purpose is to inform the learners and students of banking about various aspects of present-day banking in the country. However, banking is a very vast subject and everything cannot be put in one book.

The book tries to explain in simple language the intricate financial aspects of banks, their systems, their working, and their control. It explains many terminologies used in banking: Information on many new developments in banking and on the latest products and services has also been provided.

Banking is explained as a business of accepting deposits from the public and giving loans to those who need it. It is a simple and truthful definition of banking. It is financial intermediation as banks help in pooling the deposits from some and then allowing others to use it. But this simple enough process has great impact on the economy.

The book in the beginning gives the basic structure of banks in our country and then proceeds to explain many relevant issues about banking. The topics are arranged in a proper manner so that the reader gets information on a particular issue or question at one place to better understand it in a holistic manner.

Information on many well-known phrases connected with banking is given in question and answer format. Information on the main organisations in the banking or connected with banking in various capacities is given in an exclusive chapter.

This book aims to inform the students of banking the present trend in banking in the country. For easy understanding and for ready reference, the information is given subject-wise under the relevant chapter headings.

An index has also been provided in the book which lists the sub-chapters of the book for ready and easy reference. An additional index is also created for the readers to help them in locating some important topics dealt with in the chapters and sub-chapters.

M.S. Shetty

Acknowledgements

I acknowledge with thanks the invaluable information provided by the Reserve Bank of India in its master circulars, database, other circulars and guidelines issued and made available at its website. There can be no better source to learn about the Indian banking and the rules governing banking practices in the country than the Reserve Bank of India, the regulator of banking sector.

I also acknowledge with thanks that the information on financial organisations, other entities and banks in India are taken from the websites of the respective organisations.

M.S. Shetty

Contents

1

Information on Indian Banking

1.1 Present Banks in the Country

There are different categories of banks in the country. Different terminologies are used to describe them which are as under.

Universal Banks

The banks which are permitted to undertake all the financial activities permissible to banks are called the universal banks. Such banks can accept deposits from public, lend both in retail and wholesale segment, and undertake all the financial services permitted by RBI for a bank. Generally, they have no restriction for their operation in any geographical area of the country. All the commercial banks (public sector banks, private sector banks, foreign banks, regional rural banks, local area banks) and the co-operative banks (urban co-op banks, dist. co-op banks, state co-op banks) and land development banks (PACRDBs, SACRDBs) are universal banks. However, there are some restrictions for area of operation for RRBs, LABs and Co-op banks.

Under universal banks, there are two main categories of banks in the country. They are the commercial banks and the co-op banks. Commercial banks are the dominant category and business share wise they control 87 to 90% of total banking business.

Commercial Banks

Commercial bank is a bank which does business on commercial line; which means that its sole purpose is to make profit. Everything is decided by such banks on the basis whether the business is commercially viable and is a paying proposition. The Public Sector Banks, Private Sector Banks, Foreign Banks, Regional Rural Banks (RRBs), Local Area Banks (LABs) are all commercial banks.

Scheduled Banks

There is another commonly used title by banks. It is known as the 'scheduled bank'. A scheduled bank is one whose name appears in the Second Schedule of RBI Act, 1934. Reserve Bank has the authority to add or delete the names of the bank from this schedule. It is based on certain conditions to be fulfilled by the bank, particularly about its capital size, maintenance of liquidity ratios (SLR and CRR) and more importantly submit itself to the supervision of Reserve Bank. In our country, scheduled status of a bank is considered as a coveted status reflecting that it is a well-disciplined and managed bank under the supervisory control of RBI. Most of the banks at present fall under this category. Even the co-operative banks can also opt for this status and most of the larger urban co-operative banks and some of the state co-op banks are under this category.

Scheduled Commercial Banks (SCBs)

These are the commercial banks which are also scheduled banks. All the commercial banks in the country, except four small and old commercial banks, are in the scheduled category which includes public sector banks, private sector banks, foreign banks, RRBs, LABs, small finance banks, and payments banks. As a group, SCB is the major group of banks and they control nearly 90% of total banking business of the country.

Public Sector Banks and Nationalised Banks

Another distinction between banks is based on the ownership pattern of the banks. The banks fully or substantially owned (with over 51% stake) by governments are called as the 'public sector banks'. Again under this, some banks are known as 'nationalized banks' which denotes that these banks were existing earlier as private banks and subsequently government took over (nationalised) these banks. There was two-time nationalization of banks in India, first one in 1969 when 14 banks were nationalized and again in 1980 when six more banks were nationalized. Nationalised banks are also called the public sector banks.

The banks started by the government under any special statute, or banks promoted by public sector undertakings are known as public sector banks and they are not called the nationalized banks. These banks are the SBI, subsidiaries of SBI (5 banks—since merged with SBI), IDBI bank, Bharatiya Mahila Bank (since merged with SBI) and India Post Payments Bank. They are Government banks from the day one of their existence.

Bharatiya Mahila Bank and the five subsidiary banks of SBI were merged with SBI from 1-4-2017. After this merger and starting of India Post Payments Bank there are now 22 public sector banks as at June 2017.

Foreign Banks

Another classification of banks is known as the 'Indian bank' and 'foreign bank'. A bank which is largely owned by the government or the other residents of the country is the Indian bank. The banks owned substantially by the non-residents (foreigners) or banks incorporated outside in foreign countries are called the foreign banks. An Indian bank may become a foreign bank if the ownership of the bank passes substantially to non-residents. The status of a bank as Indian or foreign has its repercussions on the regulatory guidelines applicable to banks as many regulatory guidelines are specifically made for foreign banks. For example, foreign banks enjoy certain relaxation in guidelines for lending to priority sector particularly to agriculture sector.

There were many foreign banks operating in the country during British rule. Some of them have continued till date. Some new foreign banks have opened their branches after banking reforms were introduced. As at June 2017 there are 44 foreign banks in the country.

Exchange Banks. During the British rule, there was a category of banks in the country known as Exchange Banks who only were authorized to handle foreign exchange business. The foreign banks in India were the exchange banks and there were some Indian banks also in this category. Later RBI abolished this category of exchange banks. Foreign exchange business was allowed to banks who obtain an additional license from RBI. This license is called as Authorized Dealer (AD) license. Mostly, it is given to commercial banks and foreign banks. Now few urban co-operative banks also have this license to transact foreign exchange business.

Private Sector Banks

As discussed, banks were in private sector till such time public sector banks were created and some banks were nationalised. Private sector banks are privately owned. However, at present very few private sector banks of earlier period are continuing (12 banks in March 2015). After the introduction of banking sector reforms few new private sector banks were started (seven banks till March 2015). Two more new private sector banks were started after the March 2015 (Bandhan bank on 23-8-2015 and IDFC bank on 1-10-2015). With this, in June 2017 there are 21 private sector commercial banks in the country.

The private sector banks existing before the year 1994 are now called as the old private sector banks and the new private banks which were started from the year 1994 onwards are called the new private sector banks.

Regional Rural Banks

A new category of banks under public sector as commercial banks were started in the country from the year 1975 with government initiatives. They are known as the Regional Rural Banks (RRBs). They are created for the purpose of rural development. They are commercial banks with only restriction to the area of operation within the state at which they are incorporated. There were total of 196 RRBs existing in the year 1991. Later government initiated reforms in their structure and accordingly many RRBs were merged together to form bigger banks. In March 2015, there were only 56 RRBs due to mergers and restructuring of these banks. Their number is same now in June 2017.

Local Area Banks

After the introduction of banking reforms, in the year 1996, another category of banks was started and they are known as the Local Area Banks. They are small banks in private sector and were started with minimum capital requirement at ₹ five crores. Their area of operation is limited to three contiguous districts. These banks are required to observe the priority sector lending targets at 40% of net bank credit (NBC) as applicable to other domestic banks.

RBI issued six licences to open LABs from the year 1999 onwards. Till March, 2015 there were four banks functioning as under:

1. Coastal Local Area Bank Ltd., Vijayawada, Andhra Pradesh in 1999.
2. Capital Local Area Bank Ltd., Nakodar, Punjab in 2000.
3. Krishna Bhima Samruddhji Local Area Bank (Karnataka and Andhra Pradesh) in 2001.
4. Subhadra Local Area Bank Ltd., Kolhapur, Maharashtra in 2003/2004.

The experiment to promote local area banks was not successful and RBI stopped issuing fresh licenses. The total business size of these banks is minuscule when compared to the size of business of banking sector.

RBI under its new branch licensing policy allowed Local Area Banks to convert themselves as small finance banks by fulfilling the criteria set for small finance banks.

Accordingly one bank—Capital Local Area Bank was permitted to become a small finance bank in the year 2016 and was named Capital LAB small finance bank. Thus only three local area banks are now functioning.

Niche Banks

Besides allowing new commercial banks to be started in private sector, RBI has also decided to start new categories of commercial banks known as 'small finance banks' and 'payments banks'. These categories of banks are called the 'niche banks' as they were allowed only few banking activities earmarked for them.

Niche banks are defined as the banks that cater to and serve the needs of a certain demographic segment of the population. They typically target a specific market or type of customer, and tailor their products and services to cater the requirements of their target group.

RBI issued new licences to few promoters in September 2015 to start these two categories of new banks. These promoters were to set up these banks within 18 months' time, after seeking final approval from RBI.

Small Finance Banks

RBI in September 2015 issued 10 new licences to start small finance banks. Out of this, 7 new small finance banks became operational by the end of March 2017. They are as under:

1. Ujjivan small finance bank
2. Equitas small finance bank
3. AU small finance bank
4. Capital LAB small finance bank
5. ESAF small finance bank
6. Suryoday small finance bank
7. Utkarsh small finance bank

Payments Banks

RBI in September 2015 issued 11 new licences to start new payments banks. Till June 2017, 3 new banks have been started as under:

1. Airtel Payments Bank
2. India Post Payments Bank
3. Paytm Payments Bank

Another 4 to 5 payments banks are expected to be operational in this year (2017) itself. Newly started small finance banks and payments banks are all private sector commercial banks with the exception of India Post Payments Bank which is a public sector bank.

India Post Payments Bank is incorporated as a Public Sector Bank (with 100% GoI equity) under the Department of Posts. It started its activities on January 30th, 2017 in Ranchi and Raipur. It has a plan to open branches all over the country (See also under 1.12 for more information on these new type of banks).

Co-operative Banks

Co-operative banks are the co-operative ventures of a specific group of people to promote the welfare of its members or a particular segment of economy. It is based on co-operative movement. There are many types of co-operative banks in the country which are explained below. Constitutionally, the co-op banks are societies registered under the State Co-operative Acts.

The first co-operative bank in India was established in the year 1889 in Baroda with the name Anyonya Sahayakari Mandali Co-operative Bank Limited and later it was renamed as Anyonya Co-operative Bank Limited. This bank was in operation till the year 2007 and the bank was closed in the year 2008. It is said that this bank was also the first co-op bank in Asia.

Co-operative banks in the country fall under the dual control of RBI and the State Governments. Co-operative Acts are under the jurisdiction of State Governments. All banking policy-related areas are controlled and administered by RBI and the State Governments by virtue of State Acts control the management and internal administration of these banks. Co-op banks falls under two categories: urban co-op banks and rural co-op banks.

Urban Co-operative Banks

These are the co-operative banks started by the individual or group initiatives to provide banking services and to assist their members. They are in private sector. Mostly, these banks are in urban and metro areas. They cater to the needs of its members. They accept retail deposits from public. But their loaning activities are only for their members. Generally, the membership of these co-operative banks are open and hence one can become a member (shareholder) and then become eligible for loan assistance. As already explained, many of such banks are also have the status of a scheduled bank. The area of operation of these urban co-operative banks, in general, are restricted within the state. But, of late, RBI has allowed many urban co-operative banks to expand into other states. Such urban co-operative banks are known as multi-state co-operative banks. There are 43 multi-state co-op banks at present. Urban co-op banks can become scheduled banks by complying with the regulatory requirements. As at March 2015, there were 53 scheduled urban co-op banks. As at June 2017, there are 54 scheduled urban co-op banks.

Some prominent banks in co-operative sector (urban co-op banks) that came into existence prior to independence are:

- Shamrao Vithal Co-op Bank in 1906
- Cosmos Co-op Bank in 1906
- Saraswat Co-op Bank in 1918
- Bombay Mercantile Co-op Bank in 1939.

Urban co-op banks were not allowed to lend to agriculture till the year 1996. Now they can lend to agriculture also.

After introduction of banking reforms, one urban co-op bank has been converted as commercial bank (DCB Bank in the year 1995). The committee on reforms has recommended that the urban co-op banks be converted as commercial banks. This is now under the active consideration of government and RBI.

Rural Co-operative Banks

Rural Co-operative Banks are mostly government-owned banks created for the purpose of rural development. Government formalised the system of rural co-op banks for rural financing in 1950s and created a structure of rural co-op banks for taking up the rural financing. There were some co-op banks already in existence who were linked to the government scheme and some more new co-op banks were started.

Government created a three-tier structure for extending short-term finance to agriculture and allied activities. It created Primary Agriculture Credit Societies (PACS) at village level, District Central Co-op Banks (DCCBs) at district level and State Co-op Banks (StCB) at apex level in the states.

PACS are not banks but credit societies. They are an important link for short-term loan disbursals in rural areas. During the Second Five-Year Plan Period of 1956-61, government integrated the PACS and formalised the system for credit delivery through them. PACS are made as the delivery points for giving loans to agriculturists. DCCBs provide the funds to them for lending to farmers. Besides giving loans to members, PACS also accept deposits from its members.

District Central Co-operative Banks (DCCBs)

DCCBs were set up at districts as the banks for rural development. They act as the middle link in the three-tier rural credit dispensing system. However, they lend through PACS within their jurisdiction. Besides funding PACS, these banks are also allowed to function as a normal bank, accepting deposits and providing other banking services. They are also allowed to open branches within the district. Governments have contributed to the capital of these banks and also provide required resources to on lend to PACS.

State Co-operative Banks (StCBs)

The concept of apex co-op bank at state level came into effect from fifties. Many of the present days state co-op banks were started much earlier, from the year 1905 onwards and they were converted as apex banks in fifties. Some new state co-op banks were started as and when a new state was created.

State Co-operative Banks are conceived as apex bodies at state level for co-operative sector and are the umbrella organizations to which all the District Central Co-op Banks in the state and PACS at village level are affiliated. State Co-op Banks provide refinance support to DCCBs.

State Co-operative Banks also carries out all banking functions and services. As an apex bank of the state in the three-tier system, it can function as single office. Some State Co-op Banks have more branches as they were allowed to complement the branch network of DCCBs. In some states, there are no DCCBs and only State Co-op Bank is functioning.

State Co-operative Banks function as a normal bank and can open and maintain account with RBI. They can also become scheduled banks. As at June 2017, there are 33 state co-op banks, 19 of them are in scheduled category and 14 are in non-scheduled category.

Land Development Banks

The special banks created for providing long-term loans to agriculture were called Land Development Banks (LDBs). The first LDB was started at Jhang in Punjab in 1920. Government enacted the Land Mortgage Banks Act in 1930s (LDBs were originally called Land Mortgage Banks). After passing of this Act, LDBs were started in different states of India.

During the Second Five-Year Plan Period of 1956-61, government decided to make the Land Development Banks as the tool for extending long-term loans to agriculture and encouraged and created Land Development Banks in all the districts and states. Government created a two-tier structure for long-term credit delivery to agriculture as under:

1. Primary Land Development Bank—at district level with branches at taluka level.
2. State Land Development Bank—Central Land Development Bank at the state level with all primary Land Development Banks in the state affiliated to it.

However, in some states, there is "Unitary structure" with only State Land Development Bank operating with branches and sub-branches at all the district and talukas of the states. Even in states with two-tier structure the state level apex bank was allowed to open branches to complement the network of primary land development banks.

Traditionally, LDBs provided long-term loans to farmers for minor irrigation projects, farm mechanization and for any other permanent improvements on land. After the year 1982, at the instance of the NABARD, they diversified their activities and started financing development of wastelands, village and cottage industries, rural artisans, etc. and also started extending housing loans to farmers at villages. In view of broader role of LDBs, they are now known as Primary Co-operative Agriculture and Rural Development Banks (PCARDBs) and the apex bank at the state is known as State Co-operative Agriculture and Rural Development Banks (SCARDBs).

These banks function like normal banks and accept deposits and conduct other banking services.

The rural co-operative sector banks are under the supervisory control of National Bank for Agriculture and Rural Development (NABARD).

Number of Banks

The number of banks under different categories in the country as at March 2013, March 2016 and June 2017 are as under:

No.	Type of Banks in the Country	March 2013	March 2016	June 2017
1	**Commercial Banks**			
1.1	State Bank of India	1	1	1
1.2	Associate Banks	5	5	-
1.3	Nationalized Banks	19	19	19
1.4	Other Public Sector Bank	1	2	1
1.5	Old Private Sector Banks	13	12	12
1.6	New Private Sector Banks	7	7	9
1.7	Foreign Banks	43	44	44
1.8	Regional Rural Banks	64	56	56
1.9	Local Area Banks	4	4	3
1.10	Small Finance Banks	-	-	7
1.11	Payments Banks @	-	-	3
	Total Commercial Banks	157	150	155
2	**Co-op Banks**			
2.1	Urban Co-op Banks	1606	1574	

No.	Type of Banks in the Country	March 2013	March 2016	June 2017
2.1.1	Multi-State Urban Cooperative Banks	43	51	
2.1.2	Single State Urban Cooperative Banks	1563	1523	
2.2	**Rural Co-op Banks**		**93913**	
2.2.1	State Cooperative Banks	31	32	
2.2.2	District Central Cooperative Banks	371	370	
2.2.3	Primary Agricultural Cooperative Societies*	*92432	*92789	
2.2.4	State Cooperative Agriculture and Rural Development Banks	20	20	
2.2.5	Primary Cooperative Agriculture and Rural Development Banks	697	702	

@ India Post Payments Bank under 'payments banks' category is a public sector bank.

*PACS are not banks but credit societies.

1.2 What is Banking Business

Banking business basically is accepting deposits from the public for the purpose of lending it to those who need loans. In the process, banks earn income. The income comes from the interest on loans which is generally at higher rate than what bank pays interest to its depositors. The difference between the rate of interest a bank pays on its deposits (average cost) and the rate of interest it earns on the loans (average yield) is known as the interest spread for the bank.

Bank cannot lend all the money it receives as deposits. This is because bank has to maintain liquidity with it as the depositors, depending on the type of account and their requirement, will withdraw their money from the bank on day-to-day basis. Bank has to make all such payments. Further as per RBI regulations, bank has to maintain liquidity ratios. These are the cash reserve ratio (CRR) and the statutory liquidity ratio (SLR). Basically, these are maintained as liquidity measures but in reality it represents blocked funds as these funds are not available to banks for lending or for liquidity in the normal circumstances. They may become available only when the bank is put to liquidation.

Hence, the quantum of bank lending is dependent on the liquidity ratios to be maintained and also the liquidity required to meet normal withdrawals by the depositors. The ratio of loans to the deposits of the bank is called the credit deposit ratio. CD ratio tells how much percentage of deposits received by the bank is given as loans.

As mentioned earlier besides the liquidity ratios prescribed by RBI banks also maintain liquidity for the purpose of running their day-to-day business. This liquidity bank generally does not hold in cash. Cash is always held to the minimum required level and rest is maintained with RBI in current account. Again banks may not hold their internal liquidity only with RBI in current accounts. Generally, banks invest these funds in liquid assets like the government securities so that they can convert them back to cash anytime and till such time earn some income out of such investments.

If the loans are at low level in comparison to available surplus funds with the bank, bank may invest the funds again in government or other securities instead of keeping it idle. But a commercial bank always prefers to give maximum loans than investing it in government securities as the earning is much less in the case of government securities.

If a bank for some reason decides to cut down on its fresh loans and invest its funds in government securities which is secured investment, then the bank is said to be doing narrow banking. Narrow banking is investing depositors' money in secured investments and eschewing the risks of lending.

A. *Deposit Business*

Banks accept deposits from the public and this is the basic raw material of banking business. Deposit taking is the basic bank activity that has changed the face of modern economy and pitched the banks to the centre stage. Bank deposits now is an important component of money supply in the economy. This deposit taking enabled banks to give loans which activity is called the financial intermediation. It is taking the surplus of one and lending it to the needy. The borrower is provided with money and the depositor still has the control on his money which he can withdraw anytime he wants. This financial intermediation by the bank provides liquidity and funds to two persons based on the same money deposited with it. In the practical sense, bank created additional money on the strength of the deposit it received. Hence, banks are said to create money. The modern economy is riding on this capability of banks to create money.

Banks accept deposits basically in two types of accounts. One type is called the running account. Under this banks have savings bank accounts and current accounts. Savings bank account is for the individual for his personal transactions and current account is for the business entities. These are the running accounts and there is no promise by the account holder to retain the money in these accounts for any period. They are totally at the discretion of the account holders to withdraw it anytime without notice. Usually, the withdrawals are facilitated by issuing cheques. Generally, the account holder draws cheques and makes payment to parties and the banks pay these cheques received in clearing.

Savings and Current Accounts. These running accounts are also called the checking accounts in some other countries. The services of providing running accounts with cheque book facility is the monopoly business of banks. No other business entities can provide this service. Banks in India can only issue cheque books to its customers under RBI rules. The only exception is post office savings bank which also carries banking business of maintaining savings bank accounts for the public.

As per RBI guidelines, no interest is paid for the balance held in a current account of the customer. But for savings bank which is personal accounts, bank can pay interest. Historically, RBI use to prescribe interest rates for deposits till they were deregulated after the reforms. Banks were paying interest in the range of 3.5 to 4% on the savings bank deposits. At present it is 4% and even though banks are free to fix any rate now, no bank has changed the rates. Only Yes Bank is offering 6% now. Recently, Bharatiya Mahila Bank started offering 4.5% and 5% (for over ₹ one lac) rates on savings bank accounts (this bank is merged with SBI on 1-4-2017).

Banks were paying interest on SB accounts based on a minimum balance held between 10th and last working day of the month. And the interest is paid once in six months' time. At present after computerisation of banks and at the behest of BCSBI banks are calculating interest on the basis of daily balances held in SB account.

In the year 2016 RBI issued—Master Direction—Reserve Bank of India (Interest Rate on Deposits) Directions, 2016, on March 03, 2016 and made some changes as under:

Sec. 6 (a). Interest on domestic rupee savings deposits shall be calculated on a daily product basis as under:

(i) A uniform interest rate shall be set on balance up to Rupees one lakh, irrespective of the amount in the account within this limit.

(ii) Differential rates of interest may be provided for any end-of-day savings bank balance exceeding Rupees one lakh.

Sec. 11. Periodicity of payment of Interest on domestic savings deposits

(a) Interest on savings deposit shall be credited at quarterly or shorter intervals.

Now banks are paying interest on savings bank deposits on quarterly basis and some banks are even paying interest on monthly basis. Banks are also now allowed to pay differential rates for balance over rupees one lac in savings accounts.

Term deposits. The other type of bank accounts in deposits are called the term deposit accounts. In this the depositor places the deposit with the bank for a fixed period and these are in the form of investments by the depositor. As per present RBI guidelines, term deposits can be placed for a maximum period of ten years. There is a provision to accept deposits for longer period in case the court's order for minor's accounts. Minimum period for deposit is 7 days.

Under term deposits banks generally have three basic sub-categories. They are the fixed deposits, recurring deposits and monthly income deposits.

Fixed deposits. Fixed deposits are lump sum deposit placed for a fixed period. Interest is payable on quarterly basis or the depositor can opt for reinvestment of interest in which case he will get the entire amount on maturity. Under this the reinvested interest also earns interest increasing the yield for the depositor. Some banks call this type of deposit account as cumulative deposit or as under reinvestment plan.

Recurring deposits. Under recurring deposits scheme, the depositor can deposit a fixed amount every month for a fixed period and then on due date get back the deposit with interest. This is an attractive savings scheme which earns higher interest rate as the interest rate is same as applicable to fixed deposits depending on the period of deposit. Here the depositor gets higher interest on his monthly deposits despite the fact that the monthly deposits made in subsequent months did not remain with the bank for full period of the term.

Monthly income deposit is also a lump sum deposit for fixed period and in this bank pays interest on monthly basis. This is suitable for persons who desire to have monthly income.

Interest rates on term deposits are decided by the banks themselves as RBI has deregulated the rates from 1997. However, the interest rates of banks show very small variances.

Sweep Accounts

Banks have developed a new deposit product after computerisation. It is called the sweep account (or by some other nomenclature) which is a combination of running account and term deposit account. Under this arrangement, balance in excess of a limit set by customer in the running account is automatically swept to term deposit on daily basis and it is swept back to running account as and when required by the customer. All these transactions happen on automatic basis controlled by the computer system. This is a value added product developed for customers.

Term deposit rates offered by the bank on individual deposit is contractual and the rate cannot be changed by the bank during the currency of deposit. When bank changes its deposit interest rates, it is applicable only for fresh deposits and the existing deposits will continue at the contracted rates. Banks may also offer differential interest (higher interest) rates on bulk term deposits (deposits of ₹ One crore and above).

Joint accounts. Bank accounts of individuals can be opened as a joint account of two or more individuals. In case of joint accounts of two persons only, they can open the account with the option of making it payable to 'either or survivor', 'former or survivor', 'later or survivor'. In case of more than two joint account holders they can have the clause of 'anyone or survivor'. These clauses are useful as in case of death of any joint account holders the money will be paid to the surviving depositor as per their instructions.

B. *Loans Business* (please see chapter 2)

C. *Investments by Banks*

Banks are the financial intermediaries and the deposits they receive from the public are deployed in mainly two ways. They are the lending activity or the investments. Investment means putting the money in different types of securities which give assured returns. Government bonds, treasury bills, and company debentures are some such securities.

Generally, banks look for more of lending than the investment in securities as lending activities increase the earning for the bank. But banks are required to hold investments for the purpose of maintaining statutory liquidity ratio. Under this banks will have to invest in government securities and other approved securities.

RBI under Section 24 of Banking Regulation Act, 1949 has the authority to fix SLR to be maintained by banks up to a maximum percentage of 40% of the total of demand and time liabilities of the banks. At present (as on 08-7-2017) SLR is fixed at 20%. Thus investment in SLR securities to an extent to maintain SLR is mandatory investments for banks.

In addition to SLR investments, banks also have some portion of their resources deployed in investments of various types. Banks can invest in securities not guaranteed by government in debentures and equities of companies, mutual funds or any other type of securities. Generally, banks build up more of SLR securities over and above the prescribed ratio as it can be used as liquidity measure for borrowing from RBI under repo option. Banks also lend or borrow in interbank call money market to deploy surplus funds with them or to manage liquidity.

There are few more money market instruments available for banks to invest like the CBLO, certificate of deposits and commercial papers.

RBI has allowed banks to participate in rupee derivative products. They are also money market-related products. These products are introduced to increase the depth of money market and also to enable banks to hedge against interest rate risk in their portfolio.

Trading in two types of rupee derivatives are allowed for banks from the year 1999. They are:

Forward Rate Agreement (FRA)—This is a financial contract between two parties to exchange interest payments for a 'notional principal' amount on settlement date, for a specified period from start date to maturity date.

Interest Rate Swap (IRS)—It is a combination of FRAs in which a fixed interest on a notional principal is exchanged for a floating interest rate equal to the reference rate at periodic intervals over the tenure of the contract.

As said earlier these are basically for hedging the interest rate risk and it can be used for speculative purpose also. Banks and primary dealers can participate in this trade. However, speculation is allowed for the market makers only.

In a typical hedging case, a bank if it has taken a loan at floating rate it can hedge it by entering into an interest rate swap which will offer it a fixed rate. The bank and the counterparty can enter into an agreement which will be based on a notional amount (in this case the loan amount of the bank) and they will exchange the interest flows. The bank will pay the fixed rate it has agreed and bank will receive floating rate from the counterparty for the contracted period. With fixed rate swap bank is covered for the risk in movement of the floating interest rates over the period.

Banks can also invest in shares but there are no assured returns, even though the returns from good company shares can be high. Further there are also some statutory and regulatory restrictions on banks in investing in shares.

D. *Other Business of Banks*

Other business of banks is as under:

1. Remittances and fund transfer. Banks are providing remittance facilities for transfer of money from one centre to another centre. During earlier period this was conducted by issuing bank drafts, mail transfers and telegraphic transfers. Now with new technology, money transfer is made through electronic fund transfer systems. Bank draft is still in use but mail transfer and telegraphic transfers have been discontinued. In their place customers are now offered electronic fund transfer systems like NEFT and RTGS systems managed by RBI for remittance to other bank customers. These systems transfer funds on the same day to the credit of beneficiary. For fund transfers between the accounts of same bank, the core banking system of the bank effects fund transfer instantly between the branches.

2. Issuing LCs and bank guarantees. Letters of credit are issued by banks to facilitate the trade in goods. By issuing a letter of credit, bank becomes a party to the transaction of sale and assures the seller the payment of his bill. Letters of credit are more used in import and export business and LC removes the exporter's risk involved in receiving payment for the goods exported by him (see under LC in chapter 2.23).

Bank guarantees are issued by the banks on behalf of their customers to third parties for indemnifying that party for any default committed by the customer in his dealings. Bank guarantee acts as a security and it facilitates business transactions like the performance of contract, performance of service, etc. Guarantees are also issued for the purpose of security deposits and as guarantee for the tax liabilities (see under BG in chapter 2.24).

3. Collection of cheques, instruments and bills for the customers. Banks are offering their services for collection of outstation cheques, bills or any other type of instruments for a charge. Collection of outstation cheques were an important service earlier but with development in technology the collection of outstation cheques have been eliminated to an extent by alternate systems. RBI had introduced speed clearing system in all MICR centres and the outstation cheques at these centres are collected and paid as local cheques using core banking system of banks. Now RBI has introduced cheque truncation system and has set up three national grids. Cheque truncation system allows banks to truncate the cheques and send only the electronic image of the cheque to the paying bank, thereby eliminating the physical movement of the cheque. Under this new system, the outstation cheques are presented in CTS clearing and paid like local cheques. More than 80% of outstation cheques are now collected as local clearing.

4. Demat account services. Reforms and technological developments in capital market has converted the shares and securities trading as paperless. Now these securities are not held by the investors in physical form instead securities are held in electronic form in demat account. Demat stands for dematerialisation of securities. Central Depository Services Limited (CDSL) and National Securities Depository Limited (NSDL) are the two central depositories in the country who hold the demat securities as trustees. These depositories have allowed banks, brokers and few others to join them as depository participants (DP) and the DPs will maintain the individual accounts of the customers. This system enables paperless electronic trade in securities.

Banks are acting as DP under this system and maintain individual accounts of the investors where various types of demat securities are maintained as a running account permitting credits or debits. Now trading in securities can be done on online basis and under this, customer can have a trading account with a broker and link it with his demat account and SB or current account with the bank. This linkage enables the customer to trade in securities on line and the sale/purchase transactions are put through simultaneously and settlement of payment for the trade is made in the bank account of the customer.

5. Distribution of third party products like insurance, mutual funds. Banks are allowed to distribute third party financial products like insurance and mutual funds as corporate agents for the respective providers of these services. This helps the customers as they can purchase these products and services at the banks. Banks are also allowed to have joint ventures for insurance business both in life and non-life category with insurance companies or others. Many banks have started insurance joint ventures.

6. Merchant banking activities. Merchant banker is defined as under:

> A Merchant Banker means any person who is engaged in the business of Issue Management either by making arrangements regarding selling, buying or subscribing to Securities as Manager, Consultant, Adviser of rendering Corporate Advisory Service in relation to such Issue Management.

Merchant banking is a combination of banking and consultancy services. Banks are providing many related services to capital market. Such services include public issue management as managers, as bankers or as underwriters and also provide consultancy services. These services are generally managed by merchant banking divisions of the banks.

7. Credit card business. Credit cards business is allowed for banks and after technological upgradation banks have started issuing credit cards. But comparatively few banks, are active in this business mainly the foreign banks (Citi Bank, Standard Chartered Bank, American Express Bank), private sector banks (ICICI Bank, HDFC Bank, Axis Bank) and State Bank of India.

8. Prepaid card/instruments business. In 2009, RBI issued guidelines for the business of prepaid card/instruments and allowed banks to start this business. As the name denotes, these are prepaid by the customers and the amount is stored in the card which can be used to make payments similar to debt and credit cards.

The prepaid instruments can be issued as smart cards, magnetic stripe cards, Internet accounts, Internet wallets, mobile accounts, mobile wallets, paper vouchers and any such instrument which can be used to access the prepaid amount. The prepaid payment instruments that can be issued in the country are classified under three categories, viz. (i) Closed system payment instruments, (ii) Semi-closed system payment instruments, and (iii) Open system payment instruments.

9. ATM cards and debit cards. ATM cards are issued by the banks to the customers which enable customers to draw cash from ATMs. Banks are now issuing ATM-cum-debit cards which can be used both at ATMs and also at point of sales (POS) for purchases.

10. Safe custody services. Banks can offer the services of safe custody of documents or articles for a charge and issues a receipt for it. Nomination facility is also available for this service and the depositor can nominate a person to receive back the items from the bank in case of death of the depositor.

11. Safe deposit lockers. Banks provide safe deposit lockers facility on annual rental basis. Banks create a strong room for keeping the safe deposit vaults and individual lockers in the vault is hired out to customers. A lease agreement for the hire is executed. Customers can keep their valuables in it. Customers can access their lockers on bank working days at business hours of the branch. Bank records the time and date of visit of the customer to his locker and also obtains his signature on the visit record. Banks are not responsible for the items kept in the locker as it is not aware of items kept. But banks are responsible for the safety of lockers and the strong room. Nomination facility is available for locker accounts.

12. Sale of gold coins. Around the year 2005 RBI allowed banks to import and sell gold coins and many banks are now offering gold coins with standard purity in different weights to the public. However, the policy for gold import is subject to changes by the government and RBI. RBI placed some restrictions in the year 2013 but has not banned the sale of gold coins by banks. Banks were advised not to be aggressive in the sale of gold.

Recently in the year 2015 government has declared gold monetisation policy under which domestic gold holdings in the form of ornaments by individuals and others can be brought into banking system and monetised.

Gold is also an approved security for investment by banks for their SLR investment.

13. Foreign exchange business-trading and forwards. During British rule of the country foreign exchange business was not permitted to commercial banks and there was a separate category of banks known as exchange banks who were only authorised to undertake foreign exchange business. Generally, these were all foreign banks who have opened their branches in the country. There were few exchange banks of Indian origin also. After Banking Regulation Act, 1949 was enacted this separate category of banks was abolished and banks are permitted to carry on foreign exchange business. However, banks are required to get a separate license known as authorised dealers license from RBI to engage in foreign exchange business.

Foreign exchange business involves trading in currencies, issuing letters of credit to foreign parties, handling import and export bills, making payment for imports in foreign currency and receiving payments for exports in foreign currency and also handling permitted remittances to or from foreign countries. Besides trading in foreign currencies, banks are also allowed to enter into forward contracts with customers or other banks for trades at future dates at a predetermined contracted rate.

14. Tax payments. Tax departments of the Central and State Governments have made arrangements with the banks for payment of various taxes by the tax payers. Online Tax Accounting System (OLTAS) was introduced in the year 2004 by Income Tax Dept. and banks which enable online tax payment of direct taxes (income tax and corporate tax). Online tax payments for indirect taxes like sales tax and excise, etc. are also now available to customers.

15. Wealth management services. Many banks are now offering wealth management services to customers. This service provides counselling to customers and give recommendations for investment options to suit requirements and depending on customer's risk appetite. Banks provide market information on various investment options like bank deposits, mutual funds, insurance and other investments and advise the customer on the investment best suitable to him.

For providing all the above-mentioned services, bank collects service charges. Some services may be free also. The service charges are also called as commission except in case of safe deposit lockers where it is called rent. Generally, now banks issue ATM-cum-debit cards free of charge to its customers. Foreign exchange business is trading between Indian rupee and foreign currency. Similarly, sale of gold coin is also trading. The service charges in these cases are in-built in the exchange rates/sale price.

1.3 What is the Business Size of Banks in the Country

Business size of Indian banking is little difficult to get as it includes commercial banks and co-op banks. Data on scheduled commercial banks (SCBs) are readily available from RBI. As per information there are four non-scheduled commercial banks in the country whose business is insignificant. Data on co-op banks are generally received after some time gap.

Indian Banking System—Share by Asset Size as at March 2013

The following table gives the picture of total banking system of the country as on March 2013 based on the banking assets.

Institution	Total Assets (As on March 31, 2013) ₹ Billion	Market Share of Total Banking Assets (As on March 31, 2013) (Percentage)
Public Sector Banks	69619.67	64.4
New Private Sector Banks	15450.70	14.3
Old Private Sector Banks	4447.33	4.1
Foreign Banks	6215.63	5.8
Regional Rural Banks	2758.00	2.5
Urban Co-operative Banks	3372.00	3.1

Institution	Total Assets (As on March 31, 2013) ₹ Billion	Market Share of Total Banking Assets (As on March 31, 2013) (Percentage)
Rural Co-operative Banks	6213.00	5.7
Of which		
STCBs	1479.00	1.4
DCCBs	2573.00	2.4
PACS	1605.00	1.5
SCARDBs	294.00	0.3
PCARDBs	262.00	0.2
Local Area Banks	15.76	0.1
Total	**108092.10**	**100**

Source: Centre for advanced financial research and learning promoted by RBI.

We can observe that co-op banks account for only 8.8% share in banking assets and commercial sector has 91.2% share. Public sector banks dominate with 64.4% share. The new private sector banks who appeared on the scene only from the year 1994 onwards already have a share of 14.3%.

Commercial banks as a group, are the major players and they account for more than 91.2% of total business of the banking industry in the country in the year 2013.

Business of Scheduled Commercial Banks

(₹ in billion)

Year	Deposits	Annual growth rate deposits %	Advances gross	Annual growth rate advances %	Credit Deposit ratio %
1991	1925.41	15.3	1163.01	14.6	60.6
1995	3868.59	22.8	2115.60	28.7	54.7
1997	5055.99	16.5	2784.01	9.6	55.1
2000	8133.45	13.9	4359.58	18.2	53.6
2002	11033.60	14.6	5897.23	15.3	53.8
2005	17001.98	13.0	11004.28	30.9	62.6
2010	44928.26	17.2	32447.88	16.9	73.6
2013	67504.54	14.2	52604.59	14.1	77.9
2015	85332.85	10.7	65364.20	9.0	77.4
2016	93272.90	9.3	72496.15	10.91	77.9
2017	108,051.50	15.8	78,818.90	8.7	73.7

Source: RBI

Internationally, the banks are ranked on the basis of total assets of the banks. But in our country traditionally banks are ranked according to the deposit size of the banks.

Banking business in the country has been growing very fast and the table below gives the business growth of scheduled commercial banks in the country during the last 25 years. Scheduled commercial banks include public sector banks, private sector banks, foreign banks, regional rural banks, and local area banks.

Deposits of SCBs have increased 56 times over the 1991 figures in last 25 years. Bank advances have increased 67 times over the figure of the year 1991.

1.4 Which are the Top Ten Banks in India

The following table lists the top ten banks in India on the basis of total assets (as at March 2017). They are the top ten banks on the basis of deposits also. Three private sector banks; ICICI bank, HDFC bank and Axis bank are amongst the top ten banks.

Rank	Bank	Total Assets ₹ in crore	Deposits	Advances	Net profit	Capital + reserves	CRAR % (Basel III)	Net NPA %
1.	State Bank of India	2705966	2044751	1571078	10484	267223	13.11	3.71
2.	HDFC Bank	863840	643640	554568	14549	89462	14.60	0.30
3.	ICICI Bank	771791	490039	464232	9801	99951	17.39	5.43
4.	Punjab National Bank	720330	621704	419493	1324.8	41846	11.66	7.81
5.	Bank of Baroda	694875	601675	383259	1383	36727	12.24	4.72
6.	Bank of India	626309	540032	366481	(1558) loss	30765	12.14	6.90
7.	Axis Bank	601468	414379	373069	3967	56380	14.95	2.11
8.	Canara Bank	583519	495275	342009	214	33685	12.86	6.33
9.	Union Bank of India	452704	378392	286466	555	23435	11.79	6.57
10.	IDBI Bank	361767	268538	190825	(5158) loss	22563	10.70	13.21

Source: Annual reports of respective banks.

SBI remains the biggest bank of the country. Till the year 2010, ICICI bank was the second largest bank of the country. Though it is a new bank, the merger of its promoter ICICI Ltd (an old existing development bank) with it, made it a large bank. Another new bank in private sector HDFC bank has now emerged a big bank as many banks were merged with it. As at March 2017, HDFC bank has emerged as the second largest bank, next to SBI, in terms of total assets. ICICI bank is in the third position followed by Punjab National Bank (4th position) and Bank of Baroda (5th position).

The top ten banks of the country according to market capitalisation are given below which depicts different rankings.

Market capitalisation is the value of a company that is traded on the stock market, calculated by multiplying the total number of shares by the present share price. This reflects the market perception of these banks.

Rank	Bank	Market Capitalization ₹ in crore on 22-6-2017	Branches	ATMs
1.	HDFC Bank	435,944.78	4715	12260
2.	State Bank of India	231,391.10	*24017	*59263
3.	Kotak Mahindra Bank	188,590.10	1369	2163
4.	ICICI Bank	186,591.54	4850	13882
5.	Axis Bank	121,650.70	3304	14163
6.	IndusInd Bank	89,173.30	1200	2036
7.	Yes Bank	65,519.44	1000	1800
8.	Bank of Baroda	38,642.28	5431	9200
9.	Punjab National Bank	31,110.90	6968	9935
10.	Canara Bank	21,099.27	6083	10519

Source: For market capitalisation figures: www.moneycontrol.com

Note: *Nos. after merger of 5 subsidiaries and Bharatiya Mahila Bank with SBI

HDFC Bank has emerged as the top bank ahead of State Bank of India. Interestingly, the list has six new generation private sector banks in it and only four PSBs appear in it including State Bank of India.

Ranking of Indian Banks in the Global List of Banks

One of the objectives of the banking sector reforms was to develop few Indian banks to global size. But even now this is a difficult status for Indian banks to achieve. Only State Bank of India is in the global top 100 banks.

As per the list of 100 biggest banks in the world released by SNL Financial, based on assets as at March 2015, State Bank of India ranks 58 (assets valued at US$ 432.57 billion) in the ranking. No other Indian bank appear in the list.

State Bank of India following the merger of five associate banks and Bharatiya Mahila Bank from 1-4-2017 with it, has grown in size. It is learnt that its balance sheet size will be above ₹ 33 lakh crore. As per expectation, SBI may enter the league of 'Top 50 Global Banks' and may occupy 45th rank in the global list of banks.

According to a recent Relbanks statistics ranking banks on the basis of market capitalisation, only HDFC bank from the country is in the top 50 global banks list. HDFC bank is placed at 33rd rank with market cap of US$ 54.643 billion in 20-1-2017.

Global Banks

There are many lists ranking global banks and it is a difficult task as the countries are still following different accounting standards. The top banks are mainly from China, USA and Europe.

Top 10 Banks (asset size) in the World

Rank	Bank	Country	Total assets, US$ billion	Balance sheet
1.	Industrial & Commercial Bank of China	China	3,615.17	03.31.2017
2.	China Construction Bank Corp	China	3,149.25	03.31.2017
3.	Agricultural Bank of China	China	2,950.21	03.31.2017
4.	Bank of China	China	2,746.05	03.31.2017
5.	Mitsubishi UFJ Financial Group	Japan	2,713.44	03.31.2017
6.	JPMorgan Chase & Co	USA	2,546,29	03.31.2017
7.	HSBC Holdings	UK	2,416,47	03.31.2017
8.	BNP Paribas	France	2,348.65	03.31.2017
9.	Bank of America	USA	2,247.70	03.31.2017
10.	Wells Fargo	USA	1,951.56	03.31.2017

Source: www.relbanks.com

According to this list, China has four banks in the top ten banks of the world on the basis of assets.

To realise the size of Indian banks in comparison to global banks, we may compare State Bank of India's assets valued at US$ 432.57 billion in March 2015 with the top bank; ICBC China with assets of US$ 3320.86 billion in Dec. 2014. World no. 1 bank is nearly 8 times bigger than SBI.

1.5 What are Cheques

Banking is very old business in the human societies everywhere. In modern time, banks are unique organisations which offer cheque facility to their customers to withdraw money from the account. This facility now only banks can offer under the law.

Over the period of progress in trade and commerce, the cheque became a payment instrument. In fact, it was the only payment instrument as alternate to cash. When the cheque came into existence and use in the world is difficult to know. Probably it was present in all important developed civilisations of the world.

The ancient Romans are believed to have used an early form of cheque known as 'praescriptiones' in the 1st century BC.

In India, during the Mauryan Empire period (from 321 BC to 185 BC), a commercial instrument called 'adesha' was in use, which was an order on a banker desiring him to pay the money of the note to a third person. It was same as the modern-day cheque.

In modern era, cheques were said to be in use since 9th century by customers of banks. The Bank of England pioneered the first use of a pre-printed cheque form in the year 1717. These forms were printed on cheque paper in a numbered form to prevent fraud, and customers had to collect it personally from the bank.

In our country, it is learnt that the Bank of Hindoostan, the first joint stock bank established in 1770, introduced cheques.

Banking business world over were conducted based on the customs and practices developed in the business. The first law regarding the use of cheque was created by many countries in the world at the end of 19th century.

In our country Negotiable Instrument Act was passed in the year 1881, and this act gave legal framework for usage of negotiable instruments which are three: cheques, bills of exchange, and promissory notes.

Section 6 of the Negotiable Instruments Act, 1881 defined cheque as under (after amendment in 2002):

A "cheque" is a bill of exchange drawn on a specified banker and not expressed to be payable otherwise than on demand and it includes the electronic image of a truncated cheque and a cheque in the electronic form.

The words "and it includes the electronic image of a truncated cheque and a cheque in the electronic form" and the explanations I & II (not shown here) are inserted as amendment in the year 2002. This was effected for enabling the cheque truncation process to be introduced for clearing purposes (see under Chapter 3).

Cheque is a negotiable instrument and negotiable instrument is a wonderful concept developed by practice and customs, and it helped the commerce. Negotiation means endorsing and handing over the instrument to another person and it enables the other person to claim the amount as the owner of the amount. Negotiation of an instrument is the transfer of title to the instrument but it is slightly different from mere transfer. The basic difference is that the transferee under transfer gets the same title of transferor, i.e. if the title of the transferor is defective then the same deficiency will attach to the transferee. Whereas when a negotiable instrument is negotiated then the transferee gets a valid title devoid of any defect, if he has acted in good faith and as per the law. Clearly, there is an advantage in accepting a negotiable instrument.

In our country prior to the year 1959 even indigenous bankers were issuing cheque books to their customers for use. This was stopped by an amendment to Banking Regulation Act, 1949 in the year 1959 and a new Section 49A was inserted.

This section prohibited all others, other than banks and post office savings bank, to issue and use cheques.

Features of the Cheque

Cheque is a written order of the account holder to his bank to make the payment of the amount specified to some person as per other stipulations on the cheque. Hence, cheque has three parties involved in it. The account holder who issues the cheque, the bank on whom it is drawn and the person named therein is called the payee who is to get the payment. The account holder is the drawer and the bank is the drawee. Usage of cheques is subject to various provisions of Negotiable Instrument Act and the customs of the banks. Even the customs and practices of the banks in handling cheques have legal sanctity as the law now recognises it.

Crossing of Cheque. There is a provision under NI Act, 1881 (Section 123) for crossing of cheques. Crossing means two parallel lines drawn across the face of the cheque at any place. It can be placed diagonally or horizontally or in any other manner. It may contain the word "& co" or "& company" or without such letters. A bank's name can also be inserted in between these two lines.

Crossing of the cheque prohibits its payment in cash at banks' counters to anyone other than another bank. It means that crossed cheques will have to be collected by another bank. This makes the payee to deposit such cheques with his bank who will collect the payment from the drawee bank and credit it to his account. Thus, the account holder ensures by crossing the cheque that the payment is made to a bank only. This leaves the trail of payment, which can be traced, if found necessary for any reason subsequently.

Special Crossing. NI Act, 1881 (Section 126) also recognizes special crossing which means name of a bank has been written between the two lines. When name of any bank appears like this, the cheque is said to have been specially crossed to that bank. This means only the bank named therein can collect the payment from the drawee bank. Drawee bank cannot make payment to any bank other than the bank named therein. This provides extra safety in that the payment goes to the intended bank only.

There is a practice with banks to stamp all cheques coming into their possession with a crossing stamp. This stamp has two lines and the name of the bank and branch written between these lines. This is treated as special cross. Banks do it so that once instruments passes through their hand, it shall not be misused by anyone and find its way to another bank.

Not Negotiable Cheques. Sometimes the cheques are issued and either in the crossing or at any other place the word "not negotiable" is written. It is mandatory that such writing shall remove the negotiability of the instrument. However, transferability of it is not restricted. Then what is the significance? The payee must accept such cheques with care as his title can be affected by any existing defect of the person issuing or endorsing it (Section 130 of NI Act).

Other Features. Cheque can be issued and made payable to bearer or order. Striking out the word bearer on the cheque is treated as making the cheque payable to order. A bearer cheque can be paid to anyone who presents it for payment to the bank. But bank can make payment of order cheque only after identifying the payee.

As per usage a cheque is valid for six months from the date and bank cannot make payment after the expiry of six months. From 1 April 2012, RBI has changed this, and now cheques are valid for three months only. The cheque not presented for payment within three months are called stale cheques. Banks cannot make payment of stale cheques. The general practice is to return back the stale cheque to the issuer of the cheque and request for a new cheque. Issuer of the cheque can also revalidate the cheque.

Customer can issue post-dated cheque and it can be paid by the bank only after the date mentioned in the cheque. Customer can also write the date as pre-dated and the banks will make payment within the expiry date (three months from the cheque date).

As the cheques have become important payment instruments used in commerce and trade, government amended the NI Act in the year 1988 and made the bouncing of cheque a criminal offense. A new chapter VII was added to Negotiable Instrument Act by the amendment act and the provisions of new Sections 138 to 142 were made effective from the year 1989. There are now penal provisions in the act, for if a person issues cheques and the cheques were bounced for want of funds in the account. Punishment prescribed for the offence is fine which may extend to twice the amount of the cheque or imprisonment for a term which may be extended to two years or both.

1.6 What are the Alternate Delivery Channels for Bank Services

Banks have variety of products and services to offer to the customers/public. The medium through which these products and services are offered are known as delivery channels for bank.

Basically, banks are providing accounts services both deposit and loans, payment services for transfer of funds and some other products and services. Till the technological development, bank branches are the only channel through which bank services are provided. Now the development in communication technology has created many media through which banking services are delivered to the public. At present besides the bank branch, the following additional delivery channels are available to bank customers:

1. ATM
2. Cards-debit/credit/prepaid
3. SMS banking
4. Mobile banking
5. Internet banking

A. *ATMs and ATM Sharing Network*

Barclays Bank, a British bank, is the first bank in the world to start ATM in London in the year 1967. In India, the first ATM was set up by HSBC in Mumbai in the year 1987. Now as on August 2017 there are more than 2,22,318 ATMs in the country. The number of ATMs are nearly one and half times the number of bank branches.

ATM stands for automated teller machines that disburses cash. ATMs are generally working on all 24 hours of the day and all the 365 days of the year.

ATMs were started in large numbers in our country after the year 1994 by new generation private sector banks and the foreign banks. After computerization, the public sector banks and other banks also started setting up ATMs.

Banks can set up ATMs with prior approval by RBI which is readily available to banks. ATMs installed in the branch premises are called the onsite ATMs. The ATMs set up at locations outside from the branch is called the offsite ATMs. ATMs are connected through the telecommunication network or through satellite communication to the bank's main computer system. Banks generally provide security guard at the ATM and now video surveillance is also provided for safety purposes.

Now banks generally issue ATM-cum-debit cards to its customers which can be used both at ATMs and also at POS as debit cards for making payments.

ATM card, a plastic card issued and the customer is provided with a personal identification number (PIN) to use at ATM machine for identification and security purpose. The customer has the option to change this PIN through the ATM machines itself to guard against misuse. The validity period of the card with month and year is mentioned on the card and card may contain the name of the customer. There is provision for customer's signature on the back of the card.

Recently in order to increase the number of ATMs particularly in unbanked areas and rural places, RBI has permitted non-banking companies also to set up and run ATMs. These ATMs are called as White Label ATMs (WLAs). Eight companies were approved to start ATMs and many have already opened ATMs. These companies have opened 7100 ATMs till February 2015.

Besides cash disbursement, ATMs can also perform following other functions:

- Account information
- Cash deposit
- Regular bills payment
- Purchase of re-load vouchers for mobiles
- Mini/short statement
- PIN change
- Request for cheque book

Banks do not charge the customer for ATM card and for any number of transactions at ATMs. However, there will be a day limit for maximum withdrawal in a day.

ATM Sharing Network. Banks have started ATM sharing networks which enables the card holder to withdraw cash from other banks ATMs also. At present the biggest network of shared ATMs is the National Financial Switch (NFS) network started by RBI in the year 2004 and now managed by National Payment Corporation of India. This network has all the major banks in it and in August 2015 this network had 207919 ATMs connected to it. White label ATMs are also in the NFS network.

However, when customer uses other banks' ATMs, as per RBI directions (with effect from November 1, 2014) savings bank account holders can get three free transactions in a month in six metro cities (Mumbai, New Delhi, Chennai, Kolkata, Bengaluru and Hyderabad) and five free transactions in a month at any other stations at other bank ATMs. There will charges for additional number of transactions. There is also per transaction limit (generally up to ₹ 10000) when other banks ATMs are used.

B. *Debit and Credit Cards, Prepaid Cards*

Debit/credit/prepaid cards are also an alternate delivery channel for banking services. The main purpose and utility of these delivery channels is that it enables the bank customer to make various payments for the goods and services he buys from the market or directly from the service provider. Examples are when the customer buys goods from malls, when books his travel tickets, when he needs to pay his utility bills, when he avails catering services at restaurants, at hotels for stay, at hospitals for treatment, etc. All these require payments that also confirmed payments like cash payment. Cheques are generally not accepted for many of the payments. These are all payments for goods or services which a person has to make on day-to-day basis.

All these are the retail payments and in olden days customer is required to carry cash with him while going for these purchases. But today the technology and banks have provided the alternate mode of payment through debit and credit cards.

Debit Cards

Debit cards are only issued by banks as it is linked to the bank account. Now in India all the banks are issuing the ATM cards as a combined ATM-cum-debit card to obviate the need to issue two separate cards. Technically, both are charge cards permitting transactions if the balance in the account is sufficient. In view of this, it makes sense to have combined card which can be used at both ATMs and at POS.

Prior to the year 2012, some banks were issuing debit cards which are known as offline debit cards in association with some credit card companies. In this the account was debited for the card use after a gap of two to three days. RBI stopped the practice of issuing offline debit cards in December 2012 and advised banks to issue only online debit cards with security pin code for authentication and that the debit shall be made online instantly.

All the banks in India who are on core banking platform, now issue online debit cards to their customers Indian banks can issue co-branded debit cards and also international debit cards. International debit cards shall be subject to the directives under Foreign Exchange Management Act, 1999.

Further, according to RBI directives, POS cannot reimburse cash to the card holder and only genuine trade transactions shall be entered into at their premises. For the cash requirement, card holder has to visit the ATM.

Banks are also governed by The Banking Codes and Standards Board of India (BCSBI) code as adopted by them in handling the business of issuing ATM-cum-debit cards to its customers.

Credit Cards

Probably, Diners Club International, founded as Diners Club was the first independent credit card company in the world to start a charge card in the year 1950. Bank of America issued its credit card in 1956. Other banks like Citi Bank and American Express Bank also started their credit cards around the same time.

In India, Diners card was introduced in seventies and became popular with the elite. Later the Indian operation of this card was taken over by Citi Bank credit card.

Credit cards are generally issued by banks but it is not restricted to banks only. RBI has permitted NBFCs and also some other companies to issue co-branded credit cards with commercial banks on non-risk sharing basis. Many corporate and NBFCs have launched co-branded credit cards with commercial banks since the year 2005. There are few co-branded cards issued by petroleum companies, airlines and other companies at present.

Credit card is different from the debit card. Credit card is a credit product of the bank wherein some credit is extended to the card holder. Further credit card can be issued by banks to non-customer also, as it is not linked directly to an account of the customer. Banks cannot debit the account of the customer for the monthly bills raised, unless the customer has authorized the bank to do so.

There is a general credit to the card holder as he is billed monthly and he makes the payment after the bill is raised on him. Thus, credit card holder gets few days' interest free credit for his purchases during the month. In case of non-payment by the card holder, it becomes a loan recoverable from him.

There is also a category of credit card where the card issuing bank allows the card holder to make the payment of monthly bills in instalments. In this case, it becomes a clean advance to the customer similar to a loan taken from bank.

Hence, the bank issuing credit card is in fact making advances and this business has inherent credit risks and possible default. Issuing credit card by a bank is a credit decision and it is vulnerable business as there are no loan documentation created and no security charged to the bank like in case of regular loans. It is a clean advance for the bank.

Credit card holders are also permitted to withdraw cash from ATM for personal use up to pre-determined limit. This is in the form of clean loans to the card holders.

The rate of interest charged by the credit card issuing banks for delayed and deferred payments by customers are governed by the RBI directives on lending. Till 30 June 2010, banks were allowed to charge any interest rate as applicable to their non-priority personal loans. From 1 July 2010 onwards, the rate of interest shall be linked to the base rate of the bank concerned and made known to the customers. Banks can charge differential interest rates based on credit history of the customer but the information shall have to be given to the customer.

Banks are also governed by "Code of Bank's Commitment to Customers" (Code) issued in July 2006 by The Banking Codes and Standards Board of India (BCSBI) and as adopted by the bank. This code shall be followed for recovery of dues of credit card business and no unfair practices can be adopted by the bank in recovery matters.

Banks are issuing many types of credit cards with added benefits and features and also with enhanced credit limits. Each bank has its own nomenclature to differentiate the credit cards. Generally, following types of credit cards are issued by the banks in India. Many credit cards offer cash back incentives on the amount spent by the card holders through the cards.

Standard Credit Card: This type of card is most commonly issued and used.

Premium Credit Card: This card is in the privilege category and is generally with some incentives like travel incentives, reward points, cash back and other rewards on the use of this card.

Secured Credit Card: These are issued to who cannot be extended credit limit based on credit history but are willing to provide security deposit.

Charge Credit Card: In this type of cards no credit is allowed after the monthly bill is raised. Customer has to make full payment of the bill.

Prepaid Credit Card: These cards similar to debit cards and are loaded with money which can be used by the customer to make payments.

Not all Indian banks are in credit card business. There are only 31 banks in India who have credit card business as at March 2015 and the leaders in the business are HDFC Bank, ICICI Bank, SBI, Citi Bank, Axis Bank, Standard Chartered Bank, and American Express Bank.

Prepaid Cards/Instruments

Prepaid cards or instruments are the latest product developed as a mode of payment service by the banks. Like the credit and debit cards these may also have the tie up with the settlement providers.

RBI has allowed banks to issue rupee-denominated prepaid instruments/cards and such cards can also be issued as co-branded cards with other non-banking entities. These cards are like the credit and debit card except that the amount is prepaid and loaded on the card. It can be used just like credit or debit cards at merchant establishments for payments. RBI has permitted banks to issue the prepaid instruments as smart cards, magnetic stripe cards, Internet accounts, Internet wallets, mobile accounts, mobile wallets, and paper vouchers. RBI has classified three types of instruments in this category as under:

1. *(2.4) Closed System Payment Instruments*: These are payment instruments issued by a person for facilitating the purchase of goods and services from him/it. These instruments do not permit cash withdrawal or redemption. As these instruments do not facilitate

payments and settlement for third party services, issue and operation of such instruments are not classified as payment systems.

2. *(2.5) Semi-closed System Payment Instruments:* These are payment instruments which can be used for purchase of goods and services, including financial services at a group of clearly identified merchant locations/establishments which have a specific contract with the issuer to accept the payment instruments. These instruments do not permit cash withdrawal or redemption by the holder.
3. *(2.6) Open System Payment Instruments:* These are payment instruments which can be used for purchase of goods and services, including financial services like funds transfer at any card accepting merchant locations (point of sale terminals) and also permit cash withdrawal at ATMs/BCs.

Source: Master circular RBI/2014-2015/105 DPSS.CO.PD. PPI.No.3/02. 14.006/2014-15 July 1, 2014 (updated as on December 03, 2014)

Banks have developed different types of prepaid cards on the above lines. The main type of card is generally called a gift card which can be used to make gift and it falls under the first category. Gift cards are issued for a period of six months and the card becomes stale after that period. It cannot be revalidated. Fresh cards can be purchased. Maximum amount allowed to be loaded is ₹ 50000. These types of cards cannot be reloaded again.

Some banks have created a new type of prepaid card suitable for the corporate for disbursement of salary and reimbursements to employees. Such cards can be reloaded with amount on monthly basis (e.g.: ICICI Bank's Pay Direct Card and Meal Card, State Bank's eZ-Pay Card and Smart Payout Card).

The third category of prepaid instrument is now started and it has features of both purchases at POS and also payment facilities of fund transfer. One such new product is called the 'mobile wallet' or 'm-wallet'. As it is a prepaid instrument with the amount loaded, it is referred as wallet. It is also known as digital banking. It is a reloadable card and can be used as a mobile application.

ICICI Bank has two products falling under this category called as 'Pockets' and 'm-pesa'. State Bank of India has recently launched its m-wallet with name 'SBI Buddy'. Other banks are following as banks are now keen to enter into this new business which is seen as having great potential.

M-wallet has already been launched earlier in the Indian market by some e-commerce companies and others. Following are some of the brands of m-wallet in the market started from the year 2012 onwards.

- Payzippy (from Flipkart, a Singapore-based company operating in India)
- Paytm mobile wallet (from One97 Communication Limited)
- Oxigen wallet (from Oxigen Services India Pvt. Ltd.)
- YPayCash digital wallet (from eMudhra Consumer Services Ltd. and Karur Vysya Bank).

RBI has identified the business of prepaid cards as having great future. RBI recently permitted starting up of payments banks in the country and issued 11 new banking licenses. Payments banks are authorized to accept deposit of ₹ one lakh per customer and also can issue prepaid cards to them. It is expected that the new payments banks will grow the business of prepaid cards in the country.

1.7 How the Card Payment System Works

As the cards facilitate payment for goods and services, they are also called the plastic money. These cards are also called the electronic cards as they facilitate payment through electronic medium.

Cards (debit/credit/prepaid) work on the basis of a created and prior arrangement between the seller/service provider and bank through a payment facilitating mechanism. The sellers or service providers are called the 'point of sales' (POS) where the payment transaction is initiated for sale and purchase. POS are by arrangement registered with the banks or the settlement provider for the transactions. Registered POS is provided with card swiping machine [known as Electronic Data Capture (EDC) machine] to accept the cards. These cards are swiped in the machines and the amount of the purchase is recorded. Automatically through the communication network the transaction will be approved. Then the POS create a charge slip for the amount and get the signature of the customer on it (now with the introduction of use of PIN for card transactions, obtaining signature is generally waived). Two copies of charge slips are created and one is given to the customer for his record. POS can also compare the signature as the card contains the signature of the card holder.

The POS then sends his copy of the charge slip to the bank, if his arrangement is direct with the bank, or else to the payment intermediary with whom he is registered. POS gets immediate credit in his account for the charge slips. Generally, POS sends the charge slips in a lot every day for payment and he gets paid immediately.

For the customer the debit to his account for the payment is different on debit cards and credit cards. In case of debit card, the amount will be debited to the account immediately on line. In case of credit card, there is no immediate debit. Card holder will get his monthly bill for his total usage and then he makes the payment to the card issuing bank. For prepaid cards, as the value is stored in the card, it will be deducted from the prepaid amount.

While POS and bank linkage can be direct, in practice it is more suitable for banks and POS to be linked to an intermediary who acts as link between bank and POS. This intermediary enlarges the scope of linkage and also provides a mechanism for settlements. Some intermediaries provide tie-up within the entire country. Some intermediaries are working at global level thereby enhancing the card value and making it acceptable globally.

There are many intermediaries operating card payment settlements in India.

At international level, there are many financial companies who act as facilitators for electronic fund transfer. Two major settlement agencies for plastic cards are: MasterCard Inc. (since 1966) and Visa Inc. (since 1976) who are the biggest and worldwide organizations who provide settlement services for card use. Both these organizations were started by international banks to create a reliable system of acceptance of cards and to facilitate payment system. Under this, the parties to transactions in plastic cards are linked to these organizations, which facilitate payment and settlement between the participants (acquirers and card issuers).

Most of the banks are issuing debit and credit card have tie-up with either of these two settlement agencies and their card carries the logo of these organizations. These two bands have become the most valuable and widely accepted brands which are favored by both banks and merchant establishments (POS).

Besides these two organizations, there are two more international brands of cards, namely the American Express Cards and the Diners Club International Cards.

Under The Payment and Settlement Systems Act, 2007 enacted by Government of India, RBI is the controlling authority to oversee all the payment systems in the country. Hence, the settlement agencies for card payments also will require to be registered and approved by RBI.

In card payment segment, RBI has authorised at present following organisations to act as payment settlement agencies:

1. American Express Banking Corp., USA
2. Diners Club International Ltd., USA
3. MasterCard Asia/Pacific Pte. Ltd., Singapore
4. Visa Worldwide Pte. Limited, Singapore
5. National Payments Corporation of India (for RuPay cards).

The first four are the international agencies and the last one is the company promoted by RBI and few other Indian banks.

NPCI launched a domestic card scheme with the brand name of RuPay in March 2012. The system allows all Indian banks and other domestic entities to participate in it. NPCI is the settlement agency for this card.

Debit cards and credit cards are used in both ATMs and also at POS. The usage of debit and credit cards both at ATMs and POS are growing at fast pace since last ten years. In the year 2012, the prepaid cards have also become popular.

1.8 What is SMS Banking

SMS banking and mobile banking are the latest delivery channels developed for bank services. Telecommunication technology has made mobiles a very commonly used communication mode and it is said that by the year 2008 there were about 261 million mobiles and the market was growing by eight million every month. As the costs have come down, mobile has permeated all sections of society and has become a powerful communication mode. It is quite but natural that this medium of communication is used in banking to extend banking services to its customers.

SMS messaging has been gradually put to use by banks and in the first instance it was used to send useful messages to the customers. Slowly, banks started developing SMS banking as a delivery channel for banking services. This has necessitated the tie up with SMS service providers.

SMS banking services can be availed from the bank through any ordinary mobile connection of the customer.

SMS banking has become an accepted mode of communication between the banks and its customers. When SMS messages are sent by the bank to customers, it is called as push messages. These messages are customer, specific communication with the customer on one-to-one basis and providing information related to his accounts. At present the following types of messages are sent by banks to its customers to their mobile as SMS, who are registered with them for SMS banking;

Typical push services include:

- Periodic account balance reporting.
- Reporting of credits to the bank account from all sources.
- Reports on standing instructions of the customer.

- Successful payment of a cheque issued on the account.
- Withdrawals on the ATM or POS on a debit card.
- Large value payment on a credit card or out of country activity on a credit card.
- One-time password is communicated on mobile for using it for authentication of e-payments and Internet banking.
- Information on issue of new cheque book in the account.

Banks have generally started reporting on all credits and debits to the account over a cut of limit of few thousands.

Besides these communication banks also communicate for the following:

- Reminder for due date of term deposit of the customer.
- Reminder for loan instalments.
- Status of expiry dates for credit limits.
- Any changes in the availability bank's services—temporary or otherwise.
- Business promotion information on products and services.

These are all customer, specific information sent to the customer in SMS banking which keeps the customer acquainted with the status of his account on real time basis without having to resort to any other mode to find out the status of the account. In terms of usefulness, these services are invaluable for the customer.

In SMS banking, customers of a bank can avail some specific services by sending messages to the bank. The SMS messages sent by customer are called as the pull messages. Some examples of such messages are as under:

- Account balance enquiry.
- Request for Mini statement.
- Stop payment instruction on a cheque.
- For blocking the debit card or credit card.
- Enquiry for bank interest rates.

- Enquiry for foreign exchange rates.
- Request for issue of cheque book.

1.9 What is Mobile Banking

Mobile banking is an alternate channel for making financial transactions through the mobile. For availing the financial services under mobile banking, generally the customer needs a smart phone or a data plan activated mobile connection to access mobile banking services.

Most important services now available in mobile banking are as under:

- Utility bill payments.
- Mobile/DTH Top up.
- Fund transfer between customer's own accounts.
- Fund transfer to others in the same bank.
- Fund transfer to beneficiaries with other banks.

These services provided by mobile banking make it as an alternate channel for availing banking services for small payments. Customer can make utility bills payments, recharge of prepaid services like mobile and DTH services ('Direct to Home' service providers like the satellite channels on televisions) through the mobile. He can also transfer funds between his accounts or make third party transfers both within the bank and to other banks.

For transfer of funds to third parties in other banks, RBI has prescribed monetary limit of ₹ 50000 per day per account when messages are sent encrypted. Thus, mobile banking channel is meant for small payments.

Fund transfer to beneficiaries with other bank is provided earlier through NEFT arrangement managed by RBI.

IMPS. Now a new product known as Immediate Payment Service (IMPS) is created as an alternate to RBI, managed payment system, for use in mobile banking. National Payments Corporation of India (NPCI) has launched IMPS scheme in November 2010 and took over the settlements of mobile banking payments.

IMPS has added advantages over the system of RBI-operated NEFT. Fund transfer under NEFT is in batch mode and done on bank working days only. Under IMPS scheme the services are available on 24×7 basis throughout the year. This was facilitated by the National Financial Switch (NFS) managed by NPCI (NFS is already providing platform for sharing of ATMs of the banks). Funds are credited to beneficiaries on real time basis thus making it a very attractive remittance service. Banks authorized by RBI for mobile banking services can join the scheme of NPCI for IMPS and offer the service to its customers. IMPS handles both inter bank and intra-bank transactions.

Under IMPS scheme, customer has to register himself with his bank for mobile banking and get Mobile Money Identifier (MMID) number issued to him. It is a seven-digit random number issued by the bank and it acts as the identifying code of the customer. Similarly, the beneficiary should also register himself with his bank and collect his MMID number.

For effecting the payment, customer will also require a MPIN to be issued by the bank. MPIN is the authorization code for the transaction. Customer shall maintain the secrecy of it to avoid any misuse or fraud. For transferring funds to other bank, account number and IFSC code as required under NEFT and RTGS is not required under this scheme. MMID of the beneficiary with his mobile number acts as the identification of the beneficiary.

Customer can send SMS message to his bank as prescribed giving the details like beneficiary mobile number, beneficiary MMID, amount and his (customer's) MPIN. Money will be transferred immediately facilitated by NFS.

1.10 What is Internet Banking

Internet banking or web banking is perhaps the most powerful and all-inclusive delivery channel for banking services. The use of Internet and website for delivering banking services is started in the year 1995 in the world at United States. Wells Fargo is said to be the first bank to offer this service.

ICICI Bank was the first bank in India to introduce Internet banking services followed by HDFC Bank and others. Internet banking in India has picked up only after the year 2000 as the banks started migrating to core banking system.

Today Internet banking is one delivery channel that can perform all banking functions online. Internet banking is available round the clock with no holiday. The features of internet banking fall broadly into two categories:

Non-financial Confidential Transactions

A bank customer can perform non-transactional tasks through online banking, including:

- Viewing account for transactions and balances in the accounts.
- Downloading bank statements.
- Viewing details about the credits and debits in the accounts.
- Ordering cheque books.
- Browsing information on the bank and its products and services. (Which also gives the information on service charges and interest rates, exchange rates).
- Registering complaints for redressal.
- Submitting application for credit and debit cards.
- Submitting application for loans under different schemes of the bank.
- Banks also now provide information on tax deducted and paid to government with the linkage to the tax department website.
- Downloading applications for M-banking, E-banking, etc.
- Registering standing instructions for periodical payments.

Financial transactions handled through Internet banking are as under:

- Funds transfers between the customer's linked accounts.
- Transfer to term deposit account.
- Paying third parties within the bank.

- Third party payments to other bank through NEFT and RTGS.
- Online trading in equities and other securities held in Demat account with tie-up with relevant exchanges.
- Utility bills payments to service providers.
- Loan repayment.

All the possible payments can be made by using Internet banking. Third party transfers to any bank, Payment for utility bills, payment to other service providers, trading in shares and securities all are possible through Internet banking. Internet banking mode of payment is another alternate option for the payments through credit cards and debit cards.

Payment Aggregators. Utility bill payments are made through the linkages created by the settlement providers known as the payment aggregators. They provide the linkage between the service providers and the banks to effect payments of the bills. There are many such providers like the Bill Desk, TechProcess Payment Services Limited, HDFC Bank Payment Gateway Service and PayUmoney. They provide the linkage between the utility companies and banks and act as payment aggregators for flow of funds from bank customers accounts to utility companies accounts. Generally, the utility companies provide the link in their website for online payment through one or many payment aggregators selected by it and customer can make payment of the bills. Alternatively, bank customer can go to the Internet banking site of his bank and get the linkage to utility companies for making payment.

eMarketing. eMarketing is the process of marketing a brand using the Internet. It is a new marketing strategy developed by trade and has already picked up and further expanding. Many service providers and suppliers of goods in retail segment are adopting it. They generally tie-up with banks and payment aggregators for payment through Internet banking to enable their customers to make payment through this arrangement for the goods and services sold to them. Wherever the tie-up is in place with any bank, the customers of the bank can access to the arrangement through bank's Internet site to effect the payments.

Booking of tickets for air, train and other mode of travel also falls under this category of payments.

Fund Transfer and Third Party Payments. Fund transfer between own accounts can be made by the customer using Internet banking. Payment to third parties having accounts in the same bank can also be made through Internet banking. In both the above cases the core banking system of the bank effects the transfers instantly.

Third party payments who have accounts with other banks can be made through Internet banking. In this case, the fund transfer is routed through RBI, managed NEFT or RTGS systems.

Online Trading in Equities and Securities. This facility is also available with many banks through Internet banking and the facility is offered by banks on the basis of linkage of personal account and demat account of the customer with the bank and trading account with the broker. This linkage enables online trading and simultaneous settlements in personal and demat accounts of the customer.

Banks have generally prescribed limits for amount and number of transactions per day to be allowed under Internet banking. Limits may vary with different banks and ranges from ₹ 4 lacs to ₹ 15 lacs.

Internet banking facility is allowed to individuals and also to business entities. Individual accounts are called personal accounts and business entities are called as corporate accounts under Internet banking terminology. At the request of the customer bank provides him with security passwords which enables the customer to access the web (Internet banking) site of the bank. Customer can access this site through Internet and conduct banking transactions permissible under Internet banking facility.

Though the potential of Internet banking is tremendous, it is slow in finding acceptance from the customers. The sudden boom in information technology worldwide is slowly penetrating the populace. It is observed that the acceptance of Internet banking is more in metro cities and also with the techno-savvy younger generation of customers. It is estimated (in 2010-11) that only 7% of bank customers have moved to Internet banking channel in India whereas in the developed countries it has already crossed 50% and above. Thus viewed, Internet banking in India has tremendous potential to grow.

Internet banking has many advantages for customers as well as banks. For banks it is an effective tool to cut cost on operations as it reduces the transaction cost.

Banks are taking abundant precautions while providing Internet banking facilities and customers are given passwords and codes which requires to be changed frequently at intervals to safeguard against cyber crimes.

For the trade and commerce Internet banking and electronic payments have become a necessity for growth and progress. Governments all over the world have identified this as a growth area for the economy and are supporting it by extending legal protection. Government of India enacted the Information Technology Act, 2000 (with effect from October 17, 2000) and this act provides legal recognition to electronic transactions and other means of electronic commerce.

1.11 What are Banks. What is the Legal Constitution of a Bank

Until the enactment of Banking Companies Act, 1949 (later renamed as Banking Regulation Act, 1949), banking business was conducted by anyone in the country either as a company or partnership or as proprietary firm. Most of the indigenous bankers were partnership or proprietary firms. There was no bar for anyone carrying banking business. Many of them had named themselves as banks.

The enactment of Banking Regulation Act, 1949 changed this position. Section 5 of this Act prescribed that a company registered under Companies' act engaged in banking business only can call itself a banking company. Section 49A of Banking Regulation Act was introduced by the amendment to the act in the year 1959 which said that only a banking company can issue cheques to its customers for their use. Part V (amendment in 1965) of the Banking Regulation Act state that a Co-op bank is treated as 'banking company' defined in the Act.

In view of these provisions in the Banking Regulation Act, 1949, others who were engaged in banking business earlier, lost their recognition and status as bank or banker.

Hence, now the banks in the country are companies registered under Companies Act, 1956 or Societies registered under State Co-op Societies Acts (Co-op banks) or banks created by statutes like RBI, SBI, Bharatiya Mahila Bank, etc.

1.12 Who can Start a Bank. What is the Capital Required to Start a Bank

As per the existing law only a company registered under Companies Act or a Co-op society registered under Co-op societies act of the states are eligible to start banks.

After the banking sector reforms were introduced from the year 1994, RBI is encouraging new private sector banks to be set up in the country. Few banks were opened from the year 1994 onwards. They are all companies registered under Companies Act. But by the year 2013 only seven new private sector banks remained as many new banks merged with other existing banks. RBI wanted more universal banks to be set up in private sector and in 2013, it issued comprehensive guidelines for private promoters to start new banks. Under these guidelines, RBI has framed policy for eligibility for promoters to apply for a banking licence. The eligible promoters are named as under:

(i) Entities/groups in the private sector that are 'owned and controlled by residents' and entities in public sector shall be eligible to promote a bank through a wholly-owned Non-Operative Financial Holding Company (NOFHC).

(ii) Promoters/Promoter groups with an existing non-banking financial company (NBFC) will be eligible to apply for a bank license. NBFC can promote a bank or convert itself to a bank depending on the conditions given in the RBI guidelines.

RBI has now fixed a capital requirement of ₹ 500 crores to start a universal bank. As per the Foreign Direct Investment

(FDI) Policy, foreign investment up to 49% is allowed under automatic route and up to 74% participation is allowed under the approval route.

Based on this new policy, RBI has issued two licenses in the year 2014 to start new private sector universal banks to IDFC Ltd., Mumbai and Bhandan Financial Services Ltd., Kolkata.

IDFC Ltd. is an infrastructure development company based in Mumbai and it promoted a new IDFC Bank. The bank started operations on 1 October 2015.

Bandhan Financial Services Limited (BFSL) Kolkata, the largest Micro Finance Corporation in India, started Bhandan Bank Ltd. on 23-8-2015 at Kolkata. The bank was started with 501 branches and 50 ATMs, from the day one of its operation.

Besides allowing new entrants to start new universal banks in private sector, RBI has also decided to start two new categories of banks in the private sector to cater the needs of specific segments of the society as under:

Payments Banks. According to guidelines issued by RBI for starting of payments banks, these banks can accept deposit upto ₹ one lac from a customer. They can issue prepaid cards and conduct any payment or remittance services for the customers. They can distribute insurance and mutual fund products. Minimum capital requirement to start a bank is fixed at ₹ 100 crores. FDI investment is allowed same as in the case of private sector universal banks. They can also function as business correspondent of another bank. However, these banks cannot give loans.

As per guidelines, prepaid instrument issuers, individuals and professionals, NBFCs, mobile telephone companies, super market chains, public sector entities, etc. are eligible to seek license for starting a payment bank.

Reserve Bank of India has recently issued licenses to 11 applicants to set up payments banks under the Guidelines for Licensing of Payments Banks issued on November 27, 2014.

Small Finance Banks. As per guidelines issued by RBI, these banks are allowed to undertake basic banking activities of accepting deposits and lending. They are perceived as local banks mainly to provide banking services at hitherto unbanked areas. There is no restriction for the area of their operations but they will lend to unorganised sectors to small business units, small and marginal farmers, micro and small industries, etc.

Individuals and professionals, companies and societies, NBFCs and microfinance institutions, local area banks can apply for small finance bank license. However, all the entities mentioned above shall be of residents. FDI investment is allowed same as for private sector banks. Minimum capital requirement is fixed at ₹ 100 crores.

These banks will be governed by the rules applicable to commercial banks for CRR and SLR requirements and expected to lend 75% of their ANBC (adjusted net bank credit) to priority sector and 50% of their loans shall be in small loans category of ₹ 35 lacs and less.

The Reserve Bank of India has recently issued licenses to 10 applicants to set up Small Finance Banks under the Guidelines for Licensing of small finance banks issued on November 27, 2014.

These two new categories of banks are expected to be started in the year 2016.

1.13 Why Banks were Nationalised in 1969 and 1980

In 1950s except State Bank of India and its associate banks, all other banks were in private sector. Banks have expanded their business and their resources were increasing. But the government felt that the bank lending is not supporting the development of the economy. Agriculture was the main economic activity and it was not getting banking support. Government desired to dovetail the banking resources to the national development programs. In the year 1969, government introduced social control on banks which gave some control to government on the banking activities. In the same year, government nationalised 14 major banks of the country which resulted in nearly 90% banking business coming under public sector.

In pursuance with its development agenda, government in 1970s advised banks to mandatorily lend 40% of their lendable resources to priority sector consisting of agriculture, small-scale industries and service sector. Government also directed the public sector banks to lend to Food Corporation of India for its food procurement programmes. Banks were also given targets to lend to export business. Banks were also entrusted with the responsibility social lending under various government-sponsored credit programmes for uplifting the poor. Thus, banks were made to participate in nation-building activities. Banks were also advised to expand by opening branches at all parts of the country particularly in rural and semi-urban places. In the year 1980, government nationalised six more private banks who have grown in size, to effectively retain the control of public sector on banking industry.

Banking business remained under public sector dominance and banks' lending to priority sector and export has improved the growth in these sectors. Objectives of the government in nationalising the banks were fulfilled and public sector banks have expanded their activities to most of the areas of the country.

1.14 Why Banking Sector Reforms were Introduced

In the year 1990-91, the country faced balance of payment (BOP) crisis. Its foreign exchange reserves became precariously low, barely adequate to meet few weeks' payments, and default in international payments became a distinct possibility. To avoid the crisis, GOI approached World Bank and IMF for short-term loans to tide over the crisis. Government did get assistance from them but it appears that these world organisations analysed the BOP crisis and recommended certain corrective steps to be taken by the government to improve the economy so as to avoid future debacles. The reasons for BOP crisis was analysed as due to some external factors and also some internal factors as under:

External factors:

1. Break up of Soviet Union and German reunification which affected the rupee-denominated trade with countries in the Soviet bloc.
2. Starting of gulf war between Kuwait and Iraq which stopped the oil imports from these countries. This forced

Indian Government to buy oil at high prices in the international open market.

3. Decline in trade with USA as USA was facing economic down turn during the time.

The internal reasons:

1. Political instability in the country as during the period two governments led by Shri V.P. Singh and Shri Chandrashekhar fell and a third government headed by Shri P.V. Narasimha Rao came in.
2. Government policies on foreign investment, industry, trade were found to be restrictive for growth.
3. Country was witnessing high rate of inflation during the years (13.75% in 1991-92) and big a drop in GDP (growth rate was 1.3% in 1991-92) and industrial growth rate (0.6% in 1991-92) coupled with low foreign exchange reserves (₹ 2152 crores in Dec. 1990) of the country.

Shri P.V. Narasimha Rao Government with Dr. Manmohan Singh as finance minister decided to review government policies on the trade, industry and foreign investments and this resulted in reformation of the financial sector and the banking sector. The reforms proved successful and the economy recovered and became stronger.

Banking Sector Reforms—Narasimham Committee Report No. I and II

During the reform period starting from the year 1991, GOI appointed many committees to study various aspects of the economy with a purpose to bring in reforms. One of such committee is known as the Committee on the Financial System (CFS) formed in August 1991 under the chairmanship of Shri M. Narasimham. The committee submitted its report to the government identifying the areas of concern and gave recommendations to reform the financial sector. The committee report is known as Narasimham Committee Report I. Again in December 1997, a second committee was formed under the chairmanship of same Shri Narasimham to go into the progress of reform process undertaken in banking sector and make further recommendations. This committee is known as the Committee on Banking Sector Reforms. It submitted its report and this report came to be known as Narasimham Committee Report II.

Narasimham Committee Report I—1991

Narasimham Committee Report I made many important recommendations for improving the financial sector of the country and aligning it with the global standard. The subsequent changes effected in the financial and banking sector of the country are mainly based on this report.

Based on the recommendations of the committee, many changes were made in the financial sector of the country. The important changes introduced are as under:

- The Securities & Exchange Board of India (SEBI) which was set up in 1988 was given statutory recognition in 1992, and was made the controller of capital markets.
- In the year 1993, "the Issue of Foreign Currency Convertible Bonds and Ordinary Shares (through Depository Receipts Mechanism) Scheme, 1993" was started and the Indian companies are permitted to approach international capital market and issue Global Depository Receipts (GDR) and American Depository Receipts (ADR) to raise capital.

Particularly in reference to banking sector in the country, the Narasimham Committee identified the problem areas that are to be remedied as under:

1. RBI as the central bank has authority to fix the cash reserve ratio and statutory liquidity ratio for the banks. These are reserves meant to maintain liquidity with banks. These reserves preclude the banks from earning higher income on them as they are locked in low yielding securities or held as cash and RBI balance. Over the period RBI was using the ratios as a monetary tool to control money supply in the economy and to restrict credit expansion. Just before the crisis, it was observed that SLR was 38.5% and CRR has gone upto 15%. This seriously affected the banks as 53.5% of their resources are

blocked thus restricting their lending activities and also affected their profitability.

2. Committee also observed that government over a period has committed the banks to directed lending at concessional rates to the priority sectors, exports, etc., besides the food credit to FCI. Priority sector lending is prescribed at 40% and export finance target is 12%. These directed credit to the sectors identified by the government are crippling the banks as they are left with less resources to lend to other sectors besides the low yield and high default rate in the directed lending.

3. Banking sector in the country has given rise to large number of small banks. Even there are over 27 public sector banks and excepting SBI all others are comparatively small when compared globally. Indian banks have not become global banks and remained as small banks. It only created more competition within the country. All the commercial banks are competing in all areas amongst themselves without being able to grow larger. It is observed that banking industry has become a closed system and no new banks are coming up. RBI is involved in branch licensing for the banks. Foreign banks are not encouraged to open branches in the country. Government stand on further nationalisation of banks is not known as there is always the fear of nationalisation of banks. There is no effective competition between public sector and private sector banks.

4. Committee observed that the interest rate structure in the economy is controlled by RBI which decided the interest rates both for deposits and advances. There is no variance in interest rates across banks. Interest rate are not market driven and does not reflect the demand and supply position.

5. Committee has identified that banks are burdened with bad loans and the recovery position is weak in the country. Legal system is very slow to respond to banks recovery drives and virtually is not helping banks to recover and recycle the funds.

6. The committee observed that the public sector banks are under dual control of RBI as the monetary authority and central bank, and GOI as the owner. This is reducing the effectiveness of the bank managements.

7. The committee also found that public sector banks are suffering from lack of authority to respond to market condition due to government control on them. It is affecting their efficiency and capability to compete in the market.

The committee made many recommendations to correct the situation and to make the banks vibrant to face the market conditions. Some of main recommendations are:

1. Committee recommended that the SLR and CRR shall be brought down to realistic level of 25% (SLR) and 5% (CRR) and banks should not be burdened with excessive liquidity requirements.

2. Committee recommended phasing out of directed credit programmes of the government and banks shall be freed from obligation of lending on compulsory basis.

3. Committee recommended that the interest rates shall be freed from the administration by RBI and it should be allowed to be determined by market forces. The committee recommended phasing out the concessional interest rates for the priority sector advances.

4. Committee recommended structural reorganisation of public sector banks by merging and only three to four banks including SBI shall be created to become international banks. Other banks shall function as national banks and some as regional banks. RRBs shall focus on rural and agriculture financing. They recommended that the government should assure that henceforth there will not be any nationalization and private and foreign banks should be allowed liberal entry in India.

5. The committee recommended the establishment of an Asset Reconstruction Fund (ARF). This fund will take over the proportion of the bad and doubtful debts from the banks and financial institutes. It would help banks to get rid of bad debts.

6. Establishment of special tribunal: The committee recommended establishment of special tribunals for speedier recovery of banks/FIs loans as the proportion of bad debts and non-performing asset (NPA) of the public sector banks and Development Financial Institutes was very alarming.

7. Banking autonomy: The committee recommended that the public sector banks should be made free and autonomous. In order to pursue competitiveness and efficiency, banks must enjoy autonomy so that they can reform the work culture and banking technology upgradation will thus be easy.

8. Removal of dual control: Banks are under the dual control of the Reserve Bank of India (RBI) and the Banking Division of the Ministry of Finance (Government of India). The committee recommended that the RBI should be the only main agency to regulate banking in India.

Many of the recommendations of the committee were implemented immediately to reform the banking sector by the government and RBI. Committee recommendations on CRR and SLR, removing RBI control on interest rates, allowing new banks and foreign banks to expand were taken up immediately and implemented.

The major changes made in banking sector was in opening of the sector and allowing new private sector banks. Interest rates were freed and CRR and SLR ratios were reduced. Besides these changes, RBI and government also took the initiatives to implement the global standards prescribed for banks by the international authorities. These are the prudential norms for banking, capital requirement for banks and also the KYC standards and anti-money laundering measures which were not implemented by our country till then. RBI and government also took measures to push the technology upgradation in banking operations.

With all these changes, the banking sector in the country was strengthened and the results were clearly seen in the next 5-7 years. By the years 1997-98 there was sea change in banking scene for good.

Narasimham Committee Report II

In 1997, the government appointed another committee under the chairmanship of same Mr. Narasimham. It is also known as the Banking Sector Committee. It was told to review the progress of banking reforms and design a programme for further strengthening the financial system of India. The committee focused on various areas such as capital adequacy, bank mergers, bank legislation, etc. The committee submitted its report in 1998, called as the Narasimham Committee Report II.

The report was submitted to the government in April 1998 with the following major recommendations:

- Strengthening Banks in India. The committee considered the stronger banking system in the context of the Current Account Convertibility (CAC). It thought that Indian banks must be capable of handling problems regarding domestic liquidity and exchange rate management in the light of CAC. Thus, it recommended the merger of strong banks which will have 'multiplier effect' on the industry.
- Narrow Banking: Those banks which have become weak due to high level of non-performing assets (NPAs) may be rehabilitated and such banks may be asked to do 'Narrow Banking' where they will be allowed to place their funds only in short-term and risk free assets.
- Setting up of Assets Reconstruction Company (ARC) which can take over NPAs of the banks thus enabling the banks to clean their balance sheets.
- Interest subsidy: The interest subsidy element in credit for the priority sector should be totally eliminated and interest rate on loans under ₹ 2 lakh should be deregulated for scheduled commercial banks.
- Capital Adequacy Ratio: In order to improve the inherent strength of the Indian banking system, the committee recommended that the government should raise the prescribed capital adequacy norms. Committee recommended the minimum capital to risk assets ratio be increased to 10% from its present level of 8%.
- Asset quality of banks: Committee made many recommendations for improving asset quality of banks and by and large they were also part of asset liability management guidelines issued to banks. The committee recommended that the objective should be to reduce the average level of net NPAs for all banks to below

5% by the year 2000 and to 3% by 2002. Committee recommended requirement of a general provision on standard assets. In the committee's view, a general provision, say, of 1% would be appropriate and that RBI should consider its introduction in a phased manner.

- The risk weight for a government guaranteed advance should be the same as for other advances.
- Public sector banks and financial institutions have to introduce a system of recruiting skilled manpower from the open market.
- Bank ownership: As it had earlier mentioned the freedom for banks in its working and bank autonomy, it felt that the government control over the banks in the form of management and ownership and bank autonomy does not go hand in hand and thus it recommended a review of functions of Boards and enable them to adopt professional corporate strategy.
- The minimum shareholding by government/RBI in the equity of nationalized banks and SBI should be brought down to 33%.
- There should be no recourse to any scheme of debt waiver in view of its serious and deleterious impact on the culture of credit.
- Co-operative banks: The present duality of control over the co-operative credit institutions by State Government and RBI/NABARD should be eliminated and all the co-operative banking institutions should come under the discipline of Banking Regulation Act.
- Review of banking laws: The committee considered that there is an urgent need for reviewing and amending main laws governing Indian Banking Industry like RBI Act, Banking Regulation Act, State Bank of India Act, Bank Nationalization Act, etc. to bring them in line with the present needs of the banking sector in India.
- Entry of foreign banks: The committee suggested that the foreign banks seeking to set up business in India should have a minimum start-up capital of $25 million

as against the existing requirement of $10 million. It said that foreign banks can be allowed to set up subsidiaries and joint ventures that should be treated on a par with private banks.

Apart from these major recommendations, the committee has also recommended faster computerization, technology upgradation, training of staff, de-politicizing of banks, professionalism in banking, reviewing bank recruitment, etc.

Many of the recommendations were acted upon. Securitisation Act, 2002 was enacted to help banks and FIs for faster recovery of loans. Asset reconstruction companies were started to take over the impaired loan assets of the banks. Many other recommendations are also accepted and implemented over a period of time.

Narasimham Committee Reports I and II can be considered as the blue-prints based on which government and RBI undertook to transform Indian banking and bring them at par with global standards. In the process, Indian banking underwent many changes.

1.15 How Banks Maintain Liquidity

Maintaining liquidity is the most important function of the bank for its survival. Banks accept deposits from customers and the money so received bank deploys mainly in loans and to some extent as investments so that bank can earn income. Income is important as bank has to pay interest on the deposits and also meet its overheads. Banks also need to earn profits to keep them going. In all these activities, bank cannot lose sight of the fact that depositors may demand their money back anytime. Banks accept deposits in two categories: demand deposits and term deposits. Demand deposits are the savings and current accounts and in this customer is free to withdraw money as per his personal or business requirements. Term deposits are placed for fixed period and technically speaking bank has to return it on due date only. But the modern banking has evolved in such a way that it has become a practice that banks return the term deposit also before maturity if the depositor demands. Hence, the entire deposits of the bank have become demand deposits for practical purpose.

This underlines the importance for effective liquidity management. Banks know that there will be certain percentage of withdrawal on day-to-day basis. Banks may also receive fresh deposits continuously and such fresh deposits may match with the withdrawals from existing depositors. There can be seasonal demand for more money and less demand for money during off seasons.

Liquidity of the banks are crucial and the regulator (RBI) has prescribed liquidity ratios in the form of CRR and SLR to ensure that banks remain liquid. These ratios are to be maintained on ongoing basis. Though these ratios are meant to ensure liquidity for the banks, it acts as impounded money as it is not available to banks for their day-to-day use. It cannot be used even in emergencies. Hence, for all practical purposes these liquidities maintained by banks is not available to it as a running organisation. Hence, banks shall have to create their own internal liquidity system to fall back whenever there is demand for money. Loans are illiquid as it cannot be converted to cash. Investment in traded securities (in excess of SLR) can provide liquidity as it is near cash asset. Cash balance and balance with RBI (in excess of CRR) and other banks are liquid assets. Hence, banks build up some percentage of liquid assets to meet the day-to-day demands of the customers.

Banks also have borrowing route to augment their liquidity. Banks can borrow from the money market. Some borrowings are on clean basis and some are on collateral based.

Banks can also access to various refinance schemes available to it from RBI and other financial institutions. Approved but un-availed refinance can act as a reserve and liquidity buffer for the bank.

LAF and MSF Windows of RBI

RBI is the lender of last resort for banks and RBI provides liquidity support to banks under its liquidity adjustment facility (LAF) to manage liquidity on short-term basis. This was started in the year 2000. Under LAF, RBI allows banks to borrow through repo transactions. Repo is the system under which bank can borrow for short-term (overnight or for few days) from RBI by giving collateral of SLR securities held by it in excess of SLR requirement. This is a regular window that can be accessed by banks any day.

Marginal Standing Facility (MSF). From the year 2011, RBI has opened a new window: Marginal Standing Facility (MSF) for banks for borrowing from it, when the bank has exhausted all the sources for borrowing and it is an emergency situation for bank. Under the scheme, banks can borrow up to one per cent of their net demand and time liabilities (NDTL), subject to change in limit by RBI. The borrowing under the scheme is allowed for one day. This is also collaterised borrowing and bank shall give SLR securities as security. But as a special case, under emergency situation, bank can offer even the earmarked SLR securities held for the purpose of maintaining SLR. This is a special provision that helps bank in case it has no free SLR securities available with it.

Liquidity Requirement under Basel Accord

Under Basel accord prescriptions, banks are now assessing their liquidity risk in professional manner taking into account the historical trends in liquidity demands and also study the profile of banks' assets and liabilities. This is now the part of asset liability management (ALM) functions of the banks.

The study known as Structural Liquidity is made by calculating the remaining maturity period for each liability and asset. Then the assets and liabilities are segregated in different time buckets according to their expected maturities and find out the mismatches (when assets are less than the liabilities) in each time bucket and then take corrective actions. The time buckets now used are:

- Day 1,
- 2-7 days,
- 8-14 days,
- 15-28 days,

- 29 days to 3 months,
- over 3 months to 6 months,
- over 6 months to 1 year,
- over 1 year to 3 years,
- over 3 years to 5 years, and
- above 5 years.

This study reveals the liquidity position of the bank in short-term, medium-term, and long-term perspective. This liquidity assessment is a proactive measure as it enables banks to identify and to carry out fundamental corrections in their asset-liability mismatch rather than just wait and face the liquidity problem as and when it occurs.

Liquidity risk of the banks are now also a regulatory area under the Basel accord III implemented from the year 2013. Banks are now required to arrange their assets and liabilities in such a way that for the liabilities maturing on at any time period, banks shall have adequate matching maturing assets to meet those liabilities. Banks now take special care to ensure that they have no short-term liquidity mismatches (up to three months' period) which is the most critical area for banks.

1.16 What Happens if a Bank Fails

Many banks in our country have failed in the past. Even now banks are failing, though it is few and mostly from the urban co-op banks category.

When a bank fails, since it is a company, the bank will undergo liquidation process prescribed in the companies law. If the bank failed is a co-operative bank, then the law governing co-operative society in liquidation will apply.

Banks fail when they make huge loses or the money is lost due to bad loans or due to mismanagement and intentional diversion of funds. Under all these circumstances, the assets will be eroded and becomes less than the liabilities. Hence, the failed bank obviously cannot repay its depositors in full. In liquidation, the owners or shareholders are paid in the last, if anything is left after paying all other liabilities. Deposits are the liabilities of the bank and the depositors will have to wait till the liquidation process is completed and the assets are converted to cash. This is a long-drawn process of law. Then also depositors may get only a portion of their deposit back that also after a long wait.

For all practical purpose, the depositor loses their money when a bank fails.

Generally, when a bank is in difficulties and the news spreads, the bank may face a run on the bank. All the depositors may flock in to get back their money. This will force the bank to close down. Alternately, when RBI has detected the bankruptcy of a bank, it has powers to impose moratorium on the bank restricting the payments to depositors and avoid the run on the bank for the time being. Then RBI will decide the future course available mainly with a view to protect depositors' interest. RBI has powers under the law (since 1960s) to work out some bailout package. Generally, RBI was favouring takeover of the banks by bigger banks and save the liquidation. A bigger bank can assess the failed bank as a going concern and value it and also value the goodwill and infrastructure of the bank to form a decision. In such cases, generally the depositors are protected and the big bank takes over the assets and liabilities of the failed bank. RBI also has the powers to compulsorily merge the bank with another bank, if in its view it is feasible. RBI in such cases can stipulate the terms and conditions for merger. In compulsory mergers, generally public sector banks are forced to take over the failed bank. In our country since 1960s, many banks were merged with nationalised banks and some banks have been merged with private sector banks also.

Government introduced deposit insurance scheme for bank depositors in the year 1962 when it created Deposit Insurance Corporation under the aegis of RBI. Later this corporation is merged with Credit Guarantee Corporation to form Deposit Insurance and Credit Guarantee Corporation (DICGC). This insurance scheme is compulsory for banks to join and banks shall have to pay the premium which shall be borne by the banks only. The insurance coverage at present per account is

₹ one lac. This insurance cover is available per customer for all his accounts with the failed bank. Amount in excess of ₹ one lac is not insured. In today's standard this insurance cover only protects small depositors of the banks.

The banking history of the country shows that after 1960s no major commercial bank was closed. Weak and failed banks were merged with other banks and depositors were protected. But there were many failures in co-op banking sector. Even now the failure of co-op banks is a persisting feature, though such cases are very few.

DICGC has settled many cases of failed banks and paid maximum ₹ one lac per depositor. Mostly, these were the cases of co-op banks which have failed.

Government ownership of the banks gives a sense of security in case of public sector banks. However, there is no express guarantee from the government or RBI about the safety of deposits with these banks. Public sector banks are also covered by the insurance coverage to the extent of ₹ one lac per customer. But we can presume that government has the moral responsibility and that it cannot disown its own banks. Hence, public sector banks are considered as safe for depositors.

1.17 What is the Interest Rates Banks Pay on Deposits

Till the year 1996, the interest rates on deposits were prescribed by RBI and all banks were offering the same rate of interest. From the year 1997, deposit interest rates (except interest on savings banks deposits) were decontrolled and banks were allowed to fix their own rates. Savings interest was also decontrolled in October 2011. Thus, the banks are now free to determine their interest rates as per the recommendations of the Narasimham Committee and the rates are now market driven.

Bank term deposit interest rate is one of the key interest rates of the economy as it represents the rate of interest for safe investment in the economy. Some key interest rates of the economy are given in the following table:

Select Interest Rates				
Year	Interest Rates on			Bank Rate/ Repo Rate (from 2006) %
	Savings Bank %	Bank term Deposits Maximum/ range%	Central Government Securities Range%	
Mar-91		9.00-11.00	10.50-11.50	10.0
Mar-92		12.00-13.00	10.50-12.50	12.0
Mar-93		11.00-11.00	12.00-12.75	12.0
Mar-94		10.00-10.00	12.00-13.40	12.0
Mar-95		11.00-11.00	11.00-12.71	12.0
Mar-96		12.00-13.00	13.25-14.00	12.0
Mar-97		11.00-13.00	13.40-13.85	12.0
Mar-98		10.50-12.00	10.85-13.05	10.5
Mar-99		9.00-11.50	11.10-12.60	8.0
Mar-00		8.50-10.50	10.73-12.45	8.0
Mar-01		8.50-10.00	9.47-11.70	7.0
Mar-02	4	7.50-8.50	6.98-11.00	6.5
Mar-03	3.5	4.30-6.30	6.57-8.62	6.25
Mar-04	3.5	4.00-5.50	4.62-6.35	6
Mar-05	3.5	5.30-6.30	4.49-8.24	6
Mar-06	3.5	6.00-7.00	6.70-7.79	6.50
Mar-07	3.5	7.50-9.00	7.69-8.75	7.75
Mar-08	3.5	7.50-9.00	7.55-8.64	6.0
Mar-09	3.5	7.80-8.80	5.44-10.03	5.0
Mar-10	3.5	6.00-7.50	6.09-8.43	5.0
Mar-11	3.5	8.25-9.00	5.98-8.67	6.75
Mar-12	4	8.50-9.25	7.80-10.01	8.5
Mar-13	4	8.50-9.00	7.86-8.82	7.5
Mar-14	4	8.50-9.25	7.16-9.40	8.0
Mar-15	4	8.25-8.75	7.65-9.42	7.5

Source: RBI.

The interest offered by banks on term deposits varies from bank to bank as it is now fixed by the individual banks. However, the range of difference is small. Savings bank interest has been decontrolled from the year 2011 but all banks are continuing with the RBI prescribed rate in 2011 (4%) without change. Only one private sector bank (Yes Bank) has offered 6%

interest rate on savings bank. One public sector bank (Bharatiya Mahila Bank) is now offering 4.5% and 5% (over ₹ one lac) for savings bank accounts.

The above table also gives the interest rates on Central Government securities and bank rate/repo rate of RBI. We may observe that these rates are very close to bank deposit rates. Government securities are also secured investments and their interest rates tend to be close to bank deposit rate. Bank rate or repo rate is the rate at which RBI lends to banks and hence it acts as a reference rate for banks to decide on their deposit interest rates.

Though the interest rates on deposits are market driven, the economic principles for determining the interest rates on deposits or investments is that it shall be linked to the inflation rate of the economy. This is because the incentive to save for individuals is dependent on the 'real return on investment' (adjusted to inflation) and hence the interest rate shall be more than the corresponding inflation rate.

1.18 How Banks Treat their Customers

What are Customer-friendly Measures of the Banks

Banks are service organisations and they are economic backbone of the society. As service organisations, banks are expected to be customer friendly and transparent in their dealings with customers. Banks are not expected to exploit the weak status of the customer as compared to its own high and important status. These thinking are based on the principle that customers are very important for the banks as banks depend for its survival on the goodwill of the customers.

In the modern society, customer care is an important area developed as a progressive measure to create an atmosphere of mutual trust and care. The onus is more on the banks to take initiatives to reach out to the customers and be responsive to their problems or issues.

RBI has been active in promoting many customer-centric systems to help bank customers.

Creating Awareness

One important aspect of banker-customer relationship is creating awareness about the relationships and informing the customer about the norms for delivery of banking services. Awareness for customer means he should know the type of services available, the norms and standards for such services and his rights as a customer while dealing with a bank. He should know what he can expect from the bank in terms value return and in terms of time required for delivery of service.

This requires customer education on many aspects of banking services particularly in relation to the service charges payable by the customer and also the time norms for delivery of services.

Banks are now displaying in the bank premises the Time norms for different services at the counters of banks to make the customer aware and the staff accountable to attend. Service charges for different types of services are now standardized and displayed at the branches for the information of customers. Banks are now required to be prompt in delivering the services and be transparent in their charges and no hidden charges are to be levied. All this information is also to be provided in the websites of the banks.

Banks were advised in 1997 to bring out 'citizen charter' defining the rights of the customer and duties of the bank and make it available to customers. Most of the banks created and issued this document around the year 1997. In the year 2000, Indian Bankers' Association (IBA) reviewed the charters of different banks and brought out a uniform 'Model Citizen Charter' explaining to the customers what they could expect from the banks as a matter of right. Banks are now periodically updating this document and making it available to customers and public.

IBA brought out its "Bankers' Fair Practice code" in July 2004 and all member banks have adopted it voluntarily. IBA also came out separately with "Fair Practice Code for Credit Card Operations" and "Model Code for Collection of Dues and

Repossession of Security" to address specific concerns voiced by customers about banking practices in these areas. These also have been implemented by member banks.

Subsequently, Banking Codes and Standards Board of India (BCSBI) was formed in the year 2005, as a voluntary organization.

Banking Code and Standards Board of India (BCSBI)

BCSBI is an autonomous body created for setting up and promote code and standards for banks so that the customers of the banks get fair treatment in their dealings with the banks. It is for overseeing and prescribing customer protective measures. BCSBI is registered as a society under the Societies Registration Act, 1860 in February 2006. The membership of the society is voluntary and open for commercial banks, regional rural banks and selective urban co-op banks. The members by joining BCSBI bind themselves to the discipline of banking code and standards prescribed as a proactive and progressive measure to give fair treatment to their customers.

The main objectives of the BCSBI are:

- To plan, evolve, prepare, develop, promote and publish comprehensive codes and standards for banks, for providing for fair treatment to their customers.
- To function as an independent and autonomous body to monitor, and to ensure that the codes and standards adopted by banks are adhered to, in letter and spirit, while delivering services to their customers.

Two codes: 'Code of Bank's Commitment to Customers' and the 'Code of Bank's Commitment to Micro and Small Enterprises' have been developed by BCSBI in collaboration with the Indian Banks' Association (IBA) so far. These codes set the minimum standards of banking practices for member banks to follow when they are dealing with individual customers and micro and small enterprises. These codes are also subject to periodical review and revision. BCSBI is continuously monitoring the implementation of these codes by banks with an objective of promoting cordial banker-customer relationship.

The codes lay great emphasis on transparency and providing full information to the customer before a product or service is sold to him. They are the commitments of banks to their customers and can be considered as a 'Charter of Rights' for the customer. These codes set the minimum standards of customer service and aims to make the customer aware of what he can expect from the bank in his dealings with the bank.

The Board also has the powers to impose sanctions on the defaulting bank for breaches of the code and standards. These sanctions may be

- publication of banks name in the annual report of BCSBI,
- issue directions to the bank for future conduct,
- issue warning and reprimand,
- cancellation or suspension of membership,
- public censure by notifying the media.

When a sanction is imposed on any member, the BCSBI shall inform the Reserve Bank of India the details of the breach and the sanctions imposed. Thus, the prospect of sanction by BCSBI will put the bank on guard to mend its ways and comply with the codes and standards.

Reserve Bank is also keen to ensure that the bank customers are fairly treated by banks. As per RBI advise, banks shall make the customers aware of products and services. Banks shall observe time norms for services and stick to it. Banks shall be transparent in levying service charges and there shall not be any hidden charges. The rate of interest should be clearly informed and banks shall not mislead customers on yield based on compounding of interest.

Banks are to have time norms for disposal of loan applications and dispose them as per norms. Banks shall also provide copies of loan agreements to the borrowers for their reference. RBI frowns upon teaser rates on advances where the customers are told that the loans will be cheaper (but only for a short period) thereby misleading the customer.

1.19 What is the Redressal of Grievances Mechanism in Banks

For a service organisation like bank an effective and quick redressal of grievances mechanism is very important to ensure that customers get justice quickly for any faults or wrongful deeds of the bank. It reassures the customer about the commitment and the fair dealing of the bank.

Redressal of grievances has two components. One is the internal system of the bank wherein the customer can approach some authority in the bank itself for redressal. The other system is by making complaints to an outside authority for redressal.

Internal Systems of Banks. All banks have internal complaint redressal system in place and a senior officer of the bank at head office is nominated as designated officer for looking into the complaints. His name and address is displayed at all branches for the notice of customers. Customer can make the complaint to the branch. Customer can also send his complaint directly to the regional/divisional manager or the designated senior officer of the bank at head office. Now complaints can be lodged on-line also.

Branch manager is the first authority to look into the complaint and redress it. The complaints are recorded and the controlling offices like the regional/divisional offices of the bank and also the head office monitor the progress of the complaints to ensure that they are redressed speedily in a time-bound manner.

Banks are advised by BCSBI to have a compensation policy in place under which banks shall acknowledge liability and compensate for certain deficiencies identified while extending the services to customers. Under this policy, even cases of wrongful debits to customers' accounts shall be dealt with and they are compensated at the earliest.

Internal Ombudsman Scheme

Some banks have started internal ombudsman scheme since the year 2012 and have appointed internal ombudsman (an outsider) to study the customer complaints and decide on the matter. This was started with a view to provide redressal system within the bank so that the complaints to banking ombudsman appointed by RBI is contained to the minimum.

In May 2015, Reserve Bank of India has advised all public sector banks and some private sector and foreign banks to appoint an internal ombudsman. The internal ombudsman is to be designated as Chief Customer Service Officer (CCSO). The CCSO shall be an outsider and who has not worked in the same bank. The concerned banks are now in the process of appointing such internal ombudsman. It is expected that the internal ombudsman will act similar to banking ombudsman and can make awards upto a limit lesser than the financial limit of the banking ombudsman. This is another step taken by RBI for resolution of customer complaints in banks and to reduce the number of cases coming to banking ombudsman.

External Systems

RBI has taken many measures to ensure that customer is heard and his grievances are redressed.

Banking Ombudsman Scheme

The Banking Ombudsman Scheme is introduced under Section 35A of the Banking Regulation Act, 1949 by RBI with effect from 1995. Banking Ombudsman is a senior official of RBI appointed by the Reserve Bank of India.

Under Ombudsman Scheme complaints can be referred to Banking Ombudsman (BO) for deficiencies in service by banks and BO shall decide the matter. The purpose is to provide customers an inexpensive forum for resolution of complaints relating to certain services rendered by banks. RBI has appointed fifteen Banking Ombudsmen with their offices located mostly in state capitals. At present, BO can try cases which involves compensation upto ₹ ten lacs and banks are bound by his order. Under the scheme, Deputy Governor of RBI is the appellate authority. The Banking Ombudsman Scheme was revised during the years 2002 and 2006. The Banking Ombudsman Scheme (BOS) 2006 covers all commercial banks, regional rural banks and scheduled primary co-operative banks under its scope.

The customers can complaint to the Banking Ombudsman against deficiency in almost any banking services, including credit cards, after exhausting the channel available with the bank concerned for resolving their complaints. Customer can also lodge a complaint for deficiencies in Internet banking and also for non-adherence by the bank to the BCSBI codes and standards for customer service. The Banking Ombudsman tries to resolve the complaint through conciliation or mediation and if it does not work out then pass an award which is binding on both parties.

The parties can prefer appeal against the award of the Banking Ombudsman to the Deputy Governor RBI. Earlier the appeal was allowed only against the award of the Ombudsman and in case the complaint is rejected by the Ombudsman appeal was not available. Now the scheme allows the customer to file appeal in cases where the complaints are rejected by Banking Ombudsman.

Consumer Forums

GOI enacted Consumer Protection Act in the year 1986 and bank customers are covered under the act. Banking services have been brought under the purview of consumer protection act as customers avail banking services and pay for it. Customer can approach consumer forums for redressal of any breach or deficiency in service. Banks will have to defend themselves before the consumer forums.

Consumer forums are quasi-judicial bodies set-up in each districts, states and an apex body at national level to provide inexpensive, speedy and summary redressal of consumer disputes. At districts they are known as District Forums, at state level it is known as State Consumer Disputes Redressal Commissions and at national level it is known as the National Consumer Disputes Redressal Commission (NCDRC) at New Delhi.

A written complaint can be filed before the District Consumer Forum for pecuniary value of upto ₹ 20 lakh, State Commission for value upto ₹ 1 crore and the National Commission for value above ₹ 1 crore (as per the jurisdictions of these forums), in respect of defects in goods and or deficiency in service. However, no complaint can be filed for alleged deficiency in any service that is rendered free of charge or under a contract of personal service.

Appeals can be filed with State Commissions against the decisions of District Forums and appeal against State Commissions' decisions can be filed with National Commission.

At present, there are 629 District Forums and 35 State Commissions with the National Consumer Disputes Redressal Commission (NCDRC) at the apex.

Other Options for Customers

Public sector banks are accountable under the Right to Information Act (RTI Act), 2005 and any citizen can file application under the act for information. Bank is bound to provide the information sought as per the provisions of RTI act. An application under RTI Act may sometime provide redressal for some type of grievances. Strictly speaking, RTI Act is not a complaint redressal system but entitles citizens to get information from the governments and public sector.

Customers of public sector banks can also file their complaints under the Public Grievance Redressal System of Government of India. The Department of Administrative Reforms and Public Grievances, GOI, is the nodal agency to receive the complaints. The Director, Public Grievance will forward the complaint to the Ministry or the government office concerned for redressal and will monitor the action taken on it. Now the complaints can be lodged online also.

1.20 What is Financial Inclusion

Financial inclusion or inclusive financing is defined as the delivery of financial services at affordable costs to sections of disadvantaged and low-income segments of society.

After nationalisation of banks, the number of branches of the banks have increased tremendously. Further government has also involved banks in rural lending. Banks were encouraged to open more branches in rural and semi-urban areas. While there is good progress in all these measures still it is realised that a big portion of rural population and also a big portion of poor people in urban areas have remained out of banking reach due to various reasons. According to a RBI study about 40% of the population still do not have bank accounts. Another study estimated that of the 24.67 crore households in the country, 10.19 crore do not have access to banking services. In rural areas, 44% households and in urban areas 33% still do not have a bank account.

Government and RBI have identified the task of bringing everyone in the country into banking fold as an important task to eradicate poverty and improve the lives of the poor. When a poor man remains outside the banking system, he cannot get the benefits of modernisation and share the progress.

The important reasons for financial inclusion have been identified as under:

- To inculcate the poor to the banking habits and bring him into the economic mainstream. He is to be encouraged to save whatever he can for his future.
- With a bank account in place he can be linked to the credit programs available to poor for any economic activity that he may engage in and derive benefit.
- Government subsidy and other assistances can directly reach him through the bank account avoiding intermediary agencies or persons.

Thus, financial inclusion of everyone in the country has now thought as the most important task to reach the poor and bring them into the economic mainstream.

RBI has taken many proactive steps in this direction. When KYC norms were introduced for the banking, RBI made special provision for opening accounts for the poor with simple rules bypassing the strict requirements under KYC regime. Simplified KYC procedures have been given to banks. Banks were also asked to have a new category of savings accounts known as 'no-frills account' for this purpose. This account is designed to give only basic banking services free of cost without insisting for any minimum balance. The purpose is to allow the poor to have bank accounts without any cost and condition.

Opening of branches by commercial banks in all the villages of the country is still not feasible as it is unviable. In view of this, RBI introduced a scheme in the year 2006 for banks to appoint business correspondents who can conduct transactions with the villagers on behalf of banks. Banks are already allowed to have satellite offices (that work only few days in a week) and mobile banking units (bank on the wheels) to establish contacts with villages having no bank branches.

Another step taken for financial inclusion is introducing the bank linkage of self-help groups (SHGs) in the year 1991 and formalising the credit delivery to poor through this mechanism. Under this linkage programme, the NGOs and micro-finance companies are now involved to identify and help in forming self-help groups in villages. Micro-finance companies are also provided with bank finance to on lend to SHGs.

In the year 2014, government announced a massive programme for financial inclusion in the name of Pradhan Mantri Jan Dhan Yojana (PMJDY) to open bank accounts of people who have no bank accounts. The scheme was launched by the Prime Minister. This scheme has the attraction of insurance benefits and overdraft facility from banks. Public sector banks have made good efforts in opening new accounts. It is reported that 19.02 crore bank accounts were opened by 28 October 2015 and around ₹ 25913.56 crores were deposited in these accounts. It is a highly successful scheme for achieving maximum financial inclusion in a very short time.

Government's target is 100% financial inclusion of all the households in the country and RBI and banks are supporting it. It is a very challenging target to achieve given the diversity of population and also the geographical challenges in reaching everyone in all corners of our vast county.

1.21 What is No-Frills Account (now BSBDA-Small Account)

In 2006, RBI issued guidelines for banks to have a special category of savings bank accounts and named it as 'no-frills accounts' or 'basic banking account'. This is meant to help poor people who have no identity papers. The purpose is to enable financial inclusion of the poor and link them to some government-sponsored credit programs. Since bank account is necessary for them to collect government aid, RBI permitted banks to open accounts as 'no-frill accounts' with or without introduction and without insisting for documents or proofs for identification. Banks were advised that they need not extend all the facilities to them except for few basic facilities to enable them deposit and withdraw money from the accounts. It was also stipulated that total credits of ₹ one lac per year can be allowed excluding government aids and the balance in the account can be up to ₹ 50,000 at any time. Accounts were allowed to be opened with zero balance in the beginning.

Banks were given a simplified KYC procedure under the KYC guidelines for opening 'basic banking accounts' or 'no-frills accounts'. Slowly, banks started helping these customers with free cheque books and even with free ATM cards.

In the year 2012, RBI issued fresh guidelines for these accounts and changed name to 'Basic Savings Bank Deposit Account' or 'BSBDA-Small Accounts' and advised banks to convert all the existing 'no-frills accounts' into this new category.

As per Government of India notification dated December 16, 2010, BSBDA-Small Accounts would be subject to the following conditions:

1. Total credits in such accounts should not exceed one lakh rupees in a year.
2. Maximum balance in the account should not exceed fifty thousand rupees at any time.
3. The total of debits by way of cash withdrawals and transfers will not exceed ten thousand rupees in a month.
4. Foreign remittances cannot be credited to small accounts without completing normal KYC formalities.
5. Small accounts are valid for a period of 12 months initially which may be extended by another 12 months

if the person provides proof of having applied for an Officially Valid Document.

6. Small accounts can only be opened at CBS-linked branches of banks or at such branches where it is possible to manually monitor the fulfilments of the conditions.

This scheme is also aimed at furthering financial inclusion of those who may not have officially valid documents necessary for opening bank accounts. Simplified KYC procedures for them is continued.

Banks are now required to provide free services to these account holders for deposit and withdrawal of cash receipt/ credit of money through electronic payment channels and use of ATMs for withdrawing cash.

Under the present rules, these accounts can be allowed to run for a year and can be allowed extension for one more year, if the account holder has already applied for obtaining some officially valid documents. Once a valid officially document is submitted, the account can be treated as KYC compliant account similar to other normal accounts.

1.22 What is NRI Deposit

Non-resident Accounts

In seventies, government had realised that non-resident Indians are a good source for foreign exchange as they generally remit to their families in India and also are interested to maintain their roots in the country. Then existing exchange control rules provided that NRIs can have Non-Resident Ordinary accounts (NRO) with banks which are similar to domestic accounts. However, NRIs could not take back the balance in those accounts.

Realising the importance of NRI funds, government then started to woo the non-residents to remit their savings into the country by giving tax breaks and repatriation options. Besides NRIs, Persons of Indian Origin and Overseas Corporate Bodies predominantly owned by NRIs were also allowed to open accounts under various schemes. These three categories are identified as under:

Non-resident Indian (NRI)

An Indian citizen who stays abroad for employment/ carrying on business or vocation outside India or stays abroad under circumstances indicating an intention for an uncertain duration of stay abroad is a non-resident. (Persons posted in UN organizations and officials deputed abroad by Central/State Governments and public sector undertakings on temporary assignments are also treated as non-residents.)

Person of Indian Origin (PIO)

For the purposes of availing of the facilities of opening and maintenance of bank accounts and investments in shares/securities in India: a foreign citizen (other than a citizen of Pakistan or Bangladesh) is deemed to be of Indian origin, if,

1. he, at any time, held an Indian passport, or
2. he or either of his parents or any of his grandparents was a citizen of India by virtue of the Constitution of India or Citizenship Act, 1955 (57 of 1955).

Note: A spouse (not being a citizen of Pakistan or Bangladesh) of an Indian citizen or of a PIO is also treated as a PIO for the above purposes provided the bank accounts are opened or investments in shares/securities in India are made by such persons only jointly with their NRI spouses. Non-resident foreign citizens of Indian origin are treated on par with non-resident Indian citizens (NRIs).

Overseas Corporate Body (OCB)

Overseas Corporate Body (OCB) means a company, partnership firm, society and other corporate body owned directly or indirectly to the extent of at least sixty per cent by Non-Resident Indians and includes overseas trust in which not less than sixty per cent beneficial interest is held by non-resident Indians directly or indirectly but irrevocably, which was in existence as on September 16, 2003 and was eligible to undertake transactions pursuant to the general permission granted under Foreign Exchange Management Regulations.

Types of accounts NRI/POI/OCB can open with banks

NRO Accounts. Banks can open accounts for NRI/PIO/OCB and such accounts are known as non-resident ordinary account (NRO). When a resident becomes a non-resident, his existing account is also branded as NRO account. These accounts can be savings, term deposit or recurring deposit accounts. The balance held in these accounts cannot be repatriated.

Now RBI has allowed limited repatriation of the funds held in these accounts upto one million US dollar per year. The interest earned on these deposits are also repatriable. Repatriation means the liberty to take the money out of the country by converting it to any other foreign currency without requiring permission from RBI.

Interest rates on these accounts are deregulated and banks can offer the rate similar to domestic deposits.

NRE Deposit Scheme

Non-resident external accounts (NRE) scheme was introduced in the year 1970, wherein the repatriation of the balance was guaranteed without seeking any permission from Reserve Bank of India. Non-residents were allowed to open savings, current as well as fixed deposit accounts. Interest earned was also repatriable and tax-free. However, there is exchange risk for the non-residents. Interest rates on NRE deposits were as prescribed by RBI and were almost similar to domestic deposits. Hence, NRE account though carried exchange risk on repatriation, it earned higher interest than it would have at other countries.

This special status continued for many years and when domestic deposit interest rate was freed, RBI allowed the banks to decide on NRE deposit rates also. In the year 2003, RBI prescribed interest rate ceilings on NRE deposits and linked it to LIBOR/SWAP rates.

As per present directives from RBI, with effect from March 1, 2014, interest rates offered by banks on NRE deposits cannot be higher than those offered by them on comparable domestic rupee deposits.

FCNR Deposit Scheme

Reserve Bank of India came out with foreign currency non-resident deposit scheme (FCNR) in the year 1975 under which deposits of the non-residents were held in either US dollar or Pound Sterling. Now these deposits can be held in USD, GBP, EURO, CAD, JPY, or AUD. As the deposits are held in foreign currency, the exchange risk is eliminated for NRIs. These deposits are held only as term deposit accounts. Deposit can be opened either individually or jointly with other NRIs/PIOs/OCIs. Both principal and interest are payable in foreign currency.

When the scheme was started, RBI bore the exchange risk by purchasing these currencies from banks and returned it to banks on maturities at the same rate.

The interest rates for FCNR were attractive as it was better by at least 2% over what non-residents would have got in their countries. Loans were also allowed against these deposits. This scheme attracted lot of deposits and inflow of foreign exchange improved.

In the year 1993, RBI discontinued FCNR deposit scheme and in its place allowed FCNR-Bank scheme on similar line. Banks were allowed to retain FCNR-B deposits, hold foreign exchange assets and use the same as per their requirement and as per guidelines of RBI for the same. Banks were also allowed to lend foreign currency to its customers mainly exporters.

As per RBI directives, with effect from March 1, 2014 interest on these deposits are as under:

- deposits of one year to less than three-years maturity, interest shall be paid within the ceiling rate of LIBOR/SWAP rates plus 200 basis points;
- deposits of 3-5 years maturity, interest shall be paid within the ceiling rate of LIBOR/SWAP rates plus 300 basis points.

Deposits can be accepted on floating interest rate basis also and on floating rate deposits, interest shall be paid within the ceiling of SWAP rates for the respective currency/maturity plus

200 bps/300 bps as the case may be. For floating rate deposits, the interest reset period shall be six months.

There were two more deposit schemes for non-residents which were subsequently discontinued as under:

NRNR Scheme

At the height of foreign exchange crunch in the year 1991, RBI introduced another deposit scheme for non-residents called non-resident non-repatriable rupee deposit scheme (NRNR). The scheme came into effect from 15th June, 1992. Under this, banks accepted term deposits from 6 months to 3 years and the rate of interest was very attractive. Later when forex reserve position has improved substantially, RBI withdrew the scheme w.e.f. 1st April NRSR scheme 2002.

RBI introduced with effect from 15 April 1999, a new type of account, viz. Non-Resident (Special) Rupee (NRSR) Account for NRIs and PIOs who would voluntarily undertake not to seek repatriation of funds held in these accounts. This facility was not available to overseas corporate bodies.

Non-resident special rupee (NRSR) account schemes were discontinued with effect from April 1, 2002 along with NRNR scheme. Balance in these accounts were allowed to be credited to NRO account.

At present only NRO, NRE and FCNR schemes are continuing.

NRI Deposits

NRI deposits are a source of foreign exchange inflow into the country and government encourages it. During the crisis period, NRI deposits were of great help to the government. Now also NRI deposits play major role in foreign exchange position and helps the country.

The share of NRI deposits in total deposits of banks is sizeable as can be seen from the table below. In early nineties, NRI deposits were pursued to ease balance of payment shortfall and in 1993; share of NRI deposits was highest at 17.50% of total deposits of scheduled commercial banks. The share remained above 10% until the year 2004 and thereafter it came down to 5.05% in 2010. It has gone up to 8.45% in the year 2015.

₹ in crores

Year (end-March)	Total deposits of scheduled commercial banks	Total NRI deposits	% age of NRI deposits to Sch. Commercial banks deposits
1993	268572	46992	17.50
1995	386859	54066	13.98
2000	813345	94544	11.62
2005	1700198	144282	8.49
2010	4492826	227078	5.05
2013	6750454	385202	5.71
2015	8533285	720997	8.45

Source: RBI-Note: NRI deposits figures is for all banks including co-op banks whereas total deposits of scheduled commercial banks are only taken for arriving the share of NRI deposits in total deposits.

1.23 Which are the Important Laws Affecting Banking Business

The important laws affecting banking business are listed as under:

(i) **The Negotiable Instruments Act, 1881**. This act defines the negotiable instruments and gives the rules applicable for cheques, bills of exchange and promissory notes. The act was last amended in the year 2002 to enable cheque truncation.

(ii) **Bankers Book Evidence Act, 1891.** This is the act which exempts banks from having to submit their books and ledgers to legal authorities as it will cripple the operation of banks and put customers into difficulties. The act prohibits any authority including courts of law to call for the original books of the banks. It prescribes that only copies of the books and accounts certified by the banks officials shall be accepted in all litigations.

(iii) **The Reserve Bank of India Act, 1934.** This act created RBI as the central bank of the country and the functions and authority of RBI as the banking regulator. This act mentions about the obligation of RBI to be the banker for Central and

State Governments and also to manage public debt. The currency note issue and management of forex reserves are entrusted to RBI under this act. It also empowers RBI to lend to banks. The act empowers RBI to prescribe CRR and SLR for banks. Section 31 of the act says that only RBI or Central Government can issue bearer promissory notes and others are prohibited. Cheques are excluded from this prohibition. This is because the currency notes issued by RBI are the bearer promissory notes and there can be no other bearer promissory notes issued by anyone competing with it.

(iv) **The Banking Regulation Act, 1949.** This act was first enacted as the Banking Companies Act, 1949 and later renamed in 1966 as the Banking Regulation Act, 1949. This act defines banking companies and banking activities and regulates their activities. It authorises RBI to issue regulation over shareholding and voting rights of shareholders; to supervise the appointment of the boards and management of banking companies. RBI is given power to issue licenses to banks for starting operations. The act authorises RBI to exercise control on banks in their various areas of operation. The amendment to the act in 1965 made the act applicable to co-op banks. The act lay down instructions for audits; moratorium, mergers and liquidation of banks; and empowers RBI to issue directives in the interests of public good. RBI is also given the power to impose penalties on banks for breaches.

(v) **The Limitation Act, 1963.** Limitation Act is an important act which lays down the rules for the time limits within which civil and money suits shall be filed in the court of law for enforcing the right or/and recovering money.

The preamble of the act says: "An Act to consolidate and amend the law for the limitation of suits and other proceedings and for purposes connected therewith".

This is an important law affecting banks as the bank suits are money suits for the recovery of loans from the borrowers when borrowers fail to pay in time. The Limitation Act specifies the time period within which banks or any others can file suits in the court for recovery. In case the suit is not filed within the limitation period for the suit, the dues will become time-barred and legal recourse for recovery will be lost.

In most of the cases, the limitation period is three years, with few exceptions. For loans secured by mortgages the limitation period is 12 years. Section 18 of the act says that the acknowledgement in writing of the dues by the borrower/ parties will extend the limitation period.

Banks need to keep in mind the rules while obtaining security documents from the borrowers and also keep track of limitation period for each type of loan documents to ensure that they have legal recourse available to them.

(vi) **Unlawful Activities (Prevention) Act, 1967 (UAPA).** Its main objective is to empower Government of India to deal with activities directed against the integrity and sovereignty of the country more particularly in relation to terrorist activities. This act was amended in 2008 and a new Section 51A was inserted. This new section empowered Government of India (GOI) to freeze or attach properties/funds held in the names of individuals or entities who are declared connected with terrorist activities as per the sanction list issued by UN authorities. Under the rules of this act banks are required to keep watch on the sanction list of UN and not to open accounts for such persons or entities. In case banks are having the accounts, then the funds are to be blocked immediately under intimation and confirmation from Government of India.

(vii) **The Recovery of Debts due to Banks and Financial Institutions Act, 1993 (DRT Act).** The act provided for the establishment of tribunals (Debt Recovery Tribunals) for expeditious adjudication and recovery of debts due to banks and financial institutions (FI). Under the act all recovery cases for amounts ₹ ten lacs and above are to be filed with DRTs and the civil courts will have no jurisdiction to try the bank and FI cases. DRTs are dedicated tribunals for banks and FIs and under the act. Debts Recovery Appellate Tribunals (DRAT) are also created for appeals. At present there are 33 DRTs and five DRATs in the country.

(viii) **The Foreign Exchange Management Act, 1999.** This act replaced the earlier Foreign Exchange Regulation Act, 1973. The act is controlling the foreign trade and financial transactions involved in foreign trade and for the purpose of orderly development and maintenance of foreign exchange market in India. This act is important act for banks which lays down the rules for foreign exchange business.

(ix) **Securitisation and Reconstruction of Financial Assets and Enforcement of Security Interest Act, 2002 (SARFAESI Act).** SARFAESI Act which is especially created for banks and financial institutions (FIs) to help them in recovery of bad loans. This act empowers banks to seize the securities (both moveable and immoveable except agricultural land) upon loan default, without intervention of the court, and then auction the securities to recover the dues. This act is created to help banks and financial institutions to speedily recover the bad loans without requiring them to go to the civil courts for recovery of dues.

The act also provided for the formation of asset reconstruction companies (ARC) specifically for the purpose of taking over the distressed assets of banks and financial institutions so that the banks and FIs can get rid of NPAs from their books.

Under the provisions of this act, 'Central Registry of Securitisation Asset Reconstruction and Security Interest of India' has been created in March 2011. Central Registry is a government company with a shareholding of 51% by the Central Government and the rest by few public sector banks and the National Housing Bank. The company now maintains and operates registration system for creation of security interest in favour of banks and FIs over the property (security) for the loans given by them. Registration with Central Registry acts as a public notice as anyone can make a search and inspection and find out the charges created on the properties in favour of banks and FIs.

(x) **The Prevention of Money Laundering Act, 2002 (PMLA).** This is the anti-money laundering act which especially tries to prevent money laundering. It is new legislation but has great relevance to banking. KYC rules for customer identification has originated from this act and banks are made responsible for it. The act also gives reporting requirements for the banks and FIs to Financial Intelligence Unit-India (FIU-IND), set up under the act. The act also prescribes rules for maintenance and record keeping of information on transactions and the banks books.

(xi) **Payment and Settlement Systems Act, 2007 (PSS Act, 2007).** The PSS Act, 2007 provides for the regulation and supervision of payment systems in India and designated the Reserve Bank of India as the authority for that purpose and all related matters. The Reserve Bank is authorized under the act to constitute a Committee of its Central Board known as the Board for Regulation and Supervision of Payment and Settlement Systems (BPSS), to exercise its powers and perform its functions and discharge its duties under this statute.

Settlement system exists in all the payment segments like the cheque clearing, card payments, electronic clearing, money market operations, fund transfer systems, etc. Under the provisions of this act only RBI or RBI-authorised entities can operate any payment settlement systems in the country. The settlement conducting agency is called the system provider. The purpose is to ensure stability in the financial markets by providing reliable and safe systems for settlements. The act also recognises the net settlement basis adopted in all settlements (except RTGS system).

Besides the above laws, banks are also governed by many other laws of the country in the conduct of their business. Some commercial laws of the country are very pertinent in banks' workings. They are:

1. Sales of Goods Act, 1930
2. Indian Contract Act, 1872
3. Transfer of Property Act, 1882
4. Indian Stamp Act, 1899 and state stamp acts
5. Indian Registration Act, 1908
6. Companies Act, 1956
7. Income Tax Act, 1961

The first five of the above acts are relevant as the securities for bank loans and the legal requirements for charging of securities are mostly governed by these acts. Companies Act is important as the banks are companies. Income tax act has many rules and provisions regarding cash transactions and bank accounts.

1.24 What is the Nomination Facility for Bank Accounts

Nomination Facility. Nomination facility for bank accounts and safe deposit articles, safe deposit lockers were introduced in the year 1985. Banking Laws (Amendment) Act, 1983 amended the Banking Regulation Act, 1949 and introduced new Sections 45ZA to 45ZF for this purpose.

Under the rules bank depositor having deposit account, safe custody article, safe deposit locker in his single name, can nominate an individual as a nominee to receive deposits, articles in safe custody, contents of the locker after his death.

If the deposits are held in joint accounts, all the joint account holders together can nominate only one person as nominee to receive the deposit amount after death of all joint holders. The deposits held in joint account with either or survivor or other clauses will be paid to survivors and nominee can be paid only after the death of all joint account holders.

Nomination facility is not available for safe custody articles left with the bank by persons jointly.

In case of safe deposit lockers held in joint names and operated jointly by them, all the joint account holders can nominate one or more persons to receive the contents of the lockers jointly with the surviving locker account holders.

Nomination facility is available for accounts in individual names or for sole proprietary concerns. Nominee also should be individuals. Nominee can be a minor also. The account holders can change the nomination made, any time later and can make fresh nomination for the accounts. Under the rules, the nomination form signed by the depositor does not require any witness. But in case account holder is placing his thumb impression for the nomination then it shall be witnessed by two persons.

Under the provisions of nomination rules the nominee will not become the owner but he receives the money or articles as trustee. He is accountable to the legal heirs of the deceased.

Nomination rules are made to facilitate the withdrawal of money or articles from bank after death without having to resort to death claim application procedures which are generally time consuming and in some cases can be prolonged also. Nomination enables banks to return the money or articles to the nominee with minimum formalities of identifying the nominee.

As per RBI guidelines, banks should settle the claims in respect of deceased depositors and release payments to survivor(s)/nominee(s) within a period of 15 days from the date of receipt of the claim in normal circumstances.

Banks now allow premature withdrawal of term deposits by survivors/nominees/legal heirs in case of death of the depositor.

1.25 How Banks Deal with the Deposits/Lockers of Deceased Customers

This is an important area of the banking business. Till the nomination facilities were introduced to bank accounts, banks were paying the deposits to the successors or legal heirs as recognised by the law. These successors or legal heirs were required to file a death claim with the banks. Strictly speaking, succession certificate issued by competent court is required to claim the money belonging to the deceased. But the practices accepted by the law permits the legal heirs to the deceased to claim money belonging to the deceased.

Banks also accept the claims by the legal heirs as provided in the personal law applicable to the deceased. These personal laws are based on the religion the deceased belonged to. Hence, there is Hindu law, Muslim law, Buddhist, Sikh or Jaina, Parsi laws in the country to be followed in case of followers of those religions. The provisions of the Indian Succession Act, 1925 is applicable in other cases. However, under the Indian Succession Act, 1925, State Governments, at their discretion can allow exemptions to the communities and sects from the applicability of this act.

Generally, in all the personal laws applicable, legal heirs are the spouse and the children of the deceased with some changes and additions of other relatives.

Claim application shall be signed by all claimants and the copy of death certificate shall be attached. Banks process the claim application and depending on the deposit amount the authority to approve claim payments rests with different levels of officials of the banks. Banks settle claims on execution of indemnity by all legal heirs and may ask for surety also for the payments. Banks generally do not insist for production of succession certificate by the legal heirs. But banks may insist for it where there are disputes and/or all legal heirs do not join in indemnifying the bank or in certain other exceptional cases where the bank has a reasonable doubt about the genuineness of the claimant/s being the only legal heir/s.

Banks now allow premature withdrawal of term deposits by survivors/nominees/legal heirs in case of death of the depositor.

In case of joint accounts, traditionally since long banks were guiding the joint account holders for the payment clause to be added in case of death of any joint account holder. Accounts in joint names are generally accepted with clauses like either or survivor, former or survivor, latter or survivor or any one of the survivors. These are considered as the written mandate of the joint account holders and banks are honouring it and making the payment to the survivor. It is a banking practice since long and this practice has been accepted by the law. Banks are encouraging this practice as it obviates the procedure and delay for settling the death claims.

The legal heirs of the deceased depositor cannot claim the money in the joint account from the bank when mandate as discussed above are given by all joint account holders to the bank. Even courts will not stop the payment by banks to the survivors. Legally, it is an accepted position now that the banks can make payment to the survivor on the basis of mandate it has from the joint account holders. But the survivor does not become the owner of the money. He has the right to receive it as a trustee. As the estate of the deceased passes to legal heirs, the survivor is accountable to the legal heirs of the deceased joint account holder for the money.

1.26 What are KYC Guidelines

KYC guidelines are introduced in the year 2002 by RBI in the aftermath of many terrorist attacks and also to tackle effectively the problem of money laundering.

In view of increased threats posed by money laundering and terrorist activities, Financial Action Task Force (FATF), an international body of nations, made certain recommendations in the year 1990 to control the menace of money laundering and terrorist financing by better control on banking operations and by legal provisions to bring the culprits to books. It was felt that there is a nexus between money laundering and terrorist activities.

FATF observed that the existing practice of the banks in opening accounts for customers and handling their financial transactions is inadequate to check the misuse of banking channel by these elements. Hence, some changes in the legal system and the changes in the banks' approach towards customers are recommended. FATF recommendations are the basis on which the know your customer (KYC) norms were developed later.

Subsequently in the year 2001 the Basel Committee on Banking Supervision also issued a paper on Customer Due Diligence (CDD) for banks, with indicative suggestions. Banks are advised to relook at their practices in accepting the accounts of new customers and to ensure that a proper policy framework on 'Know Your Customer' is put in place.

The changes are necessitated by the fact that the banker customer relationship by tradition is based on trust and confidentiality. Banks are not to divulge the financial dealings of their customer to anyone as the information is considered as confidential. This practice also had legal recognition.

The practices of banks world over in identifying and accepting new customers was observed to be weak by the

FATF. In our own country, banks were opening new accounts for customers and the practice was to obtain an introduction of the new customer from an existing customer of the bank. But banks hardly knew or understood the business dealings of the customers. The introduction route followed by banks and accepted by the law was a proxy identification of the customer and banks generally do not make any independent verifications about the new customer.

All these views about the practices of banks and the problems faced by law enforcing agencies came into sharp focus again after the 9/11 terrorist attacks on US in 2001. The United Nations Security Council immediately issued guidelines to the governments to arm themselves with suitable legal provisions to control money laundering and terrorist activities.

In view of the above developments, GOI enacted Prevention of Money Laundering Act, 2002 (PMLA, 2002), a new legislation to fight against money laundering and created FIU-IND (Financial Intelligence Unit of India), a statutory body under Ministry of Finance to implement the provisions of PMLA.

RBI also first issued guidelines to banks on 'Know Your Customer' (KYC) in 2002 and then issued detailed guidelines in the year 2004 advising banks to have 'Know Your Customer Policy' in line with the guidelines.

RBI has stated the objectives of the KYC guidelines as under:

> The objective of KYC guidelines is to prevent banks from being used, intentionally or unintentionally, by criminal elements for money laundering activities. KYC procedures also enable banks to know/understand their customers and their financial dealings better which in turn help them manage their risks prudently.

Under the guidelines, for the purpose of KYC Norms, a 'Customer' is defined as a person who is engaged in a financial transaction or activity with a reporting entity and includes a person on whose behalf the person who is engaged in the transaction or activity, is acting.

Thus, the banks are not only to check the antecedents of the bank customers having accounts with them but also to check on persons who conduct any financial transactions with the banks directly or through a third person.

As per guidelines, now banks have their own Board-approved KYC policy covering following areas:

- Customer Acceptance Policy;
- Customer Identification Procedures;
- Monitoring of Transactions; and
- Risk Management.

Customer Acceptance Policy. Under this banks now have a clear defined policy for opening accounts for individual and entities and have prescribed documents required from different types of customers for opening accounts. Further banks shall not open accounts for persons and entities as under:

1. Accounts in anonymous or fictitious/benami name.
2. Account where the bank is unable to apply appropriate customer due diligence.
3. Account for person or entity, identity of which match with any person or entity, whose name appears in the UN sanction lists circulated by the Reserve Bank of India.

Customer Identification Procedures. Under this it is now the responsibility of banks to identify the persons or entities desiring to open accounts on the basis of officially valid documents (OVDs).

Officially valid document (OVD) means;

- Passport,
- Driving Licence,
- Permanent Account Number (PAN) Card,
- Voter's Identity Card issued by the Election Commission of India,
- Job Card issued by NREGA duly signed by an officer of the State Government,

- Letter issued by the Unique Identification Authority of India containing details of name, address and Aadhaar number,
- Or any other document as notified by the Central Government in consultation with the Regulator.

RBI has also given a simplified measure of KYC for enabling persons belonging to weaker section of the society to open accounts with banks and the following two documents are deemed as OVDs for them.

1. Identity card with applicant's photograph issued by Central/State Government Departments, Statutory/ Regulatory Authorities, Public Sector Undertakings, Scheduled Commercial Banks, and Public Financial Institutions;
2. Letter issued by a gazetted officer, with a duly attested photograph of the person.

Under KYC guidelines banks may accept some other documents like utility bills, property or municipal tax receipt; bank account or post office savings bank account statement; and few other documents, only for the limited purpose of residential proof.

Monitoring of Transactions and Risk Management: Under the KYC guidelines banks now have the responsibility to monitor the transactions in the account. This monitoring is based on information collected at the time of opening the account about customer's business, viz. source of income, the level of business, the type of business, etc. Banks are monitoring the transactions in the account with this information to ensure that the transactions are in agreement with the profile of the customer.

Banks now categorise the customers according to the risk profile as low risk, medium risk and high risk customers. This categorisation enable banks to apply the required monitoring standards according to the risk profile of the customer.

Risk categorization is based on the expected level and the expected/known sources of funds. A customer with known means and small resources is placed in the low risk category as the transactions in the account will not be large. (The accounts of governments and legal bodies are also considered low risk category as they require minimum monitoring.) A customer with known means and identity but with large level of business is placed in medium risk category. High risk customers are those with multiple and unknown means, whose transactions also cannot be predicted.

Banks in India are now following the KYC guidelines and also the provisions of PML Act, 2002. Bank accounts are now opened strictly as per KYC guidelines.

2

Banking – Credit

2.1 To Whom Banks can Give Loans

Bank loans are subject to the credit policy and guidelines issued by RBI under Section 21 of Banking Regulation Act, 1949. Credit policy contains certain statutory and some regulatory prohibitions for lending by banks.

The policy stipulates the purposes for which loans can be given. Credit policy also contains some broad guidelines for security and margin requirements for loans. Prior to 1994 even the rate of interest on loans are prescribed by the credit policy.

Restrictions for Sanctioning Loans

The restriction on banks for lending is in two categories. One is the statutory restrictions as stipulated in laws of the country. Other is the regulatory restrictions stipulated by RBI from time to time. Some statutory restrictions are as under:

- Section 20(1) of the Banking Regulation Act, 1949 lays down the restrictions on loans and advances to the directors and the firms in which they hold substantial interest.
- In terms of Section 20(1) of the Banking Regulation Act, 1949, a bank cannot grant any loans and advances on the security of its own shares.
- In terms of Section 19(2) of the Banking Regulation Act, 1949, no banking company shall hold shares in any company, whether as pledgee, mortgagee or absolute

owner, of an amount exceeding 30 per cent of the paid-up share capital of that company or 30 per cent of its own paid-up share capital and reserves, whichever is less,

Some of the Regulatory restrictions are:

- Restrictions on Granting Loans and Advances to Relatives of Directors.
- Restrictions on Grant of Loans & Advances to Officers and Relatives of Senior Officers of Banks.
- Restrictions on Grant of Financial Assistance to Industries Producing/Consuming Ozone Depleting Substances (ODS).
- Restrictions on Advances against Sensitive Commodities under Selective Credit Control (SCC).
- Restrictions on Loans against Certificate of Deposits (CDs) as banks cannot grant such loans.
- Restrictions on Advances for purchase of Gold and lending against Gold Bullion/Coins/Primary gold. However, there are exemptions from this rule for gold loans to individuals and loans to jewellery manufacturers.

These are the restricted areas for bank loans. Subject to these restrictions and some other stipulations in the credit policy, banks can give loans to persons or entities based on their own commercial judgment. At present banks are permitted to extend loans to all segments of the economy including personal loans to individuals.

Banks are giving loans for all economic purposes like industry, trade, services, exports, agriculture and allied activities, fishing, cold storage, real estate development, infrastructure development etc. Banks are also giving personal loans for different purposes like housing loans, vehicle loans, education loans, loans for consumer durables, loans against properties or gold or against other securities and also clean loans.

Banks are prohibited from giving loans for speculative purposes. For example, banks shall not lend for the purpose of investing in stock market to brokers or others. However, for individual investors there is some exemptions as they can avail small personal loans upto limit fixed by RBI from banks against the security of stocks. There are certain restrictions for giving loans against some selective commodities covered by the selective credit control guidelines of RBI as mentioned earlier.

Public sector banks are under statutory obligation to lend to FCI for its food procurement programme and it is called the food credit. It is a charge on the credit of the banks. RBI has also prescribed mandatory lending of 40% of the credit to priority sector including agriculture (40% is calculated on the basis of previous year end advances of the banks). Banks are also required to lend 12% of their credit to export purposes. Hence, about 50% of bank credit thus falls under directed lending category.

Prior to the year 1994, interest rates on advances were as prescribed by RBI and banks were following it. After the banking reforms were introduced, RBI deregulated the interest rates and allowed banks to fix their own lending rates. Banks were asked to fix their prime lending rate (PLR) and link the rate of interest to PLR. In the year 2003 Bench-mark prime lending rates (BPLR) system was introduced for banks. This was again replaced in the year 2010 by Base Rate System. Base rate system was again replaced by MCLR system from the year 2016.

Under RBI guidelines for marginal cost of funds based lending rate (MCLR), banks are required to fix their MCLR and offer interest rates on loan to different categories of borrowers which is linked to MCLR. Banks generally cannot lend below its own MCLR.

Banks can sanction loans either with fixed rate of interest or with floating rate. For loans sanctioned under fixed rate system, the rate of interest cannot be changed at future date. For loans sanctioned with floating rate of interest, the rate changes as and when the bank changes its MCLR for advances. Generally, the fixed interest rates for the loan offered by banks are little higher than the rates under floating interest rates.

Earlier in 1970s banks were charging interest on loans on monthly basis and in 1990s RBI changed the system to charging of interest on quarterly rests. Now again from April 1, 2002 RBI allowed the banks to charge interest on monthly basis.

2.2 What are the Types of Loan Accounts

Banks sanction loans in different type of accounts to suit the requirement of the borrower or depending on the nature of loans. Generally, following types of loan accounts are in use.

Demand Loan/Fixed Loan Account. It is a fixed loan given in lump sum to the borrower against any type of security or on clean basis. A loan account is created in the books of the bank with the debit for the loan amount disbursed. Thereafter, this loan shall be repaid as agreed either in instalments or at a time as decided at the time of giving the loan. Generally, short-term loans with maturities up to three years are given as demand loan. This can be against the securities like the pledge of deposits, immoveable properties, consumer durables, vehicles, education loan, etc.

Banks may take loan documents like demand promissory note or loan agreement and security charging agreements.

Term Loan Account. This type of loan account is opened when the loan is given for long duration like loans to acquire business assets, a project finance or housing loan. These are the one-time loan and after the loan is disbursed only repayments will be allowed in the account. No fresh loan can be drawn from this account.

Term loans are generally allowed for acquisition of all kind of business assets or in individual cases, for acquiring immoveable (house) and moveable (vehicle, equipment, consumer durable) assets. Though it is also a fixed loan, it is called a term loan because the term for repayment is fixed as monthly, quarterly, half yearly or yearly instalments. The repayment is worked out on the basis of repaying capacity of the individual borrower taking into account his present income level and in case of business entities, on the basis of expected income from the business. In case of term loans to business, banks analyse the financial statements of the borrower and work out debt service coverage ratio (DSCR) to ensure that the business will have adequate surplus to repay the loan.

The term loan also may be disbursed in instalments depending on the payment schedule for acquisition of the assets.

Generally, banks use the nomenclature of term loan or demand/fixed loan based on loan documentation obtained by them. In case of a term loan bank gets a term loan agreement executed by the borrower. The term loan agreement acknowledges that the loan is to be repaid in instalments over a period as agreed between the parties. In view of this clause, bank cannot make a demand on the borrower for total loan outstanding but can demand only the instalment that has fallen due. However, there may be a clause in the agreement which enables bank to make demand for total dues in case of continued default by the borrower in payment of instalments.

In case of a demand/fixed loan, bank obtains either a demand promissory note (DPN) or a demand loan agreement executed by the borrower which empowers bank to make demand for the total dues in the loan account any time it chooses.

Overdraft Account. Overdraft account is a loan account where bank has allowed loan facility as a running account facility. In an overdraft account, bank fixes a limit which is marked in the account and borrower is free to use the amount anytime upto the limit. Borrower can also deposit back the amount as per his cash flows and again draw the loan amount from the account for his next requirement. There is no restriction for number of transactions both credit and debit in this account except that the balance when in debit cannot exceed the limit fixed. This type of arrangement is useful for business people as it acts as combined current account and a loan account. Overdraft accounts are generally secured by some securities or it can be on clean basis also. In this type of loan account, the loan given cannot be separately identified because of various debits and credits in the account over the time and the loan agreement provides that the loan amount is the balance outstanding in the account at any given point of time.

Cash Credit Account. Cash credit account is same as an overdraft account. It is a type of overdraft account. The differentiating factor is that in a cash credit account the security given is the stocks and receivables of a business concern.

Bill Purchase or Discount Account. This is the loan account allowed by the banks against the bills of the customer raised on his clients. Generally, the documents submitted by the customer will have a bill of exchange and also the receipt for goods in transit in the form of railway receipt, transport receipt or bill of lading (for export bills). This is a separate loan account and the bank purchases (demand bills) and or discounts (usance bills) the bill and debits the amount to this bill account and credit the same to customers running account. When the payment of the bill is received, the debit in the loan account is reversed as paid.

Packing Credit Account. This is a pre-shipment credit facility allowed to the exporter to procure goods and organise exports. It is maintained as a separate account. Under this the facility can also be released as demand loans separately for each export order and the loan amount is credited to running account of the customer. On export and payment of export bill, this loan is adjusted. For some regular large customers instead of sanctioning separate loans, banks are allowing packing credit facility on running account basis where only one loan account is maintained in which all the individual loans for each export order are debited.

Working Capital Loans

The business and industries may also require bank finance to help them in their day-to-day business of manufacturing and trading activities on a continuous basis. This requirement is known as working capital requirements and banks finance the borrowers by creating overdraft, cash credit, bill purchase or packing credit accounts as discussed earlier. These accounts enable the borrowers to draw, deposit back and again draw as per their requirement. Only maximum limit is fixed up to which the borrower can draw at any time. These working capital limits are generally sanctioned for a period of one year and can be renewed thereafter. The renewal will be based on the financial performance of the borrower during the previous year. Bank may agree to renew the limit, increase or decrease the limits depending on the level of business and few other factors.

2.3 What are the Terms and Conditions for Bank Loans

Under Section 21 of Banking Regulation Act, 1949, bank loans are under the regulatory authority of RBI and RBI advises banks from time to time about its credit policies that will govern the loans given by banks.

Loans can be sanctioned by banks on some terms and conditions as stipulated in the credit policy guidelines issued by RBI. The credit policies of RBI now only specify the broader parameters and allows maximum discretion to banks to decide on details within the policy framework. Banks are practically free to give loans to anyone or for any purpose with minimum regulatory and supervisory restrictions.

Bank loans are as discussed earlier is under two categories.

- Fixed or term loans, and
- Working capital loans.

Fixed loans are given for many purposes. Term loans are given when the borrower like to invest in fixed assets. The loan is for acquiring the asset concerned. Once disbursed thereafter the loan will have to be repaid in instalments fixed for repaying the loan.

Working capital facility are given as a running facility and for the purpose to meet day-to-day requirement of the borrower. These are generally given to industry, trade or business to manage the working capital requirements.

The main terms and conditions for loans are as under:

Purpose. While sanctioning loans, banks look into the purpose of loan whether it is for industrial or business purpose or for personal purpose. Business loans are preferred as they are for productive purpose and increases production and employment for the country. Now personal loans are also encouraged as these loans creates demand for goods and services. Housing loans under personal loan category is given priority status also. Banks can give loan for any type of economic activity but banks are prohibited to give loans which are used for purely speculative purposes and for illegal activities.

Security. Banks will generally require securities to secure the loans. The type of securities bank accepts and how they are charged to banks is discussed separately. Further as per the credit policy of RBI, banks shall take the securities of the assets acquired through bank finance. The securities created from the loan funds are called the primary security. Besides primary security banks may also take additional securities to secure the loans and such securities are called the collateral securities.

Margin. While sanctioning any type of advances, banks insist for some minimum contribution for acquiring asset or for working capital facilities from the borrower and it is called the margin. It means that banks do not give 100% loan for any purpose. There may be a very few exceptions to this general rule.

Repayment. All bank loans are repayable within a stipulated period. Term loans are repaid in a short-term (less than three years), medium-term (three to seven years) and long-term (over seven years) period. The working capital limits are allowed for one-year period and generally banks may renew the limit depending on assessments. Bill advances are to be repaid on their due dates.

Repaying capacity. Banks sanctioning loans particularly the fixed/term loans shall have to make assessment of repaying capacity of the borrower to repay the loan over loan period. This is very important as the repayment can come from the income. In case of loan to industry, trade, and business, these business entities shall be assessed for their future income-generating capacities based on many factors like the prospects of business, the expected cash flows of the business, the expected turnover and profits, etc. to satisfy that the loan can be repaid with interest in time. In case of other loans like personal loans to individuals, their existing income will be checked to ensure that they have the capacity to repay the loan in time. Further in case of fixed loans against securities like fixed deposit receipt, other liquid securities the repayment can be accepted on the basis of such securities maturing.

2.4 How Banks take Credit Decisions—Analysis of Financial Statements of the Borrowers

Firstly, banks apply know your customer guidelines to identify the borrower and also make market enquiry about the creditworthiness of the borrower.

For business loans, banks generally collect financial statements of the borrowers for minimum past three years to analyse the balance sheets and profit and loss statements for the purpose of knowing the financial strength and the status of the business. Studying three years statements reveal the trend in business whether it is growing or losing.

Profit and loss account is a statement of business activity for the year and gives the turnover, the expenses incurred and the net profit or loss earned. Balance sheet is as on a particular date (usually year end date) and is the statement of the assets and liabilities of the business on the given date.

Balance sheet reveals all the assets and liabilities of the business. It is presented as per the accounting standards and audited in most of the cases. But banks may have to regroup the various assets and liabilities to analyse the balance sheet. This regrouping is done on the following pattern:

Assets Side

- Fixed assets (land, bldg., plant & machinery, spares, equipment, fixtures & furniture's vehicles all used for the business activity).
- Current assets (cash and bank balances, investments in marketable securities, stocks of raw materials, work-in-process, finished goods, receivables, prepaid expenses, advances to suppliers—current assets are considered as those assets which can be turned into cash within the financial year).
- Miscellaneous assets (any type of assets, moveable or immoveable owned which have no bearing to the business activity).
- Intangible assets (assets like goodwill, patents, accumulated losses—they do not represent any physical asset).

Liabilities Side

- Capital and reserves.
- Long-term loans (long-term borrowings from any source including bank/FI term loans).
- Current liabilities (short-term borrowings from any source, bank borrowing for working capital, sundry creditors, creditors for expenses, advance from buyers, tax liabilities due-current liabilities are all the liabilities accruing due for payment in the financial year).

Banks calculate net working capital as under;

Net working capital =

1. (capital and reserves + long-term loans) – (fixed assets + miscellaneous assets + intangible assets)

   Or

2. Current assets – current liabilities

Net working capital represents the portion of long-term sources of the business that is available for day-to-day working (working capital) of the business. It acts as the margin for working capital limits sanctioned by bank.

Ratios

While analysing the balance sheet banks work out some critical ratios which are considered very important and banks have some benchmarks fixed for these ratios. These ratios indicate the financial strength, the liquidity position and income generation capacities of the borrower. Some important ratios are:

Debt Equity Ratio. This is the ratio between the owned funds of business and its long-term borrowings. It is calculated as:

Debt equity ratio = long-term borrowings/capital plus reserves.

The ratio is mentioned as 3:1 or 2:1 etc. and reflects how much is the long-term loans (debt) in relation to the capital (equity). Capital in the ratio is constant at 1. Debt in the ratio can be more than one or even less than one or even zero.

General benchmark acceptable to banks are 3:1 ratio meaning thereby that long-term debt can be three times the equity. Banks may also accept higher ratio for some specific borrowers like infrastructure segment.

Leverage Ratio. This is the ratio between the owned funds to total outside borrowings (long-term + short-term). It is calculated as:

Leverage ratio = total outside borrowings/capital plus reserves

This is higher than the debt equity ratio as it includes all borrowings of the borrower from all sources.

Current Ratio. Current ratio is the ratio between current assets to current liabilities of the borrower and is worked out as under:

Current ratio = current assets/current liabilities

It is expressed as 2:1 or 1.33:1, etc. where the current liability is constant at 1.

This is an important ratio to be considered while assessing working capital limits which reveals the liquidity position of the borrower. Ideally, the current assets shall be more than the current liabilities which means the business can meet all its current liabilities. If the current assets are less than current liabilities, then the business is illiquid as it has not enough current assets to pay off the current liabilities. This also indicates that the business has no net working capital (NWC) available to it and that its owned funds are blocked in fixed or other assets.

Since from long time banks use to insist for benchmark current ratio of 1.33:1 which gives the margin of 25% for working capital loans. At present RBI has allowed banks to accept even little lower current ratio based on their prudent assessment of limits.

Quick Ratio—Quick Ratio is a refinement of current ratio. It is also called as 'acid test ratio'. It reveals the short-term liquidity of the business and is worked out as under:

Quick ratio = (current assets – stocks)/current liabilities

Current assets – stocks, means that current assets like cash and equivalent, marketable securities and receivables of the business are only taken in to account to calculate the liquidity. Stocks are removed as they are considered as illiquid to some extent. A good or positive quick ratio reveals that the business is highly liquid and sound.

Debt Service Coverage Ratio (DSCR)

It is an important ratio calculated by banks while assessing term loan or project finance. This ratio reveals whether the borrowing entity will have sufficient income to service the loan interest and also the loan repayments. In case of a business enterprise, term loan is given to acquire the fixed assets (plant, machinery & equipment, other assets) to start a new venture or to increase the production of existing venture. The new business will generate income and the banks will be assessing the level of projected future income and the loan repaying capacity. The ratio is calculated as:

DSCR = Net operating income/Total debt service

Total debt service means the total of interest on loan plus the loan repayment due during the year. Net operating income in case of a new venture will be projected figures. Hence, the basis for projections and their reliability will have to be considered. For bigger projects banks call for technical feasibility reports also for study. Generally, banks consider the net income of the business as per the prevailing accounting standards and add back the interest charges (because it is shown as expenses in the accounts) and arrive at DSCR as under:

DSCR = (Net profit + yearly interest on loan)/(yearly interest on loan + yearly loan instalments payable)

The ratio shows whether the business can service the interest and instalments from its earnings. If the ratio is 1 then the earnings are just sufficient to take care of debt servicing. Since the projected figures are considered, ratio of 1 is not considered safe. It should be more than 1 so that there is margin and cushion available to the business in case of stress. Banks consider DSCR of 1.75 as the ideal ratio. Further, bank also needs to consider income-tax liability of the business on the net profit as it will reduce the funds available and also reduce the DSCR ratio after tax.

Besides these important ratios, banks may also analyze few other ratios like turnover ratios and profit ratios. Turnover ratio is also called the inventory turnover ratio and it is arrived by dividing the net sales by average stock holding. This reveals how many times the stocks were 'turned' or sold during the year.

Under profit ratios generally return on assets (ROA) and return on equity (ROE) are calculated which reflects the percentage earning of the business on total assets and on total capital of the business.

2.5 How Banks Assess the Loan Requirement

Loan requirements of an individual or an entity is for two purposes as under:

- Term or fixed loan
- Working capital loan

Term or fixed loans are considered by banks when the borrower wants loan to acquire some fixed assets like premises/ factory, machinery, equipment, etc. or requires the loan for the purpose of investments or personal expenses on medical, social functions, etc.

Under term loan or fixed loan, the borrower requires the loan amount immediately for spending it for the desired purposes mentioned above. Hence, banks sanction the loan in lump sum and allow it to be drawn by the borrower.

In case of term loans to business or industry, banks will look at the purpose and the type of fixed assets proposed to be acquired. Generally, borrowers in case of setting up a new business or industry are asked to submit a project report giving the details of the assets proposed to be acquired, its requirement for the business and its cost. Bank will also study the business projections in the project report and find out whether the business/industry will have adequate future earnings to repay the term loan by working out DSCR.

In case of existing business/industry for expansion, banks will study the financial statements of the borrower along with the expansion project proposed, to assess the term loan requirement and its repaying capacity.

For term loans to individuals like housing loan, vehicle loan, etc. banks will make the assessment based on the existing income level of the individual and his repaying capacity.

Term loans are generally considered for medium-term (three to seven years) and the long-term loans are considered only in case of infrastructure projects and housing loans.

Generally, borrower will have to bring in his contribution as margin for the term loan. Margin requirement may be up to 25% or more of the cost of assets to be acquired depending on specific case and also depending on the type of asset. In exceptional cases particularly under priority sector lending, margin requirement may be reduced or waived. In term loans, the assets acquired from the loan funds will have to be necessarily charged to the bank as security and it is called the primary security for the loan.

Fixed Loan. Fixed loan is also disbursed similar to term loan by opening a fixed loan account. The difference with term loan is that fixed loan can be allowed for any approved purpose, with or without security, with or without margin, and the repayment can be flexible. Fixed loan can also be allowed against some maturing assets of the borrower like a FD with the bank or some other securities. This type of loans is sanctioned with a margin stipulation on the security value and in such cases the loan repayment can be flexible and borrower may repay the entire loan in one lump sum on the maturity of his securities.

Working Capital Loans

Besides loans for the purpose acquiring assets for setting up the business, the borrowers also need bank loans to assist them in their day-to-day business. Working capital for a business is the amount of funds required by it to run business activities, viz. to maintain stock, for extending credit to buyers, to meet running expenses, etc. Total requirement will be based on the size of the business. Business entities may find it difficult to arrange funds from their own source to run the business. When bank finances them for the purpose of running the business, it is called a working capital loan.

Business cycle is normally considered as annual and banks finance the business for working capital on short-term basis maximum upto a year. But as the business will continue year after year for indefinite period, banks also review the limits annually and renew the limits after making fresh assessments.

The important aspect of this type of loan is that it is not allowed as one-time loan but as a running facility. Under this, bank opens a cash credit or overdraft account for the borrower and a maximum limit will be fixed. Borrower is free to draw any amount and deposit any amount and again draw the amount within the limit fixed as per his day-to-day requirement. Bank gets cash credit or overdraft agreement executed by the borrower to facilitate this arrangement.

Overdraft accounts are also allowed for individuals depending on their requirements for running account loan facility.

For assessing working capital limits for industry, trade and business banks are using three methods as under:

MPBF Method of Lending—Tandon Committee, Chore Committee

This method was introduced in the year 1975 based on the Tandon Committee Report. It was originally prescribed for industrial units to make assessment of working capital limits on the basis of inventory norms. Inventory norms are the acceptable levels for build-up of stocks and receivables (calculated in terms of months) for the industrial unit. Tandon Committee Report recommended inventory norms for 17 basic industries.

Inventory norms were introduced to ensure that the industry does not hold unduly large inventory more than what is required to carry on manufacturing activity smoothly. If the inventory levels are very high, it will amount to hoarding which is not a desirable feature for the economy. High level of inventory also results in banks sanctioning higher working capital limits than warranted. By first fixing the inventory norms, banks can assess and sanction working capital limits as the Maximum Permissible Bank Finance and it is called the MPBF method.

This method of assessing the limits was made as a standard model for assessing the working capital limits for all industrial/ business units. Under this method, banks first fix the required inventory levels and then assess the working capital limits on this level of inventory as the permissible bank finance. For the inventory build-up, borrower is required to bring adequate margin in the form of net working capital (NWC) in the business. NWC is that portion of capital which is available for the day-to-day workings to the business and is worked out as under:

Net Working Capital = Capital from long-term sources (capital, reserves and long-term loans) – investment in the fixed and miscellaneous assets of the business.

The committee recommended three formulas for calculating permissible bank limits known as the first method, second method and third method of lending.

Later, in the year 1979 another committee known as Chore Committee, reviewed these inventory norms and methods of assessments. This committee recommended continuance of assessments based on inventory norms and for calculating permissible bank finance, and recommended only the second method prescribed in the Tandon Committee Report to be made applicable. Other methods are withdrawn.

Under the second method, NWC shall be minimum 25% of the total inventory which translates to minimum current ratio of 1.33:1. RBI has withdrawn this stipulation in 2005 and banks are allowed to decide the minimum margin requirements. Banks are also allowed to have flexible inventory norms.

The above assessment now is known as Traditional or MPBF method and is used for all working capital loan assessments.

Turnover Method of Lending—Nayak Committee

In the year 1991, Nayak committee reviewed assessment of working capital limits for small-scale industries and it concluded that the MPBF method is rigid and does not allow flexibility to SSI units. The committee recommended Turnover method as a simple and practical solution. Under this, the working capital assessment is based on projected turnover of the unit. Working capital requirement is assessed at 25% of the projected turnover and 20% of projected turnover is sanctioned as limit with the condition that 5% shall be brought in by borrower as margin. Under this system, banks need not fix inventory norms as in the MPBF method. This method is now made applicable to all borrowers belonging to various categories and is applicable for limits upto ₹ 5 crores.

Cash Budget Method of Lending

The MPBF and the turnover methods are used to assess the working capital limits but for few segments of borrowers these methods were not providing a need-based assessment of limits. The requirements of seasonal industries and software companies and few others could not be properly assessed under these methods.

In view the difficulties faced by these segments of borrowers, RBI in the year 1997, permitted banks to assess the limits by a third method of lending called as Cash Budget Method. Under this, cash budget of the borrower is worked out taking into account the periodical cash inflow and outflow of the business. The gap between the inflow and outflow is financed by the bank in the shape of working capital limit. Thus, this assessment is not based on inventory norms or turnover norms.

At present all the three methods of assessing working capital limit for business ventures are permitted by RBI and banks are free to determine the method that is suitable for the borrower. Turnover method is generally used for assessing the limits upto ₹ five crore ands banks make assessments on both MPBF and turnover methods and if the limits assessed are higher under turnover method then the higher limits are fixed.

2.6 How Banks Create Securities for Loans—The Type of Charges Created

Banks are giving loans and in order to safeguard the banks' interest and also to ensure that the borrowers stick to their commitments, banks create securities for the loan lent. These securities are fall backs in case of need and by creating security; the bank gets specific rights over the assets under its charge and can claim the asset for liquidation of loan in preference to any other general creditor of the borrowers.

In the ordinary course of business, securities are generally moveable assets, immoveable assets, and actionable claims. Depending on the type of security offered, bank creates charge on the asset as appropriate and recognized by law. These charges can be created as per provision of any particular Act, then only it becomes enforceable legally through court of law. There are many laws applicable to different kind of assets. For example, immoveable property is governed by Transfer of Property Act. Goods are covered by the Sale of Goods Act and also Indian Contract Act. Assignments are recognized under various acts. Before accepting any security bank shall have to ensure that the asset can be legally charged under some provision of the relevant act. Then only a legally enforceable charge can be created and bank is said to have secured the loan.

The words 'lien' and 'charge' are also used as general terms sometime to explain the right of the bank against the particular asset. However, it is important for the bank to create charge on the security in an appropriate manner.

Different types of creation of charges commonly in use are:

Lien. Lien is a right given to another by the owner of property to secure a debt. Liens fall into two categories: particular lien and general lien. In case of banks law permits general lien in favor of banks and further as per customs and practice, bankers lien is recognized as implied pledge which enables banks to dispose of the security to recover the loan. Lien is generally used to charge the deposits of customers for giving loan against those deposit accounts.

Assignment of Actionable Claims

The term 'Actionable Claim' has been defined in Section 3 of the Transfer of Property Act, 1882. As per this section, actionable claim means a claim to any debt, other than a debt secured by mortgage of immovable property or by hypothecation or pledge of movable property.

Way of creating security on actionable claims is by assignment. Actionable claims are those claims wherein the person who has to receive certain amount from another person can transfer his right to receive the payment to some third party.

The person who has to pay, generally, has no say in the matter and he is bound by the assignment and has to accept it. The debt or beneficial interest may be existing, accruing, conditional or contingent.

In banking business, three types of securities fall under this category. They are the beneficial interest in LIC policies, book debts of the borrower and the government supply bills raised by the supplier on the government depts. LIC policy has a provision for assignment of the policy. Governments also accept assignments in favour of banks. Book debts of the borrowers are also assigned to the lending bank which gets a legal charge on the book debts.

Pledge. Pledge is a common type of charge created on moveable assets to secure the bank loan.

The Indian Contract Act, 1872, Section 172 defines pledge as "The bailment of goods as security for payment of a debt or performance of a promise is called pledge".

Pledge is a way of creating security on moveable assets and the essential feature of the pledge is the physical possession of the asset is given to creditor/bank. Thereafter, the asset remains in the custody of bank till such time the loan is repaid. Pledge is a fixed charge on specific assets and in case of bank, bank has the authority to dispose the asset after giving notice to the party. All moveable assets can be pledged and also the securities like bonds, shares, deposit receipts, warehouse receipts, transport or railway receipts, bill of lading, etc. In case of paper securities, besides handing over the possession, the borrower shall also have to complete some other formalities like endorsing or signing the transfer deeds etc. In case of paper securities, the pledge agreement gives 'constructive possession' of assets represented by the paper security.

Hypothecation. Hypothecation is a type of charge created on moveable assets to secure the bank loan. The charge is similar to pledge but unlike pledge, the possession of the asset remains with the owner (borrower). It is also known as floating charge on the asset and banks have a right to crystallise the charge and take possession of the assets. This type of charge is created on the basis of the practices of the banks and is recognised by the courts.

In the year 2002, the Securitisation and Reconstruction of Financial Assets and Enforcement of Security Interest Act, 2002 (SARFAESI Act) gave a legal definition of hypothecation as under:

> Hypothecation means a charge in or upon any movable property, existing or future, created by a borrower in favour of a secured creditor without delivery of possession of the movable property to such creditor, as a security for financial assistance, and includes floating charge and crystallization into fixed charge on movable property.

Banks generally create hypothecation charge on stock-in-trade, receivables, plant & machinery, equipment, vehicles, fixtures & furniture and any other fixed assets of the business other than immoveable property.

In case of fixed assets hypothecated though it remains in the custody of borrower, he cannot dispose it without banks permission. The charge of the bank is specific to that particular asset and it cannot even be replaced with similar assets without bank's consent. In case of vehicles, the charge is hypothecation and as per Motor Vehicles Act, it is compulsory for the bank to register the charge with the vehicle registering authority-RTO. When the hypothecation charge is created on moveable assets of a company, the charge shall have to be registered with Registrar of Companies (ROC).

Now under the provisions of SARFAESI Act, 2002, a central registry has been created in the year 2011 and banks can now file their security interest on the assets of borrowers with this registry. This registration of charge with central registry acts as a public notice about banks interest in the securities.

Hypothecation charge is a floating charge when the stock-in-trade is hypothecated to bank. In this the borrower has the authority to sell the goods and replace it with fresh goods as per business requirement. Under this practice and system, the stocks that remains with borrower at any time is deemed to be under the bank's charge but when the borrower sells some stock in his ordinary course of business, the sold stock is free from bank's charge. This floating charge can become a fixed charge if bank crystallises the charge and take possession of stock-in-trade currently held by the borrower.

Mortgage

Under the Indian Transfer of Property Act, 1882 the term "mortgage" is defined under Section 58(a) as follows:

> A mortgage is a transfer of interest in specific immovable property for the purpose of securing the payment of money advanced or to be advanced by way of loan, an existing or future debt or the performance of an engagement which may given rise to a pecuniary liability.

There are different kinds of mortgages recognized by the law. They are:

- Simple mortgage
- Mortgage by conditional sale
- Usufructuary mortgage
- English mortgage
- Anamalous mortgage
- Mortgage by deposit of title deeds/equitable mortgage

Banks in India generally use two types of mortgages; simple mortgage and equitable mortgage. In simple mortgage, mortgage deed is prepared and it will be registered with sub-registrar's office. Simple mortgage is also known as registered mortgage. The equitable mortgage is created by a simple procedure of depositing tittle deeds of the properties by the borrower with the banks. This type of mortgage can be created only in notified towns (notified by State Governments for this purpose).

Under equitable mortgage as provided in Transfer of Property Act only deposit of title deed of the property is to be made by the borrower (owner) with the bank within the notified towns. This transaction does not require creation of any written agreement and hence there is no requirement of stamp duty and registration. As per practice of banks, banks on their own make a book entry in bank's book recording the transaction of deposit of title deeds with it. Banks are also taking a letter of confirmation subsequently from the borrower. But presently the procedure to create equitable mortgage has undergone many changes due to changes made by many State Governments in their state laws. These changes are mainly in relation to stamp duty payable and registration requirements for creating equitable mortgage within the states concerned.

Personal Guarantees

Banks generally take personal guarantees of third parties to secure the loan collaterally.

Guarantees are governed by the Indian Contract Act, 1872 and guarantor is called surety. The Chapter VII of the said Act defines the rights and liabilities of surety. Banks take continuing guarantee from the guarantor. Continuing guarantee is defined by the Section 129 of the Act as "A guarantee which extends to a series of transaction, is called, a continuing guarantee".

There is no bar for accepting guarantee from anyone either related or otherwise and the contract of guarantee need not have any monetary consideration for binding oneself. It is presumed that the promise made for the benefit of principal debtor is sufficient consideration as per Section 127 of the Act.

According to the Act, liability of the surety is coextensive with the principal debtor. This means the surety is liable for anything owned by the principal debtor and to the same extent. For whatever the principal debtor is liable the surety is also liable.

Corporate Guarantees

Besides individuals, all legal entities can also execute contract of guarantees. Generally, banks are taking corporate guarantees from corporate to secure loans sanctioned to other corporate borrowers. Examples are when bank accepts corporate guarantee of the holding company for sanctioning loan to a group company. Similarly, banks also accept corporate guarantee from a company to secure loan sanctioned to its associate or group company.

2.7 What is Food Credit for Indian Banks

Food Credit

Food Corporation of India (FCI) was created in the year 1964 to hold buffer stock of food grains that can be used in time of famine and other natural disasters. FCI's objective is food security for the country. GOI authorized FCI to avail credit from banks under a consortium led by SBI. Public sector banks are obliged to provide credit to FCI based on its requirement. This credit by banks is called Food Credit and is shown separately by banks and monitored separately.

In fact, the statistics release from RBI divides the total bank credit into two heads: food credit and non-food credit of the commercial banks. All the analysis of bank credit is based on only on the non-food credit of the banks. Total of food credit and non-food credit is referred as gross bank credit.

The following table shows the food credit and non-food credit of commercial banks for few select years from 1969-70 to 2016-17.

Food Credit by Commercial Banks

(Crores)

Year	Food Credit	Non-Food Credit	Bank Credit	Food credit to total credit %
1969-70	56	3915	3971	1.41
1974-75	613	8149	8762	7.00
1979-80	2100	19437	21537	9.75
1984-85	5665	43287	48953	11.57
1989-90	2006	99446	101453	1.98
1994-95	12275	199286	211560	5.80
1999-00	25691	410267	435958	5.89
2004-05	41121	1059308	1100428	3.74
2009-10	48489	3196299	3244788	1.49
2014-15	99400	6003000	6102300	1.63
2015-16	105253	7144362	7249615	1.45
2016-17	53930	7827960	7881890	0.68

Source: RBI.

2.8 What is Social Lending by Banks

In our country, public sector banks like SBI and its associates were created and some banks were nationalised in the years 1969 and 1980 with a purpose to divert banks resources to development activities of the nation. The concept of priority sector was formulated and banks were given target to lend to these segments. Agriculture, small-scale industries and small enterprises were identified as the target group. The purpose was to create self-employment for the people so that they can be gainfully occupied.

In 1969, lead bank scheme was launched covering all the districts of the country and the scheme is still continuing. Under this, banks are advised to finance all the credit needs of population in the districts, particularly the poor, and help them to get involved in some gainful employment.

Besides, the government from time to time sponsored new loan schemes for financial assistance to particular sections of poor for their self-employment and/or starting some economic activities. Under these schemes, government gave subsidies as a percentage to the cost involved in starting the economic activities and advised banks to extend loans to the beneficiaries identified under the schemes. These government-sponsored schemes are in operation since 1970s and are still continuing. Many of the schemes were revised or merged to form new schemes over the period.

The first such scheme was known as the Integrated Rural Development Programme (IRDP), a rural development programme of the Government of India launched in the financial year 1978 and extended throughout the country. It is a self-employment program for the target group consisting of small and marginal farmers, agricultural labourers and rural artisans living below the poverty line. Under the scheme, the government gave subsidy of 25 per cent for small farmers, 33-1/3 per cent for marginal farmers, agricultural labourers and rural artisans and 50 per cent for Scheduled Castes and Scheduled Tribes families and physically handicapped persons. Banks were advised to extend the full loan and then appropriate subsidy released by government as margin. This program is implemented in all the blocks of the districts in the country. The scheme has been merged later in the year 1999, with another new scheme launched by GOI named Swarnajayanti Gram Swarozgar Yojana (SGSY).

Under SGSY scheme, self-help groups (SHGs) of the identified beneficiaries are financed. SGSY scheme was restructured in the year 2013 and GOI launched a new programme known as National Rural Livelihoods Mission (NRLM). This programme is now continuing.

The Government of India also launched a scheme known as Swarna Jayanti Shahari Rozgar Yojana (SJSRY) in 1997 for the poor in urban areas on similar lines with SGSY scheme. This scheme also has been restructured in the year 2013 and launched as the National Urban Livelihoods Mission (NULM). NULM scheme is now continuing.

Another important scheme in the name of Prime Minister Rozgar Yojana (PMRY) is introduced in the year 1993. The scheme is designed to create and provide self-employment opportunities to unemployed youth in the country. The scheme was made applicable in all the areas of the country. In the year 2008, Government of India merged another scheme; Rural Employment Generation Programme (REGP) with PMRY and introduced a new scheme, called Prime Minister Employment Generation Programme (PMEGP). This scheme is now continuing.

Government of India introduced a scheme known as Self Employment Scheme for Rehabilitation of Manual Scavengers (SRMS) from January 2007, with the objective to rehabilitate remaining manual scavengers and their dependents. The scheme has been revised in 2013 and is now a continuing scheme.

These are the main loan schemes sponsored by GOI and there are many other schemes also in operation. In all these schemes, government is providing subsidies and asking banks to provide loans. All these loans are for the social cause to uplift the poor above the poverty line. Loans to these categories of borrowers cannot be assessed by commercial standards as the credit absorbing capacity of the poor are weak and the likely default rate is high. These are all social lending for the banks.

Education Loans. Another type of loan is the education loan which the banks are asked to provide the students for pursuing higher education without the security of collaterals. This loan scheme was started from the year 2001. This is also aimed to provide loan assistance to students from poor families. Education loan is also included under the priority sector.

Within the priority sector, a category was identified as 'weaker section' on the basis of economic and social backwardness. There are many sub-categories under weaker section. This segment is financed by all banks on easy terms and sometimes on unsecured basis. All beneficiaries under the government-sponsored loan schemes discussed above are under the weaker section category.

Similarly, a segment called as DRI scheme beneficiaries was created who are the poorest of the lot. Banks were asked to finance them at a concessional interest of 4% (please see under DRI advances at 2.9).

A new category of finance known as micro finance has been formally identified from the year 1991 and banks are asked to participate in financing beneficiaries under self-help groups (SHGs) mechanism.

Micro finance is described as financial assistance to low income individuals who do not have access to normal banking services. The loan assistance per person is generally upto ₹ 50000 and such loans are disbursed through self-help groups of such persons created for the specific purpose. There are also many micro finance companies now in the country who finance this type of borrowers with social objectives. Banks are also asked to provide financial support to such companies (please see under priority sector and micro credit below for more details).

In lending to priority sector, the driving force is not always the commercial consideration and judgment. It is with a social objective to uplift the poor and improve their lives. Particularly for borrowers who are below the poverty line, it is based on social and humanitarian considerations. Banks are accepting and absorbing the default risk in these loans which is known to be high for various reasons. Thus, broadly speaking, loans sanctioned by banks with social objectives to improve the living standards of the poor fall under the concept of social lending.

However, it may be noted that the lending to many activities under priority sector and particularly to the medium- and big-sized category of borrowers under it, are commercially viable and they merit for loans even without adding the tag of social lending.

2.9 What is Priority Sector Lending

In the year 1969, government introduced social control on banks and also nationalised 14 major banks of the county as it wanted the growing resources of the banks to be used for national development programmes.

At that time government identified some sectors as very crucial for the development of our economy. Agriculture is the backbone of the economy and large population depended on it for livelihood. There was shortfall in food grain production and country was importing the same. However, farmers were exploited a lot and they were not getting financial support. Hence, agriculture was recognized as the first priority for bank loans.

At the time of independence, country was industrially backward and government had the task of promoting industries in the country. Government started many large basic industries. It was felt that setting up of large industries alone will not suffice. Private entrepreneurs were also to be encouraged. Small industrial units were to be encouraged to promote entrepreneurship. Such smaller units were best suited for employment generation and also contribute significantly to the production of goods and services. Government policy was to promote smaller units along with large industries.

On this backdrop, Reserve Bank of India formally came up with definition of priority sector in the year 1974 as the preferred target group for providing bank finance. Priority sector was mainly divided to three sub-sectors. They are the agriculture, small-scale industries and tertiary sector comprising retail trade, transport, professional services, small business and enterprises. All these activities are identified as the priority areas of the economy.

Nationalised banks started lending to the priority sector as identified and advised by RBI. Then RBI fixed a target of 40% of aggregate bank advances to be deployed in priority sector advances and advised the banks to achieve it by the year 1985. Sub-targets were also fixed for lending to agriculture and the weaker sections within the overall target. Banks achieved the targets in the year 1985 and thereafter the same percentage-wise target was continued till date. As the quantum of bank advances grew over the years, so the quantum of advances to priority sector also went up.

Reserve Bank started Agriculture Refinance Corporation in the year 1963, which later became ARDC in the year 1975, to provide refinance to banks for their agriculture lending. In the year 1982, NABARD was created by an Act of Parliament to support the agriculture sector for all its requirements and it took over ARDC and also some functions from RBI.

RBI was issuing new guidelines from time to time for inclusion of certain activities within the definition of priority sectors and also making changes in the eligibility conditions for the advance to be included in priority sector classification. RBI also fixed many sub-targets within the overall target for priority sector lending.

DRI Advances: In the year 1972, RBI created a special segment of borrowers under priority sector who are below the poverty line (whose annual family income is below ₹ 24000 in urban area and ₹ 18000 in rural areas) and banks were asked to extend 1% of their total credit to this segment of borrowers at a special concessional rate of interest of 4%. These advances are called DRI (differential rate of interest scheme) advances. The maximum assistance per beneficiary has been now fixed at ₹ 15000 for productive purposes. In addition to this, physically handicapped persons can avail of assistance to the extent of ₹ 5000 (maximum) per beneficiary for acquiring aids, appliances, or equipments. Housing loan upto ₹ 20000 per beneficiary over and above the loan of ₹ 15000 is permissible under the scheme. DRI advances are treated as advances to weaker section.

Weaker sections within priority sector: RBI created a weaker section concept within priority sector who are identified based on economic and social backwardness and banks were advised to take care of their credit needs on top priority basis. Guidelines were also issued to earmark sub-limits for them within the overall limit for priority sector. At present 10% target is fixed.

As per the latest guidelines issued by RBI in the year 2015, Priority sector loans to the following borrowers is considered as Weaker Sections Category Advances:

No.	Category
1.	Small and Marginal Farmers
2.	Artisans, village and cottage industries where individual credit limits do not exceed ₹ 1 lakh
3.	Beneficiaries under Government-sponsored Schemes such as National Rural Livelihoods Mission (NRLM), National Urban Livelihoods Mission (NULM) and Self Employment Scheme for Rehabilitation of Manual Scavengers (SRMS)
4.	Scheduled Castes and Scheduled Tribes
5.	Beneficiaries of Differential Rate of Interest (DRI) scheme
6.	Self-Help Groups
7.	Distressed farmers indebted to non-institutional lenders
8.	Distressed persons other than farmers, with loan amount not exceeding ₹ 1 lakh per borrower to prepay their debt to non-institutional lenders
9.	Individual women beneficiaries up to ₹ 1 lakh per borrower
10.	Persons with disabilities
11.	Overdrafts upto ₹ 5,000 under Pradhan Mantri Jan-Dhan Yojana (PMJDY) accounts, provided the borrowers' household annual income does not exceed ₹ 100,000 for rural areas and ₹ 1,60,000 for non-rural areas
12.	Minority communities as may be notified by Government of India from time to time

In terms of achievement, it is to be noted that priority sector lending was a success story and banks have contributed to very large extent to support the target groups.

Banks and other institutional lending to agriculture have brought in "green revolution" in the country. The Green Revolution resulted in a record grain output of 131 million tons in 1978-79. This established India as one of the world's biggest agricultural producers.

In the year 2005, Government of India came out with concept of small & medium enterprise (SME) and banks were asked to encourage these sectors.

On this line, RBI made changes in the categories under priority sector and created the concept of micro and small enterprises (MSE) in place of existing SSI sector. Thus, the definition of priority sector advances underwent some major changes in the year 2005 and following sub-categories were prescribed:

1. Agriculture,
2. Micro & small enterprises,
3. Micro credit (up to individual limit of ₹ 50000 to SHGs or MFIs),
4. Education loans,
5. Housing loans.

The definition of MSE included both manufacturing and service units. Any enterprises providing some services is eligible for treatment as MSE under priority sector and get favourable treatment by banks. Thus, the tertiary sector as defined earlier has now been merged with small enterprises.

Targets/Sub-targets

From the year 2005, under priority sector, RBI has fixed overall target and sector-wise sub-targets to be achieved by commercial banks and foreign banks. Agriculture has a separate target of 18% within the overall target of 40% for priority sector. Within agriculture, targets have been fixed for direct lending and indirect lending. In case of advances for micro & small enterprises, sub-targets have been fixed for micro manufacturing enterprises. Besides these targets, 10% target for weaker section advances and 1% target for DRI advances have also been fixed.

New RBI Guidelines Issued in April 2015

RBI reviewed the priority sector classifications and issued fresh guidelines to banks in April 2015. These guidelines have again modified the definitions of priority sector and introduced some changes. Under the present guidelines, the sub-categories of priority sector are given as under:

Categories under priority sector:

(i) Agriculture
(ii) Micro, Small and Medium Enterprises
(iii) Export Credit
(iv) Education
(v) Housing
(vi) Social Infrastructure
(vii) Renewable Energy
(viii) Others

Export credit, social infrastructure, renewable energy are the new additions to priority sector advances under these new guidelines.

Now RBI has added export advances upto ₹ 25 crores per borrower in the priority sector. However, this is calculated on incremental basis over the previous year.

Social Infrastructure. Bank loans upto a limit of ₹ 5 crore per borrower for building social infrastructure for activities, namely schools, health care facilities, drinking water facilities and sanitation facilities in Tier II to Tier VI centres are now included in priority sector.

Renewable Energy. Bank loans upto a limit of ₹ 15 crore to borrowers for purposes like solar-based power generators, biomass-based power generators, wind mills, micro-hydel plants and for non-conventional energy-based public utilities, viz. street lighting systems and remote village electrification, and for individual households (the loan limit will be ₹ 10 lakh per borrower) are now included under priority sector.

Under the category of 'Others', few types of loans not covered in other sub-sectors are included. The overdraft facility of ₹ 5000 to be allowed under the newly introduced Pradhan Mantri Jan Dhan Yojna is included in this head.

Under agriculture RBI has dispensed with the existing sub-categories of direct and indirect finance and made it a single category.

Priority Sector Targets Fixed in 2015

Categories	Domestic scheduled commercial banks and Foreign banks with 20 branches and above	Foreign banks with less than 20 branches
Total Priority Sector	40 per cent	to be achieved in a phased manner by 2020
Agriculture	18 per cent Within the 18 per cent target for agriculture, a target of 8 per cent is prescribed for Small and Marginal Farmers	Not Applicable
Micro Enterprises	7.5 per cent	Not Applicable
Advances to Weaker Sections	10 per cent	Not Applicable

Banks, particularly the foreign banks, are given some time (upto 2018/2020) to achieve the targets and sub-targets.

The percentages are now calculated on the Adjusted Net Bank Credit or Credit Equivalent Amount of Off-Balance Sheet Exposure, whichever is higher. The current year's targets for priority sectors and sub-targets will be computed based on Adjusted Net Bank Credit (ANBC) or credit equivalent of Off-Balance Sheet Exposures of banks on March 31st of the preceding year.

Priority sector advances of banks are shown in the following table.

We may observe that priority sector advances of banks in the year 2015-16 accounted for 34% of total non-food credit of the banks. As informed earlier the target 40% fixed is in relation to the previous year's closing Adjusted Net Bank Credit (ANBC) of the banks. Generally banks have been achieving their priority sector targets in all the years.

Sectoral Deployment of Non-Food Gross Bank Credit (Outstanding)
(Part table showing total non-food credit and priority sector advances)

(₹ Billion)

No.	Sector	Outstanding as on						
		2009-10	2010-11	2011-12	2012-13	2013-14	2014-15	2015-16
	Non-food Credit (1 to 4)	30396.15	36673.54	42897.45	48695.63	55296.01	60029.52	65469.03
5	Priority Sector	10921.79	12624.45	14210.45	15397.96	18297.24	20103.24	22259.07
	Memo:							
5.1	Agriculture & Allied Activities	4157.41	4806.34	5466.26	5899.14	6659.79	7658.80	8825.90
5.2	Micro & Small Enterprises	3735.30	4428.48	4986.25	5622.96	7078.13	8003.43	8475.87
5.2(a)	Manufacturing	2064.01	2102.06	2366.57	2843.48	3481.94	3800.28	3714.67
5.2(b)	Services	1671.30	2326.42	2619.69	2779.47	3596.18	4203.14	4761.20
5.3	Housing	2178.77	2391.05	2658.51	2672.03	3020.07	3223.86	3422.76
5.4	Micro-Credit	217.99	192.31	160.24	165.07	172.13	177.01	188.46
5.5	Education Loans	362.47	425.89	480.67	526.12	578.88	591.84	601.37
5.6	State-Sponsored Orgs. for SC/ST	12.34	0.87	1.79	1.24	3.28	3.48	5.14
5.7	Weaker Sections	1891.64	1906.13	2333.59	2733.98	3860.00	4048.84	4773.97
5.8	Export Credit	302.00	318.21	391.00	422.34	483.13	426.26	423.82

Note: Data are provisional and relate to select 47 banks, which account for 95 per cent of total non-food credit extended by all scheduled commercial banks. For 2013-14, 2014-15 and 2015-16 it is related to 46 banks.

Source: RBI

2.10 What if a Bank Fails to Achieve Priority Sector Target

RIDF

Priority sector target was made mandatory from the year 1995-96 and banks were penalised for not achieving the targets set for agriculture lending. Under the penalty provision, banks are required to deposit amount equal to the shortfall (every year) with NABARD in its Rural Infrastructure Development Fund (RIDF) at low interest rates. This is to make the banks lend directly to priority sector to avoid the penalty. The first RIDF was established with NABARD in 1995-96. The funds are utilised to provide loans to the State Governments for financing rural infrastructure projects.

As banks who were failing in fulfilling the targets are obliged to deposit default amount in RIDF every year, RIDF became the main instrument to channelize bank funds for financing rural infrastructure.

RBI also has the discretion to direct the banks to deposit the shortfall in lending, with few other development agencies besides with NABARD. RBI, at its discretion, can direct the banks to deposit the shortfall amount with SIDBI, National Housing Bank (NHB) and Micro Units Development & Refinance Agency (MUDRA Ltd.). RBI uses this discretion to channelize funds to these development agencies.

2.11 What is Credit Guarantee Schemes Available for Priority Sector Advances

Historically, advances to priority sector and to export sector are considered as vulnerable areas for lending due to various reasons. The chances of default are high in these loans due to uncertainties.

To encourage banks to lend to priority sector, two guarantee schemes were launched—one for small-scale industries and another for other priority sector advances. These schemes gave some relief to banks by settling claims in case of loans becoming non-recoverable. Claim was generally restricted to average of 70-75% except in very few cases. Guarantee scheme for SSI was administered by Reserve Bank of India since the year 1960 on behalf of the government and for other guarantee scheme, Credit Guarantee Corporation of India was formed in the year 1971.

In the year 1978, Credit Guarantee Corporation and the Deposit Insurance Corporation (established in 1962 as Deposit Insurance Authority) were merged to form the Deposit Insurance & Credit Guarantee Corporation (DICGC), a fully owned subsidiary of Reserve Bank. The credit guarantee scheme for SSI operated by RBI was also taken over by DICGC from the year 1981. Later, banks were given the choice to opt out of credit guarantee schemes but not from deposit insurance scheme. Banks opted out of credit guarantee schemes due to unsatisfactory claim payment record and that the scheme did not provide support to banks for bad loans in priority sector as intended. At present no bank is availing credit guarantee from DICGC.

CGTMSE

In the year 2000, government with SIDBI started another credit guarantee scheme under the aegis of a trust named Credit Guarantee Trust for Medium and Small Enterprises (CGTMSE). Under this scheme, banks are encouraged to lend without insisting for collateral securities. The credit facilities provided by the lending institutions to Micro and Small Enterprises without any collateral security and/or third party guarantees are covered under this guarantee scheme. Guarantee cover on eligible borrowers upto one crore is available to commercial banks and in case of RRBs the cover available is ₹ 50 lacs. This scheme is at present operative as it has many attractive features like online claim lodging and settlement system.

Credit Guarantee for Export Finance

Export Credit Guarantee Corporation of India Ltd. (ECGC) is a Government of India enterprise which was originally started as Export Risk Insurance Corporation (ERIC) in the year 1957 as insurance provider for export business. It provides insurance coverage to exporters directly and also to banks for exports.

ECGC has evolved various export credit risk insurance products to suit the requirements of Indian exporters and commercial banks as under:

- It provides insurance policy/cover to exporters/banks to protect the Indian exporters against unforeseen losses due to non-payment for any reason (like failure of the buyer or bank or problems faced due to government policies at buyer's country etc.).
- It also issues surety insurance cover for bankers to facilitate banks to sanction adequate bank finance to the Indian exporters.

ECGC insurance cover is generally upto 75-80% of loses. ECGC issues whole turnover policies for pre-shipment and also post-shipment credit to banks under which all advances of the bank can be covered. It also issues individual specific policies to banks and exporters. ECGC insurance cover has become a necessity in export finance and banks generally insist for it. Claim payment record of the ECGC is also very good and it provides security to exporters and banks.

2.12 What is Lead Bank Scheme

Lead bank scheme was introduced in the year 1969 by the government and RBI as novel scheme to implement the credit plans in each district in the country. Banks are made as the coordinators for the credit planning for the district.

It is a decentralised system of credit planning taking into account the government plan for the district and then aligning and dovetailing the bank and institutional credit sanctions to support the government's district development plan. It will take in to account the all the government-sponsored loan schemes for the poor allocated for the district and also other development schemes and plan of the government for the district. It will also include the credit plan of all banks in the district for their mandatory lending to the priority sector and other sectors and also the development schemes or plans of any other financial institutions in the district.

After the district credit plans for each district in the state is finalised, a state credit plan will be prepared by aggregating all the district credit plans. All the states and also the union territories in the country are covered under this scheme.

Under the scheme, RBI appointed the lead bank for each district amongst the banks present in the district. Generally, the bank which has large number of branches and high level of business is selected as the lead bank. The lead bank has to appoint a lead district manager (LDM) from the bank who shall be the coordinator for the scheme. The lead bank role is to act as a consortium leader for coordinating the efforts of all credit institutions in the district.

Under the lead bank scheme, lead bank is required to prepare a Potential Linked Credit Plans (PLPs) for the district. The planning process starts with the lead district manager (LDM) convening a special Block Level Bankers' Committee (BLBC) meeting at each block of the district where the Branch Credit Plans will be discussed and aggregated to form the Block Credit Plan. Then LDM aggregates all the Block Credit Plans of the district to form the District Credit Plan. This plan shall be ready in August every year for the next financial year.

The District Credit Plan will be placed before the District Consultative Committee (DCC) by the LDM for final acceptance/approval. DCC is the common forum in the district and the District Collector is the Chairman of the DCC meetings. All banks in the district, RBI, NABARD and various State Government departments and allied agencies are the members of the DCC. The Lead District Officer (LDO) from RBI represents the Reserve Bank as a member of the DCC.

DCC is also the reviewing body under the scheme which periodically reviews the implementation of the credit plan and the performance of each member banks.

At state level, there is a state level bankers' committee and RBI has appointed a bank as the SLBC convener. SLBC convenorship is also generally given to a bank which has large presence in the state. For Union Territories there are union territory level bankers' committee (UTLBC).

All the District Credit Plans will be eventually aggregated into State Level Credit Plan to be prepared by SLBC convenor bank and to be launched by 1st of April every year.

The SLBC is an apex inter-institutional forum in all states, to oversee the development of the state under lead bank scheme. SLBC is chaired by the Chairman & Managing Director (CMD)/Executive Director of the convenor bank. It comprises representatives of all banks in the state, RBI, NABARD, heads of government departments, representatives from National Commission for Scheduled Castes/Tribes, National Horticulture Board, Khadi & Village Industries Commission and some other invitees. The SLBC meetings are convened by the SLBC convenor bank of the state on quarterly basis. SLBC meetings are for the purpose of coordination between the banks, government departments and other agencies involved in the implementation of district credit plans.

Lead bank scheme is a novel scheme aimed to involve banks, other credit agencies and the district administration in preparing a district credit plan in a synchronised manner with all the participants in the plan supplementing others efforts in the development of the district economy. It also leads to the state credit plan implementation on the same basis.

2.13 What is Micro Credit

Micro finance concept is said to have originated in Bangladesh with the institution of Grameen Bank in 1983. The founder and originator of this concept is Muhammad Yunus (born on 28 June 1940) a Bangladeshi social entrepreneur, who was awarded the Nobel Peace Prize for founding the Grameen Bank and pioneering the concepts of micro credit and micro finance.

Micro finance is a broader term which explains extension of banking service to those who are not availing any banking service from the banks. This includes the savings, loan, remittance and other facilities made available to the poor by creating a linkage with them as groups.

Micro credit refers to only to the informal small loans to the poor for any purpose under the concept of self-help groups

(groups of persons from same locality or vocation) which creates a social collateral by peer monitoring within the group. Women groups are mainly targeted in this model. This model of extending credit is referred as linkage of SHGs with banks.

It started in India in the early 1980s by forming informal self-help groups (SHG) to provide access to much-needed savings and credit services to the poor. Non-governmental organisations (NGO) took the initiative for the same. Subsequently, RBI and NABARD took up the matter and many studies were made on the subject. It was realised that in rural area, informal credit still plays an important role, and the formal credit delivery structure put in place through banks and RRBs, are not enough. Poor households still depend on this informal credit and it was accepted that there is a need to bring this system of credit delivery through SHGs into the mainstream. Based on the experiences of many other countries like Bangladesh, Indonesia, Thailand, and Bolivia, it was decided that credit linkages to SHGs be provided by banks to encourage the system.

In 1991-92, a pilot project for linking about 500 SHGs with banks was launched by NABARD in consultation with the RBI, which advised the banks to actively participate in it. In 1994, RBI advised that the banks' financing of SHGs would be reckoned as part of their lending to weaker sections and as priority sector lending. RBI made formal policy announcements in 1999.

Keeping in view of the importance of micro credit, a separate category under priority sector was created. Loans of very small amounts, not exceeding ₹ 50,000 per borrower provided by banks either directly or indirectly through a SHG/joint liability group (JLG) mechanism for on-lending, is considered as priority sector advance.

Banks were urged to make all out efforts for providing micro credit and forging linkages with SHGs, either at their own initiative or by enlisting support of NGOs.

A new breed of organisations called Micro Finance Institutions (MFIs) have made their appearances and are now allowed to play a role in providing linkage between banks and

SHGs. Even foreign investments in MFIs are encouraged. These MFIs are non-deposit taking non-banking financial companies (NBFCs).

Under the latest guidelines issued by RBI in the year 2015, the micro credit extended by banks directly to borrowers, or through SHG/JLG or through MFI are all treated as weaker section advances under priority sector. In case of lending to MFI for on lending to the beneficiaries, the limit is now increased up to maximum ₹ One lac per borrower.

NABARD provides refinance support to banks for their loans under micro credit through SHGs. Micro credit is picking up very fast with the active support of RBI. NABARD and banks as can be seen from the table below:

Self-Help Group-Bank Linkage Programme

(Amount in ₹ Billion)

Year (end-March)	No. of SHGs Linked		Bank Loan		Refinance Assistance	
	During the year	Cumulative	During the year	Cumulative	During the year	Cumulative
1998-99	18678	32995	0.33	0.57	0.31	0.52
1999-00	81780	114775	1.36	1.93	0.98	1.50
2000-01	149050	263825	2.88	4.81	2.51	4.01
2001-02	197653	461478	5.45	10.26	3.96	7.97
2002-03	255882	717360	10.22	20.49	6.22	14.19
2003-04	361731	1079091	18.56	39.04	7.05	21.24
2004-05	539365	1618456	29.94	68.98	9.68	30.92
2005-06	620109	2238565	44.99	113.97	10.68	41.60
2006-07	1105749	–	65.70	–	12.93	54.53
2007-08	1227770	–	88.49	–	16.16	70.68
2008-09	1609586	–	122.54	–	26.20	96.88
2009-10	1586822	–	144.53	–	31.74	128.62
2010-11	1196134	–	145.48	–	31.74	128.62
2011-12	1147878	–	165.35	–	30.73	184.80
2012-13	1219821	–	205.85	–	39.17	223.96
2013-14	1366421	–	240.17	–	37.46	261.42
2014-15	1141208	–	203.84	–	44.93	306.35

Notes: 1. Data relate to commercial banks, RRBs and co-operative banks.

2. From 2006-07 onwards, data on number of SHGs financed by banks and bank loans are inclusive of 'Swarnajayanti Gram Swarozgar Yojna' (SGSY), SHGs and existing groups receiving repeat loans. Owing to this change, NABARD discontinued the publication of data on a cumulative basis from 2006-07.

3. Data for 2013-14 are Provisional.

Source: NABARD.

In the guidelines on priority sector issued in the year 2015, RBI has created a new micro segment in priority sector as micro industries, micro enterprises, etc. These segments have now wider meaning and covers more borrowers engaged in different activities in many areas. Higher limits can be sanctioned to them as per the schemes. The new and wider micro segment under priority sector also includes the micro credit started earlier as discussed above.

2.14 What are PLR, BPLR, Base Rate and MCLR in Indian Banking

PLR

Prior to the year 1994, interest rates on advances were as prescribed by RBI and banks were following it. After the banking reforms were introduced, RBI deregulated the interest rates and allowed banks to fix their own lending rates. Banks were advised to fix their own prime lending rate (PLR) as the minimum rate of interest for advances. The prime lending rate is defined as the rate which the bank offers loans to its prime customers and that the bank cannot lend to anyone below this rate. For loans upto ₹ two lacs, banks were advised to charge only the PLR and for loans above ₹ two lacs, banks can charge higher rates than the PLR.

But RBI continued the concessional rate of interest to export finance and few loans under government schemes. These were the exempted categories. However, over the period the concept of Prime Lending Rate got diluted as there were many exemptions and also some business compulsions of the banks forced them to charge interest lower than the PLR to many categories of borrowers. Slowly, PLR lost its relevance as a bench mark rate.

BPLR

In order to streamline the mechanism of PLR system, RBI introduced in the year 2003 the concept of Benchmark Prime Lending Rate (BPLR) for banks. Under this banks were asked to work out their BPLR on a given formula and announce it.

For determining their Benchmark PLR, banks are advised to take into account the following factors:

(i) actual cost of funds of the bank,

(ii) operating expenses of the bank,

(iii) a minimum margin to cover regulatory requirement of provisioning/capital charge and profit margin.

But banks can lend at below BPLR to borrowers which shall be based on bank's Board approved policies. Thus, BPLR will act as a benchmark rate based on the economic calculation but the rates offered to borrowers will be based on bank's policies. This was prescribed to make the system transparent and allow the banks discretion to respond to the business exigencies. It was prescribed that the loans upto ₹ two lacs shall be at BPLR and for others it shall be generally above BPLR or at rates prescribed by the banks Boards (which can be below BPLR also). But all the applicable rates to the borrowers shall be linked to BPLR (as either plus or minus by a percentage) so that whenever the BPLR is changed the applicable rates to all borrowers will change.

PLR and BPLR system was introduced by RBI to make the interest rate structure dynamic and changing in tune with the changes in market conditions. As the banks are to link all their lending rates to BPLR, any change in BPLR is meant to change the interest rates for all borrowers. The economy can move in both directions depending on many factors like the demand and supply and the changes affecting the cost of funds. Ideally, BPLR should change when the cost of funds for the bank changes. RBI also expected that the bank loan interest rates shall show some movements as and when the policy rates (bank rate and repo rate) are changed by it.

But in reality this was not happening in the banks' lending rates. Banks were seldom changing their BPLR downward whereas they were increasing it with increase in costs of funds. Hence, the lending rates were generally not lowered when the costs are low or when policy rates are lowered by RBI and it was only increased when costs go up. In view of this, RBI decided to move forward and change the system by introducing Base Rate System for bank lending to bring in more transparency in the system.

Base Rate

In the year 2010, RBI introduced the Base Rate concept from 1 July 2010. Base rate is defined as minimum lending rate of the bank and bank cannot lend below this rate. RBI advised banks to adopt any methodology to calculate the base rate for the bank and gave one illustration which is not made compulsory as under.

Illustrative Methodology for the Computation of the Base Rate:

(a) Cost of Deposits/funds

(b) Negative Carry on CRR and SLR

(c) Unallocatable Overhead Cost

(d) Average Return on Net Worth

But banks were free to adopt any other methodology. Banks were also directed to announce their base rates on their websites with the objective of making lending rates more transparent.

Under this scheme, all categories of loans were to be priced only with reference to the base rate. Banks cannot lend at below the base rate. With this change, the earlier stipulation under BPLR scheme for loans upto ₹ two lacs was withdrawn. RBI also issued separate guidelines applicable for export credits. However, the following categories of loans were exempted which could be priced without reference to the base rate:

(a) DRI advances

(b) loans to banks' own employees

(c) loans to banks' depositors against their own deposits.

Banks are required to review the base rate at least once in a quarter with the approval of the Board or the Asset Liability Committee (ALCO) and announce it. Changes in the base rate shall be applicable in respect of all existing loans linked to the base rate, in a transparent and non-discriminatory manner as all loan interest rates are linked to base rate.

All banks operating in India announced their base rates on 1 July 2010. Most public sector banks kept their rates at 8%, while most private banks, a few government-owned banks (such as SBI) and foreign banks kept their base rates at 7.5%.

In April 2015, RBI issued fresh guidelines to banks concerning the methodology of calculating the base rate. These guidelines now require banks to follow uniform methodology as suggested by RBI in the year 2010 but not made compulsory then. Now banks are asked to adopt the same methodology.

The components of Base Rate will now include cost of funds, negative carry on CRR/SLR, unallocable overhead costs and Average return on Net worth.

As per clarifications provided, Negative carry on the mandatory CRR arises because there is zero return to banks for maintaining cash balance with RBI. Negative carry on SLR balances may arise if the actual return thereon is less than the cost of funds. The unallocable overhead costs is explained as the costs incurred for the bank as a whole, which is not allocable to any particular business activity/unit.

The new guidelines also stipulated fixing of spreads by the banks while offering interest rates on loans. The component of interest which is above the base rate, in the interest rate charged to a customer is called the spread. Banks are advised to fix the spread applicable to each type of borrowers taking into account the credit risk in a transparent manner and as a policy approved by the Boards of the banks.

MCLR (Marginal Cost of Funds based Lending Rate)

As further refinement to arrive at benchmark lending rates for banks, RBI introduced the concept of the MCLR methodology for fixing interest rates for advances and made it effective from April 1, 2016. This new methodology replaces the Base Rate system introduced earlier in July 2010.

The MCLR comprises of:

(a) Marginal cost of funds;

(b) Negative carry on account of CRR;

(c) Operating costs;

(d) Tenor premium.

(a) The marginal cost of funds will comprise of marginal cost of borrowings and return on networth. It will be calculated as under:

'Marginal cost of funds = 92% × Marginal cost of borrowings + 8% × Return on networth.'

The marginal cost of borrowing refers to the average rates at which deposits of a similar maturity were raised in the specified period preceding the date of review, weighed by their outstanding balance in the bank's books.

RBI has explained the methodology of calculating in its circular RBI/2015-16/273

DBR.No.Dir.BC.67/13.03.00/2015-16 dated December 17, 2015.

(b) Negative carry on account of CRR is same as prescribed for calculating base rate earlier.

(c) Operating costs are explained as 'all operating costs associated with providing the loan product including cost of raising funds will be included under this head'.

(d) Tenor premium as explained by RBI—'these costs arise from loan commitments with longer tenor. The change in tenor premium should not be borrower specific or loan class specific. In other words, the tenor premium will be uniform for all types of loans for a given residual tenor'.

RBI has further explained that 'Since MCLR will be a tenor linked benchmark, banks shall arrive at the MCLR of a particular maturity by adding the corresponding tenor premium to the sum of Marginal cost of funds, Negative carry on account of CRR and Operating costs'.

Hence banks are now required to decide and publish their benchmark lending rates for following maturities:

(a) overnight MCLR,

(b) one-month MCLR,

(c) three-month MCLR,

(d) six-month MCLR,

(e) one year MCLR.

In addition to the above, banks have the option of publishing MCLR of any other longer maturity.

Banks shall quote interest rates on loans by adding 'spread' as per their Board approved policy, to their MCLR. The spread is based on many factors including the credit risk perceptions. However banks cannot lend below MCLR (except for few exempted categories). Banks are now required to review its MCLR on monthly basis.

We may observe that there are some differences in the components of base rate and MCLR. The components of Base Rate include Cost of Funds, Negative Carry on CRR/SLR, Unallocable overhead costs, and Average return on Net worth.

MCLR is based on Marginal cost of funds, Negative carry on account of CRR, Operating costs and Tenor premium. MCLR is largely determined by marginal cost of funds and especially by deposit rates and repo rates (92% weightage) and return on networth (8% weightage).

It is claimed that MCLR will be more sensitive to changes in policy rates announced by RBI from time to time, and shall help in effective implementation of monetary policy.

However base rate system will continue for old loans to existing borrowers till repayment or renewal. Existing borrowers will also have the option to move to the MCLR linked loan at mutually acceptable terms. In view of this banks are publishing both Base Rate and MCLR at present.

2.15 What is the Interest Rates Banks Charge for Loans

From the year 1994, banks were allowed to prescribe their own rates on loans on the basis of PLR, BPLR and base rates. Banks are required to announce their rates of interest on loans. PLR, BPLR or the base rates (as banks have moved from one system to another) are the minimum rates. Banks generally add a premium on this rate based on many factors like the type of loan, security position, the purpose of loan and the risk perception on the loan, etc. Banks generally add to the minimum rate any premium upto 4% and quote their interest rate for a particular loan.

The minimum rates of the banks over the last few years are shown in the table below:

Bank Lending Rates of Scheduled Commercial Banks (Excluding RRBs)

Year (as at end March)	Type of minimum rate	Lending rates* %	Weighted Average Lending Rates of SCBs excluding RRBs % (WALR)
2001-02	PLR	11.00-12.00	
2002-03	PLR	10.75-11.50	
2003-04	BPLR	10.25-11.00	
2004-05	BPLR	10.25-11.00	
2005-06	BPLR	10.25-12.75	
2006-07	BPLR	12.25-14.75	
2007-08	BPLR	12.25-15.75	
2008-09	BPLR	11.50-16.75	
2009-10	BPLR	11.00-15.75	
2010-11	BASE RATE	8.25-9.50	
2011-12	BASE RATE	10.00-10.75	12.65
2012-13	BASE RATE	9.70-10.25	12.28
2013-14	BASE RATE	10.00-10.25	12.21
2014-15	BASE RATE	10.00-10.25	12.06
2015-16	MCLR	9.30-9.70	
2016-17 (As on July 15, 2016)	MCLR	8.90-9.15	

* Data on deposit and lending rates relate to five major Public Sector Banks up to 2003-04. While for the subsequent years, they relate to five major banks.

Notes: 1. Data on lending rates relate to either Prime Lending Rate (PLR) or Benchmark Prime Lending Rate (BPLR), Base Rate or Marginal Cost of Funds Based Lending Rate (MCLR) (overnight) as the case may be for the relevant year.

2. BPLR system effective November 2003 was replaced by the Base Rate System effective from July 1, 2010.
3. Base Rate System effective from July 1, 2010 was replaced by the MCLR System effective from April 1, 2016.

Source: Scheduled Commercial Banks (Excluding RRBs) and the Reserve Bank of India.

The Weighted Average Lending Rates shown in the above table represents the average interest yield on advances to the banks. These figures are now being given by RBI from 2012.

2.16 What is Selective Credit Control by RBI

Sections 21 and 35A of the Banking Regulation Act, 1949 empower RBI to exercise control on the credit against the sensitive commodities. These commodities listed under are important as at times when there is scarcity, there is tendency by some to hoard them and create scarcity in the market.

Sensitive commodities:

(a) food grains, i.e. cereals and pulses,

(b) selected major oil seeds indigenously grown, viz. groundnut, rapeseed/mustard, cottonseed, linseed and castor seed, oils thereof, vanaspati and all imported oils and vegetable oils,

(c) raw cotton and kapas,

(d) sugar/gur/khandsari,

(e) cotton textiles which include cotton yarn, man-made fibres and yarn and fabrics made out of man-made fibres and partly out of cotton yarn and partly out of man-made fibres.

Till early 1990s there use to be many restrictions for banks to lend against the securities of these commodities. There were regulations like the higher margin requirements, higher interest rates, ceiling on limits, etc. with the purpose to curb the hoarding in these commodities as it can put the public into inconveniences. These measures by RBI is known as selective credit control.

In the year 1996, RBI withdrew all the restrictions and allowed banks to lend against these commodities at their discretion and held back only sugar under the purview of selective credit control. The change in RBI stance on these commodities is obviously based on increased production and availability of these commodities now, which were scarce in olden days.

Presently, the following commodities are covered under stipulations of Selective Credit Control:

(a) Buffer stock of sugar with sugar mills

(b) Unreleased stocks of sugar with sugar mills representing
   - levy sugar, and
   - free sale sugar.

In this also only levy sugar under unreleased stocks has the prescription of minimum 10% margin and others are free from restrictions. Banks are also free to fix their lending rates.

However, banks are advised to keep in mind the broad objectives of selective credit control concept while dealing with loan cases. Further though at present there are no stipulations on these sensitive commodities, RBI can introduce it any time as it may deem fit.

2.17 What is Kisan Credit Card

Kisan Credit Card is a credit card to provide affordable credit for farmers in India. It was started by the Government of India, Reserve Bank of India (RBI), and National Bank for Agriculture and Rural Development (NABARD) in 1998-99 to help farmers access timely and adequate credit from banks.

Kisan Credit Card is a credit delivery system for providing adequate and timely credit to farmers under single window. It is devised to take care of all the credit needs of the farmers for various purposes without requiring them to approach the bank time and again for different loans.

Under KCC scheme, credit limit is set up for the short-term credit, medium-term and long-term credit needs of the borrowers for agriculture and allied activities including a reasonable component for consumption needs.

The limit is also based on the land holding, cropping pattern, previous record of the farmer, etc. and the bank fixes an overall limit on revolving basis. It provides revolving cash credit facility allowing any number of withdrawals and repayments within the limit.

Sub-limits to cover short-term, medium-term as well as long-term credit are also fixed by the banks.

Farmers under the scheme are issued with a credit card and a pass book or a credit card-cum-pass book incorporating all the details. The limit fixed is valid for three to five years thus obviating the need to renew the limits every year. Only yearly review of the limit is conducted.

KCC is issued to following type of borrowers:

- Farmers—Individuals/joint borrowers (owner cultivators)
- Tenant farmers, oral lessees and share croppers
- SHGs or joint liability groups of farmers including tenant farmers, share croppers, etc.

KCC scheme is highly successful and maximum loans to farmers are now made through this scheme. Government has reviewed the scheme in the year 2012 and has further improved it. Now technological features have been added. Based on the review, banks are now advised to implement the changes in phased manner. The main changes introduced are as under:

1. Paper card (pass book) to Plastic card-KCC in the form of ATM-enabled debit card.
2. Wider acceptance of KCC in allowing operations through branch/cheque facility/BCs/ATM/POS/mobile handsets.
3. More liberal assessment of credit needs of the farmers.
4. Cost escalation to be built in for assessing the limit—Notional hike of 10% for fixing credit limit from second year onwards.

The progress made under this scheme is given in the table below:

	Year ended March 2010	Year ended March 2016	Half year ended # September 2016
KCCs - Total (No. in million)	24.3	47.3	46.4
KCCs -Total (Amt. ₹ in billion)	1,240.1	5,130.7	5,543.4

Provisional.

Source: Report on Trend and Progress of Banking in India 2015-16 (Table 5.1)-RBI).

2.18 What is Export Finance

In the international trade, the country exports goods and services that is available in surplus of domestic consumption and imports goods and services from other countries that is either scarce or not available within the country. Imports are possible only when country exports and earns foreign exchange which can be used to make import payments. Thus, the role of exports is critical for the country. Our country cannot do without imports of especially petroleum products. There are also many other critical import requirements.

Foreign Exchange Regulation Act which was replaced later by Foreign Exchange Management Act is enacted basically to conserve the export proceeds so that it can be used for imports.

Any type of loans given by banks to exporters for the purpose of exporting goods and services to other countries is known as the export finance.

With the intention to boost exports, Reserve Bank of India gave separate priority status to export finance by banks and advised public sector banks to achieve 12% target for export finance. Foreign banks are also given a target of 12% for finance to exports as in their case all export finance are treated as priority sector advances. The interest rates on export finance is always separately prescribed by RBI which generally is lower than for the domestic loans. Even after deregulation of loan interest rates, interest rates for export finance is fixed by RBI as an exception. Government also gave many incentives to exporters in the form of duty drawbacks and other facilities like automatic entitlement to import (replaced in 1991-92 by Exim script scheme). Government also started interest subvention scheme for banks under which for credit allowed to exporters at concessional interest rates, the government reimbursed banks some percentage of interest (interest subvention scheme was substituted by GOI by Interest Equalisation Scheme in Nov. 2015). Government created Exim Bank to finance exporters and to provide refinance to banks. Export Credit Guarantee Corporation was created to provide guarantee cover to exporters.

All these measures to promote exports and give export finance at concessional rate is based on the fact that interest rate in our country is quite high as compared to many developed countries. Exporters from those countries enjoy cheap credit from banks which in turn enable them to market their products at competitive rates. By giving benefit of low interest to Indian exporters, government is enabling them to compete globally.

Exporters can be in 100% export business or partly in exports and partly do domestic business. Export finance is always assessed on the basis of different set of guidelines issued by RBI and banks finance the domestic part of the business on usual terms. Export and domestic limits are always segregated.

Commodities exported from our country are mainly agriculture and allied products, ores and minerals, manufactured goods from leather, chemicals, engineering, textiles, gems and jewellery and handicrafts. Invisible exports are the services exported. Services comprises services related to travel, transportation, insurance, software services, business services and financial services, etc. These are the main export earners for the country.

Banks generally provide two types of credit facilities for working capital requirement; pre-shipment credit and post-shipment credit.

Pre-shipment credit is extended to the exporter to finance procuring goods and services and processing them. It is the finance given till the time of actual export. Pre-shipment credit is generally given as packing credit loan. Packing credit loan can be a fixed loan for executing a particular export order backed by letter of credit or confirmed order from the foreign buyer. Packing credit loan can be allowed as a running account facility where like in cash credit limit, limit is fixed for total export orders in hand. Here individual loan for each export order is not maintained. It is pooled.

Packing credit loan can only be repaid from the proceeds of exports. It cannot be repaid from domestic financial sources of exporter. RBI has issued guidelines as to how to treat and adjust the outstanding packing credit, in case the payment for goods exported failed due to any reason.

Post-shipment credits are allowed against the bills raised by the exporters on foreign buyers by exporting goods and services to them. These are known as export bills discount or purchase facilities. In case the export bills are drawn under LC, banks are said to be negotiating the bills. Export bills may be payable immediately (on demand) or payable after the agreed usance period.

RBI has also permitted banks to make available loans in foreign currencies to exporters for both pre-shipment and post-shipment advances. Pre-shipment credit in foreign currencies are known as PCFC loans. Both PCFC and post-shipment foreign currency loans are given by banks at LIBOR-linked rates. Earlier the interest rates for foreign currency loans were at concessional rates as decided by RBI. From May 2012 onwards, the concessional rates were withdrawn and banks are allowed to fix interest rates for foreign currency loans for exports at LIBOR plus 3.5% maximum.

Interest rates on rupee pre-shipment and post-shipment credits were also at concessional rates as decided and advised by RBI. Till June 2010, the interest rates were pegged at BPLR (of the bank) minus 2.5% for these advances. From 1 July 2010 onwards as the base rate system for banks was introduced, RBI freed the interest prescriptions for export credit and made it at base rate or above it to be determined by the banks. Base rate is the minimum rate of the individual bank for lending.

Hence at present export credit does not enjoy any concessional interest rate but it is to be provided by banks at their minimum lending rates (base rates) or little above it. For foreign currency loans also the rates at LIBOR plus 3.5% is the normal rate. Banks will have to offer rate of interest keeping in mind the priority status of export credit.

Banks also finance exporters for their term loan requirement for setting up units for processing export goods.

Banks are also financing exporters by extending temporary loans in the shape of bridge loans against their duty drawbacks receivable. Duty drawback is the rebate of duty charged on imported material or excise duty paid on material used for exports. The exporter may claim drawback or refund of excise and customs duties paid by his suppliers as an incentive for exports.

Exporters fall under two categories. One is trading exporters and the other is the manufacturing exporters. Both are covered by the export priority status. Many of the manufacturing exporters also fall under micro small and medium enterprise (MSME) category of priority sector which has separate credit target. Hence, the export finance to MSME is counted as general priority sector advances as well. In the year 2015, RBI has created export finance as a separate sub-segment under priority sector.

Export credit subsector under priority sector will have only a part of total export credit of the banks as mentioned earlier. Export credit of SCBs for last few years are given in the table below:

Outstanding Advances of Scheduled Commercial Banks to Exporters (Amount in ₹ Billion)

As on the last reporting	March	June	September	December
2016	2248.00	2286.00	–	–
2015	2291.00	2156.00	2170.00	2147.00
2014	2382.00	2237.00	2123.00	2222.00
2013	2097.00	2109.00	2197.00	2221.00
2012	1915.00	1961.00	1846.00	1983.00
2011	1678.60	1665.60	1757.00	1896.00
2010	1459.20	1453.30	1493.30	1645.00
2009	1289.40	1203.00	1266.00	1243.60
2008	1299.83	1299.56	1361.72	1374.51
2007	1049.26	1079.83	1133.73	1177.19
2006	862.07	930.67	947.73	977.63
2005	690.59	704.34	753.91	819.65

Notes: (1) Data pertain to select scheduled commercial banks (excluding RRBs) which are availing export credit refinance (ECR) facility from the RBI. Since April 1, 2004, data for export credit also include five co-operative banks, viz. (i) Bombay Mercantile Co-operative Bank, (ii) Maharashtra State Co-operative Bank, (iii) Saraswat Co-operative Bank, (iv) Thane Janata Sahakari Bank, and (v) The Cosmos Co-operative Bank which are availing ECR facility from RBI.

(2) Export credit Refinance (ECR) Facility has been withdrawn in February 2015 and merged with the system level liquidity provision.

Source: Monetary Policy Department, RBI.

2.19 What are Consortium Finance, Multiple Banking Arrangements and Loan Syndication

The general trend followed by banks is to lend to a borrower for all his credit needs and avoid financing the same borrower by more banks. This is for the purpose of monitoring and also for creation of security charge on the assets of the borrower. When a borrower is financed by more than one bank, it is called as multiple banking. Multiple banking was not allowed as a matter of rule earlier as there will be no formal arrangements between banks' lending to the common borrower. Once there are more banks financing the same borrower, credit discipline will also get diluted.

Later, when the size of the projects grew with large requirement for bank finance, banks were finding it difficult to provide entire finance, due to many constraints like fund constraints and exposure constraints and risk concentration, etc. Then the banks started accepting multiple financing system under a consortium arrangement. Under this few banks joined hands to lend to one big borrower.

Consortium Arrangement. Reserve Bank issued detailed guidelines on consortium arrangement in 1974 and revised guidelines were issued in 1987. RBI made it compulsory for banks to form consortium for lending to bigger borrowers. Under consortium arrangement, one bank having a major share in the finance assumes the role of lead bank and other banks join the consortium as members and take up their agreed share of finance. Under consortium arrangement there is commonality of approach and common documentation and regular meeting of bankers to review the account. Generally, the lead bank takes the responsibility of assessing limits and then conveys it to member banks for taking decisions. Member banks are free to take their decision and there is no compulsion on them for accepting any of the views/assessment by the lead bank or accepting any particular percentage of share in the advances. Member banks are sanctioning the limits as per their own policies and conveying it. This arrangement, helped the banks to share the risk and at the same time have common control over the account.

Multiple Arrangement. However, over a period consortium has proved ineffective as the decisions were delayed because each bank had to take independent credit decision at higher level and there were delays in conveying decisions. Borrowers had little say in such matter. Enhancements were unduly delayed due to different views of member banks. Though they are to go by consortium decision, it was taking long time. This has ultimately forced Reserve Bank to yield and agree for multiple banking arrangements. RBI allowed banks discretion to sanction loans on either consortium basis or multiple banking or as syndicated loan with a view to introduce flexibility in the credit delivery system and to facilitate smooth flow of credit. Banks started lending under multiple banking arrangement to the common borrower without forming consortium. Each bank was taking its own decision and sanctioning loan without reference to other banks. There is no binding understanding with other banks on any matter. RBI did not issue any guidelines for multiple banking arrangements other than permitting banks to sanction loans under it. However, later at the instance of Chief Vigilance Commissioner, RBI advised banks in 2001 to be vigilant about the arrangements and issued some guidelines for effective sharing of information about the credit history and the conduct of the account of the borrowers amongst various banks.

Loan Syndication is a new type of banking arrangement that developed with the banks as a modification to consortium and multiple arrangements.

A syndicated credit is an agreement between two or more lending institutions to provide a borrower a credit facility using common loan documentation. A prospective borrower intending to raise resources through this method awards a mandate to a bank as 'Lead Manager' to arrange credit on his behalf. The mandate spells out the commercial terms of the credit and the prerogatives of the mandated bank in resolving contentious issues in the course of the transaction. The mandated bank prepares an information memorandum about the borrower in consultation with the latter and distributes the same amongst the prospective lenders soliciting their participation in the credit to be extended to the borrower. The information memorandum provides the basis for each lending bank making its own independent economic and financial evaluation of the borrower, and if necessary, by seeking additional supporting information from other source as well. Thereafter, the mandated bank convenes a meeting of banks to discuss the syndication strategy and finalise the share of each participating bank in the credit. The loan agreement is signed by all the participating banks.

The borrower is required to give prior notice to the 'Lead Manager' or his agent for drawing the loan amount to enable the latter to tie up disbursements with the other lending banks. Syndication is thus very similar to the system of consortium lending and is a convenient mode of raising long-term funds by borrowers.

Borrowers now generally prefer loan syndication arrangement. This is a new service provided by many banks, or through their subsidiaries. Loan syndication is becoming popular for all big projects, which help the promoter as he need not to run after the banks to join the project. Loan syndicator does this job and may also join as lender. Once financial closure takes place, i.e. banks have taken up entire loan; the participant banks can either create a consortium arrangement and select one bank as the consortium leader or have multiple banking arrangement for monitoring the loans to the borrower.

2.20 What is Loan System for Credit Delivery

This is a new approach to extending working capital loans by banks started by RBI in the year 1995. It was to address a systemic issue faced by banks in sanctioning working capital loans.

In nineties, it was observed that banks have sanctioned working capital limits to many big borrowers and these big borrowers were not effectively utilising it. In view of lower average utilisation levels, banks had sanctioned working capital limits to many more parties to an alarming extent. This created a peculiar situation as it was observed that the total limits sanctioned were far to higher than the financing capabilities of banks. It caused concern, as banks may face problems if many big borrowers start using the limits fully at a time. Further, it was an undesirable feature as the large borrowers probably got higher limits sanctioned far in excess of their needs and retain the option to use the full facility when it suits them at the cost of banks. Keeping this problem in mind, some banks may also react by curtailing fresh sanctions. This development was hindering the free credit flow to the economy.

In order to contain this tendency, RBI introduced loan system for credit delivery in the year 1995.

Under this system, banks were advised to allow 80% of assessed working capital limits as loan component and only 20% of the limit sanctioned is made available as cash credit (running account) component. This is applicable to borrowers with working capital limits of ₹ 10 crores and above from the banking system. Borrowers are obliged to take the loan component first and it shall remain outstanding throughout the year without change. Only the cash credit component can fluctuate as per utilisation. Loan component is renewed at the time of renewal and rolled over. Borrowers are however, allowed to repay the loan component, or part of it, any time during the year in case they have liquid surplus but the limit shall not be restored again during the year. Limit can be restored only after yearly renewal of working capital limits.

In 2001, RBI permitted some relaxations on this as under:

- Banks can inter-change 80:20 ratios either way depending on their judgment. They can increase or decrease cash credit component and also the loan component. Inland bills limits are to be kept separate and continued by carving it from the loan component of 80%. Banks are advised to offer differential interest rates on the components (loan component shall have lesser interest rate).
- Banks may allow exemption from this rule to some industries and business whose working capital needs are seasonal and cannot be fixed under loan system of credit delivery.
- Limits to exporters are exempted from the loan system of credit delivery.

- Banks may encourage borrowers with less than ₹ 10 crore limit also to come under the loan system by offering little lower interest rate on loan component of the limits.

2.21 What is Bridge Loan

Bridge loans are a type of short-term loan typically taken from banks for short period as an interim financing until permanent or the next stage of financing, which is already in the pipeline, can be obtained. Banks were sanctioning bridge loans for various purposes and sometimes with no securities to back-up the loans. Credit discipline was also weak and the bridge loans became a high risk area for banks. In view of this, RBI in the year 1995 advised banks to stop the practice of giving bridge loans due to the risky nature of such loans.

In the year 1997, RBI again allowed banks to sanction bridge loans for a maximum period of one year for some specific approved purposes. Banks are advised to obtain securities for the bridge loans. Banks are also advised to monitor the end use of bridge loans. Further, banks are prohibited to extend bridge loans for any other purpose than the permitted purposes. Banks are also specifically prohibited to give bridge loans against amounts receivable from Central/State Governments by way of subsidies, refunds, reimbursements, capital contributions, etc. except for fertiliser industry.

Based on the present applicable guidelines (2015), bridge loans can be sanctioned by banks for following purposes:

- Banks may give bridge loans to fertilizer industry to finance subsidy receivable under the normal Retention Price Scheme (RPS) for periods upto 60 days.
- Banks may give bridge loans to exporters to finance against receivables from government, viz. duty draw back and IPRS, as permitted.
- Banks may give bridge loans to companies for a period not exceeding one year against expected equity flows/ issues.
- Banks may extend bridge loans against the expected proceeds of non-convertible debentures, external

commercial borrowings, global depository receipts and/ or funds in the nature of Foreign Direct Investments.

There are many other conditions and stipulations in the guidelines which banks shall have to observe while sanctioning bridge loans as above.

2.22 What is Project Finance

Project in the broader sense means setting up of a new business venture which can be an industrial unit, or a service unit. Industrial unit can be of any size; small, medium, or large. Project is conceived by an entrepreneur who with the help of professionals makes a project report. The project report is a document which explains about the project, its relevance, its products, marketing, time required to implement the project, the finance requirement for the project and future cash flows expected from the project. With this document the entrepreneur approaches banks for loan support for the project.

Banks assess the proposal to arrive at a decision to sanction loans; both term loans and working capital loans for the proposed unit. While bank makes some independent financial and technical feasibility study of the project with the help of experts, it generally relies more on the track record of the promoters and their creditworthiness. Banks generally obtain collateral securities from the promoters in the form of some tangible securities or insist for their personal guarantees or some corporate guarantees from the existing companies of the promoters.

As the economy has progressed, the size of the projects is getting bigger now. Further, infrastructure projects are now in priority as they are necessary to develop infrastructure which is the basic requirement for the growth of economy. The government departments, government undertakings and government companies are now into many infrastructure projects. Even the private sector in the country has also entered into large infrastructure projects. These projects are huge in size involving thousands of crores of investments.

At the same time, commercial banks in the country during the last 25 years have grown in size and currently they have very huge funds with them and they are capable of financing any type of viable projects that is in the interest of the economy.

For financing the large projects, it is necessary for commercial banks now to deviate from their traditional approach to financing the project on the basis of promoter's creditworthiness or the capacity of the promoters to provide comfort in the form of collateral securities. Because of the sheer size of the projects, where the loan component runs to few thousand crores, banks cannot look to secure the loan by collaterals. Banks are now sanctioning loans to such type of projects solely on the basis of the viability of the projects as assessed by itself and/or by the experts from different professions.

This type of loans sanctioned by banks solely on the merits of the projects are called the project finance. Long-term financing of the projects based upon the prospects and the projected cash flows of the project without looking for comfort from the promoters is project finance. Thus, they are generally non-recourse loans as banks will not be looking at promoters for recovery. Only the project assets will be available for recovery.

Project finance are generally long-term financing and in case of some infrastructure projects it can extend upto 25 years also. Under the project finance, all the assets created by the projects form the security for the banks. Banks will also have charge on any revenue producing agreements of the project with third agency.

RBI has allowed banks to lend to projects including infrastructure projects and sanction loans by way of working capital finance, term loan, project loan, subscription to bonds and debentures/preference shares/equity shares acquired as a part of the project finance package which is treated as "deemed advance" and any other form of funded or non-funded facility.

As the project finance is for long-term (15 to 25 years), sometimes it creates a mismatch for the banks in their asset and liability management since the banks liabilities are for maximum upto five years only. This mismatch is a limiting factor for banks in extending loans to infrastructure projects. In order to encourage banks to give project finance, GOI has created a scheme called takeout financing which is extended by the India Infrastructure Finance Company Limited (IIFCL) set up by GOI. Under this arrangement, bank can exit from the project at a later date and the loan will be taken over by IIFCL subject to certain conditions. IDFC Ltd. is another infrastructure development company in private sector which also offers take out finance arrangement to banks for their loans to infrastructure projects.

2.23 What is Letters of Credit (LC)

Letters of credit (LC) are undertaking by the bank in writing issued in favour of the beneficiary at the behest of opener of LC, wherein bank undertakes that bills drawn in conformity with terms specified therein shall be honoured by the bank on presentation. Banks in India only deal with documentary letters of credit, which means the requirement of LC is to facilitate trade and movement of goods from seller to buyer.

By issuing LC, bank lends its name and credit to the buyer in favour of the seller. Now the seller has a bank undertaking which is far safer for him. He can know about the bank issuing LC from his own bank. Hence, the letter of credit brings parties together and facilitates trade.

LC is issued both for local and international trade. In fact, it is more relevant in international trade as besides the party risk, there are other kind of risks like country risk, payment risk, etc. attached to international trade.

LCs is governed by uniform customs and practice for documentary credit (UCPDC) rules, which have been accepted internationally.

Uniform Customs and Practice for Documentary Credit (UCPDC)

Uniform Customs and Practice for Documentary Credit (UCPDC) is a set of predefined rules established by the International Chamber of Commerce (ICC) on Letters of Credit. The UCPDC is accepted by bankers and commercial parties in more than 200 countries, including India, to facilitate trade and payment through LC.

UCPDC was first published in 1933 and subsequently updated over the years. The Banking Commission of the ICC approved the latest revision in October 2006. This latest version, called the UCPDC 600, formally commenced on 1 July 2007. It contains about 39 articles extensively dealing with various issues pertaining to LCs. It creates a uniform practice to be followed by all parties.

LC Terms

The bank issuing LC is called issuing bank. The party on whose behalf and request it is issued is the opener of LC. To whom the LC has been issued, is the beneficiary. LC issuing bank, if not in the same place as the beneficiary, sends the LC to its own branch or another bank requesting that branch or bank to convey it to the beneficiary. The bank conveying the LC is called advising bank.

The beneficiary then can ship the goods and submit bills strictly as per the terms of LC to his own bank or any other bank or even to advising bank for negotiating the bill. Such bank will be called as negotiating bank. However, the LC can contain a condition to restrict negotiation by a particular bank in which case, only that bank can negotiate the bill and make payment to beneficiary and claim reimbursement for the LC from issuing bank. If no condition is stipulated for negotiation, it is open for any bank to negotiate and LC opening bank is bound by it.

LC will contain mandatory clauses like what are the documents to be submitted, latest date for shipment and negotiation. There can also additional clauses like inspection, certificates, insurance cover, packing list, etc. The negotiating bank has to check every document submitted and ensure that the LC terms are fully complied with. A small mistake anywhere may give chance to opening bank to reject the document and refuse the payment.

As per practice, banks deal with documents only and not with the actual goods. Banks have no responsibility as regards the goods and their quality. Their checking is limited to prescribed documents under LC, including the bill of lading, invoices and insurance cover and ensuring compliance of all the terms and conditions.

Generally, LC issuing bank specify the arrangement for reimbursement and the negotiating banks shall follow it.

Types of LCs

Demand LC. LC can be issued as demand LC, in which case the payment has to be made on presentation of the bills.

DA LC. LC can be issued on usance basis and it is called DA LC. The usance period can be for any period, as decided, and it may start form LC date, bill date or shipment date.

Revocable LC. LC can be issued as revocable, and in this case, the LC can be revoked by the issuing bank any time but before the actual negotiation of bills. This type of LC is generally not accepted as risky.

Irrevocable LC. Once issued this LC cannot be revoked by LC issuing bank or the opener.

Confirmed LC. If required; the advising bank can confirm the LC by adding its confirmation. Then the advising bank becomes confirming bank also. By confirming the LC, the bank takes the responsibility to honour the commitment as per LC terms. These are generally used in foreign trade as the seller of the goods may insist for confirmation of LC advising bank locally, so that he has the commitment of a bank in his country, which is very safe for him.

Transferable LC. LC can be issued as transferable letter of credit. Under this LC, the first beneficiary who is usually an intermediary may request the nominated bank to transfer credit in whole or in part to the second beneficiary. In the transferable LC, there is a right to substitute the invoice and the whole value can be transferred to a second beneficiary.

Back-to-back LC. Sometimes the beneficiary of the LC after receiving the LC may approach his bank or any bank to open a LC in favour of his supplier to enable him to procure the goods for shipment. Banks may accept this request since there is a LC and payment is guaranteed once the goods are shipped. Banks may issue LC as requested and hold the original LC in their possession. These type of LC opened are called back-to-back LC.

Revolving LC. This is a LC which can be used many times on revolving basis without the requirement for issue of fresh LC. This can be used for regular and repetitive exports and the LC issued will revolve and reinstate once the bill under it is negotiated and paid. This obviates issue of separate LCs for each subsequent shipment. This type of LC is not in common use and the UCPDC has not defined this type of LC under its rules.

Standby Letters of Credit. Some international banks are issuing standby letters of credit, which is purely a guarantee of the bank. It is not documentary credit and goods are not involved. Instead of issuing guarantees, banks are issuing standby LCs for various purposes.

Banks generally issue LCs against securities provided by the customer. Generally, some cash margin is insisted upon and for the balance amount bank may accept any other form of security. LC facility is generally not sanctioned to parties in isolation. In practice, this facility forms part of working capital requirement of the regular borrower of the bank.

LCs issued by the banks are treated as contingent liabilities of the banks and banks shall have to disclose the total of such liabilities in their annual accounts statements as the footnote to the balance sheet. It is an off-balance sheet liability of the bank which is to be accounted for many purposes including for capital requirement of the banks.

2.24 What is Bank Guarantee (BG)

Banks issue guarantees at the request of its customers. Bank guarantee is in many ways similar to guarantee issued by any one. But the banking practice has made it little different from the normal guarantees executed by others. When bank guarantee is invoked the bank shall have to make the payment on demand.

Bank guarantees play an important role in trade and commerce. Government depts., government tax depts., courts, etc. who for various purposes require to collect money from parties and keep it as deposit for some time, now prefer to accept bank guarantee instead of cash. Bank guarantees obviate them from the responsibility of accepting cash from the parties and maintaining the account and then returning it. Bank guarantee gives them the option to demand the money from bank any time it is needed.

Bank guarantees are generally of two types. They are the financial guarantees, and performance guarantees. Financial guarantees are simple money guarantees, guaranteeing the financial obligation of the customers. It is like standing as surety for the money.

Performance guarantees on the other hand are for the purpose of guaranteeing performance and in case of default or deficiencies in performance, the financial liability arises and becomes payable. Here the money claim is contingent on the performance.

Some of the type of guarantees generally issued by banks are as under:

- Bank guarantees to government depts. on behalf of suppliers or contractors for different purposes.
- Bank guarantees issued in favour of other principal parties on behalf of contractors/suppliers/agents for security deposits/due performances/retention money, etc.
- Bank guarantees to customs dept. for duty payments.
- Bank guarantees to tax departments for disputed tax liabilities under adjudication or appeal.
- Bank guarantees for disputed amount under litigation before the courts when courts direct the party to submit a bank guarantee.
- Bank guarantees on behalf of share brokers to stock exchanges, commodity brokers to commodity exchanges as security deposit or other purposes.
- Bank guarantees of different types connected with exports or imports.
- Co-acceptance of bill of exchange by a bank also is a form of bank guarantee.

Co-acceptances. Sometimes banks are called to co-accept the bills of exchanges drawn on the customers which makes the banks as sureties for the amount of the bill, in case the bill is not paid by the customer on time. RBI has permitted banks to undertake such business with a view to encourage bills market. Bill of exchange being a negotiable instrument can be discounted to raise finance. Co-acceptance of bills (bill of exchanges) makes such bills backed by bank guarantee as prime security for any lender.

In trade, the supplier of the goods or machinery may agree to extend what is known as supplier's credit to the buyer provided the bills are co-accepted by buyer's bank. When the buyer's bank co-accepts the bill of exchange, the supplier can discount the bill easily with any bank and get funds released to him. As the bills bear bank's guarantee, it is safe for the supplier and to his bank who discounts the bill. For the buyer, it is supplier's credit and he need not make payment immediately by arranging funds or by getting loan. He can pay later as per the tenor of the bills. For the bank co-accepting the bill, it is contingent liability in case the buyer fails to make the payment on due date of the bill.

Banks generally issue bank guarantees against securities provided by the customer. Generally, some cash margin is insisted upon and for the balance amount bank may accept any other form of security. Bank guarantees are issued always with an expiry date. Claim under the guarantee, if any, shall have to be made before the expiry date. Bank guarantee is for a specific sum of amount mentioned in the guarantee and beneficiary can claim only upto the amount stipulated.

BG facility is generally not sanctioned to parties in isolation. In practice, this facility forms part of working capital requirement of the regular borrower of the bank. Banks may sanction this facility in isolation if the customer does not need any working capital finance from the bank.

Bank guarantees issued by the banks are treated as contingent liabilities of the banks and banks shall have to disclose the total of such liabilities in their annual accounts statements as the footnote to the balance sheet. It is an off-balance sheet liability of the bank which is to be accounted for many purposes including for capital requirement of the banks.

Beneficiaries under bank guarantee can invoke the guarantee anytime during its currency and banks are bound to make payment on demand and without demur. Banks cannot delay or raise any dispute for payment on any pretext. By practice and convention, commitments of banks under bank guarantees are viewed as sacrosanct. This convention has legal recognition and courts usually do not interfere with the payments of invoked bank guarantees. Reserve Bank of India also has advised the banks to make the payment of invoked guarantees on demand without excuses. RBI has advised the banks to have a proper system in place for issuing bank guarantees and for honouring the commitments.

To guard against the misuse or frauds in the area of bank guarantees, banks are now issuing bank guarantees (over ₹ 50000) generally under dual signatures of bank officials and also providing confirmations to the beneficiaries about the issuance of bank guarantees.

2.25 What is an Asset Reconstruction Company (ARC)

After the prudential norms and capital standards were introduced for banks in the year 1992 in the wake of banking sector reforms, the NPA portfolio of banks came into sharp focus. Many banks including nationalised banks had huge NPAs. High level of NPAs are not only putting pressure on banks for higher provisions and higher capital requirements, they are also making the banks to go slow on advances. Slowing down of credit by banks is not desirable in the growing economy.

In view of this, Narasimham Committee II, in its report in the year 1997 recommended setting up of Asset Recovery Companies who can take over the NPAs of the banks at a discount with a purpose to find out a solution for the sickness of the units and try to turn them around. Once the NPA is removed from the banks books, bank will be free of its burden and can concentrate on its core business.

GOI accepted this recommendation and accordingly enacted the Securitization and Reconstruction of Financial Assets and Enforcement of Security Interest (SARFAESI) Act, in the year 2002. This act recognised asset reconstruction companies and defined their role as a non-banking financial company (NBFC) to undertake the asset reconstruction functions by taking over distressed assets from banks and FIs. Section 3 of the act made it mandatory for such companies to seek registration with RBI and work under the control of RBI.

As per RBI guidelines, the functions of asset reconstruction companies have the following role to play:

(i) Acquisition of financial assets (as defined u/s 2(L) of SARFAESI Act, 2002).

(ii) Change or takeover of Management/Sale or Lease of Business of the Borrower.

(iii) Rescheduling of Debts.

(iv) Enforcement of Security Interest (as per Section 13(4) of SARFAESI Act, 2002).

(v) Settlement of dues payable by the borrower.

Asset reconstruction company can take over the NPA from banks or FIs at an agreed discounted price and make payment either in cash or in bonds payable at a future date. ARC is empowered to raise funds for its acquisition of NPA under Section 7 of SARFAESI Act by offering 'security receipts' to qualified institutional buyers (other than by offer to public) for subscription. Generally, the ARC is required to maintain separate accounts as trusts for each of its acquisition by earmarking the assets.

After acquiring the assets ARC has an obligation to help the unit in distress and try to turn it around. The main aim of acquisition of distressed asset is for the purpose to nurse it back to health and reap benefit as the asset value will appreciate. If the nursing is successful then the profits made is shared between the qualified institutional buyers who have provided funds and the ARC.

In case the unit cannot be nursed back to health and is destined to be closed down, then ARC will have all the rights of the creditor to realize the securities charged to it through legal recourse under the provisions of the act. If there is loss, then the same will be shared between investors and ARC.

Asset Reconstruction Company (India) Limited (ARCIL) is first asset reconstruction company that came up in the year 2002. ARCIL was incorporated as a public limited company and it holds a certificate of registration issued by the Reserve Bank of India. It is the first and also the largest asset reconstruction company in the country. It is promoted by prominent banks, namely State Bank of India (SBI), IDBI Bank Limited (IDBI), ICICI Bank Limited (ICICI) and Punjab National Bank (PNB). ARCIL has its registered office at Mumbai, Maharashtra:

Some other ARCs in the country are as under:

- Asset Care & Reconstruction Enterprise Limited (ACRE)
- ASREC (India) Limited
- Pegasus Assets Reconstruction Private Limited
- Alchemist Asset Reconstruction Company Limited
- International Asset Reconstruction Company Private Limited.

3

Banking – Others

3.1 What is Currency Notes. How RBI Issues Currency Notes

Currency is the monetary unit of the country and it is issued by the government in the form of coins and currency notes. In India, government issues one-rupee currency notes and the currency notes of all other denominations are issued by RBI under the authority of government. RBI also manages the issue of coins on behalf of the government.

Legal currency of the country is Rupee—originally being a silver coin. Government of India (GOI) started issuing one-rupee notes later, during wartime, as silver became short in supply.

In the history of Indian banking, many banks were issuing bank notes as bearer promissory notes which were used by public as alternate to currency. The first bank to issue bank notes was the Bank of Hindustan started in 1770 by an Agency House. Few other banks of that period also issued bank notes. The three presidency banks (Bank of Bengal, Bank of Bombay and Bank of Madras) started in 1806, 1840 and 1843 were issuing bank notes. It is also known that State Bank of Hyderabad (1941) issued its currency—Osmania Sikka, in pre-independence period.

In the year 1861, government passed Paper Currency Act and took over the function of note issuing from the presidency banks. But presidency banks continued to issue bank notes on behalf of the government. Thereafter, this function was transferred to RBI after its formation. At present Issue Dept. of RBI is issuing notes. The coins are issued by RBI as per provisions of Coinage Act passed in the year 1906. The 1955 Indian Coinage (Amendment) Act that came into force with effect from 1 April 1957 introduced a "Decimal series" coins. The rupee was now divided into 100 'Paisa' instead of original 16 Annas or 64 Pice.

Section 26 of RBI Act, 1934 prescribes bank notes as legal tender and that it carries the guarantee of the Central Government. Hence, the word 'promise to pay' appearing on the bank notes has no special meaning and nobody can invoke the promise as bank note itself is the legal tender. This makes the notes issued by RBI also as currency. The word 'promise to pay' is in fact is the past legacy of bank notes when it started originally as a promissory note and contained a promise of the bank issuing it. The promise has no relevancy now.

However, Section 31 of RBI Act, 1934 prohibits others to issue any bill of exchange, hundi, promissory note payable to bearer on demand, because bank note is construed as a bearer promissory note. Cheques are exempted from this prohibition. Others can issue only order instruments. Hence, bill of exchange, hundi, promissory note issued by others are always an order instrument.

At present Government of India issues one-rupee notes containing the signature of finance secretary. RBI issues notes in the denomination of 2, 5, 10, 20, 50, 100, 500, and 1000-rupee notes. Currency notes in denomination of 5000 and 10000 were also issued earlier which were subsequently demonetized in the year 1978.

Recently on 8-11-2016, Government of India demonetised currency notes of 500 and 1000 rupee denominations. After this demonetisation a new denomination of 2000 rupee notes were issued. New series of notes of 500 rupee denomination were also issued.

RBI maintains sufficient currency in its currency chests located at cities all over the country. These chests are also attached to banks who on behalf of RBI manage the same. It is like a currency go-down. These chests are maintained to ensure that currency notes are available at every part of the country as per demand.

As per law, notes can be printed to the extent the Issue Dept. of RBI is holding equal eligible assets against such issue. However, replacements of old notes can be done by the dept. Historically, the reserves against the note issues was in the form of gold to maximum extent and other eligible securities (mostly government securities) to some extent. Now the gold reserve has become smaller in proportion to other eligible securities.

Under the law, RBI is obliged to supply rupee coins in exchange for bank and currency notes or bank and currency notes in exchange for coins.

3.2 What is Money and Money Supply in the Economy

The economic definition of money is that it is a unit of value, medium of exchange and store of value.

Value of anything is expressed in terms of the currency of the country. So money serves the purpose as unit of value. We can buy goods and services by paying the price in money, so it serves as a medium of exchange. When we store the money with us it represents the storage of value as we can use it any time in future to buy things.

Money is issued by the government or by RBI on behalf of the government. How much money is there in the country is important to know. But in modern economy it has different meaning. Money being a medium of exchange it represents the total purchasing power. In modern economy an individual deposits his money in a bank account either in SB or current account or in term deposit. So the physical money goes to bank. In view of this, the balance of individuals or entities in bank accounts are also part of money as they are free to use it for purchases whenever they like. Hence, while counting the total money these new money equivalent is also to be counted to know the actual purchasing power with the public. This total is called the money supply in the economy.

RBI publishes the position of money supply on fortnightly basis for information. There are many components of money supply as under:

Reserve Money (M0): This has three components in it as under:

1. Currency with the public
2. Bankers deposits with RBI
3. Other deposits with RBI

Narrow Money (M1): This also has three components. This is higher than the reserve money as in place of banker's deposit with RBI, it takes demand deposits of all banks in to account.

1. Currency with the public
2. Demand deposit in all banks (e.g. current account, savings account)
3. Other deposits with RBI.

M2: This is same like M1 with addition of post office savings (post office savings accounts are also demand deposits same as other banks)

- M2 = M1 + Post office bank savings

Broad Money (M3): This has four components as under

1. Currency with the public
2. Demand deposits with the banks
3. Term deposits with the banks
4. Other deposits with RBI

This is also called as 'money aggregate' and RBI regularly publishes the position of reserve money and M3. The position of M3 is given under (as per RBI publication):

₹ in billions	Outstanding as on		
Item	Mar 31, 2015	Mar 31, 2016	Mar 31, 2017
M3	105455.5	116176.2	128390.8
Components (i+ii+iii+iv)			
(i) Currency with the Public	13863.5	15972.5	12637.7
(ii) Demand Deposits with Banks	8907.5	9898.3	14095.4
(iii) Time Deposits with Banks	82538.7	90150.8	101446.8
(iv) 'Other' Deposits with Reserve Bank	145.9	154.5	210.9

Source: RBI

There is one more category of money supply which is known as M4 which is as under:

M4: M4 = M3 + total post office deposits

In this, total deposits held by post offices in savings, term deposit and recurring deposits are added but other deposit schemes operated by post office like the NSC, IVP, KVP, and public PF, etc. are not included.

Money supply thus expresses the total purchasing power with the public represented by money and money equivalents.

3.3 What is Current Account Convertibility of the Currency

Current account convertibility of the currency is the status of the country when all restrictions for international current account transactions are removed for the citizens and payments are allowed freely. This means the import and export trade in goods and also services and other payments of current nature like payment of interest on loans, etc. are freely allowed. However, this does not include the capital account items like the assets owned and other capital investments.

Current account transactions of a country are aggregated on annual basis. The difference between the value of the import and export of goods is known as the balance of trade (BOT) position. But for the country balance of payment (BOP) is more important.

The balance of payment is the record of the payments and receipts of the residents of the country in their transactions with residents of other countries. It includes import and export of goods and services and other financial and capital transactions. This account is also usually drawn on annual basis.

Though in foreign trade the transactions are entered into by citizens with foreign parties, ultimately it is the responsibility of the government to ensure that all payments due to foreign parties are made in time. To ensure payments, government has to maintain foreign exchange reserves with it. Foreign exchange reserves are built from the proceeds of exports of goods and services or by other foreign exchange inflows including the capital inflows like loans or investments.

Residents of the country are generally bound by the exchange control rules of the government for entering into any type of financial transactions with residents of other countries.

Our country since independence was facing the problem of balancing the imports and exports as imports was always higher. Country was having negative balance of trade (BOT) position almost every year. Balance of payment position was also negative. In order to manage the international payments for imports and other obligations, government was then strictly controlling the foreign exchange outflows. This has resulted in many restrictions for imports and restrictions to send any remittances abroad. Foreign Exchange Regulation Act, 1973 was a strict law which controlled the foreign exchange transactions.

The exchange rates were fixed by RBI and was known as the official rate of exchange. Historically Indian rupee was linked to pound sterling and RBI used to fix the exchange rates between rupee and sterling. Later in the year 1975, this linkage was shifted to a basket of currencies (viz. the US dollar, the Deutschmark, the British Pound, the French Franc and the Japanese Yen). All the foreign exchange received by the citizens of country were to be surrendered to RBI at official rates. There was no market rate of exchange as there was no trading in foreign currencies.

In the year 1991, foreign exchange reserves plunged to very low level, which forced the government to pledge its gold for IMF loan to tide over the situation. Government then decided to bring in reforms to correct the imbalances in the economy and to align it with global trend.

Government then introduced many reforms in the areas of the Exchange Rate Policy, Foreign Trade Policy, Industrial Policy, Foreign Direct Investment (FDI) Policy etc. to bring in changes in the economy. It also initiated reforms in financial sector and banking sector. Foreign Exchange Regulation Act, 1973 was replaced by Foreign Exchange Management Act, 1999 which is a friendly legislation compared to FERA.

Changes in exchange rates policies—In the budget of 1992-93, the Finance Minister announced the Liberalized Exchange Rate Management System (LERMS). Under this 40% of foreign exchange earning was to be surrounded at official rate and 60% can be converted at market-determined exchange rate. This meant that 60% of foreign exchange earned need not be surrendered to government and can be freely traded in the market.

Due to this change, foreign exchange market was started in the country for the first time and the banks started to trade foreign exchange in the market at market-determined rates. Later, government discontinued the dual exchange policy in March 1993 and allowed the exchange rate of rupee to be totally market determined. The system of prescribing official rate of exchange was discontinued. Citizens are no longer required to surrender foreign exchange to RBI. Thus, the rate of exchange of Indian rupee became market determined.

With the reforms and changes introduced in the economy the balance of payment position of the country improved and became comfortable. Then in August 1994 Reserve Bank accepted obligations under Article VIII of the IMF, which is a commitment by the country not to resort to exchange restrictions while managing the balance of payments.

Presently, in our country, residents are free to enter into current account transactions like import and export of goods and services and some other transactions of current nature. However, they are not free to transfer assets held in the country. Similarly, they are also not free to hold assets in other countries. Holding or disposing assets are the capital account transactions and it can be done only with specific approval from the government (through RBI) or if it falls under some exemptions permitted under the present exchange control rules.

Hence, Indian rupee is now a convertible currency for current account transactions. Current account convertibility of rupee means that the exchange rate of rupee is market determined and that the citizens are free to make payments for current account transactions with foreign parties without requiring permission or approval from government or RBI. It also means that the country is now complying with the World Trade Organisation (WTO) agreements [which in the year 1995 replaced the earlier General Agreement on Tariffs and Trade (GATT)] for the smooth conduct of international trade without creating unnecessary barriers for trade in form of restrictions for imports or in the form of high customs duties for imports.

3.4 What is Capital Account Convertibility/Full Convertibility

The ultimate aim of any developing economy is to achieve full convertibility of its currency which includes capital account convertibility. It is the stage when the economy becomes a developed economy. But it is not easy to achieve as it will require the nation to be a truly developed nation from all angles, economically and politically.

Capital account convertibility gives the option to citizens to hold assets anywhere in the world and also that the assets held in the country can be freely converted to foreign assets.

Government is thinking in terms of making rupee a fully convertible currency since the economy is growing stronger. This means besides current account convertibility, capital account convertibility will also be permitted.

Capital account convertibility (CAC) is defined as "the freedom to convert local financial assets into foreign financial assets and vice versa at market determined rates of exchange." In simple language, this means that CAC allows anyone to freely move from local currency into foreign currency and back. It means that the citizens will be free to move their assets anywhere in the world without permission. This is the highly cherished status for a currency to achieve. Very few developed countries in the world have achieved this status. There are about 18 currencies in the world which have this status and it includes US dollar, Pound Sterling, Euro, Japanese yen, Canadian dollar, Australian dollar, Singapore dollar, etc. There are no restrictions from the governments of these countries for trading in these currencies.

Even though full convertibility will enhance the status of the country and attract large funds from abroad for investment, at the same time there is also a fear of flight of capital by the residents to other countries which may affect the stability of the economy.

Reserve Bank of India (RBI) has setup a Committee on capital account convertibility under the chairmanship of former RBI deputy governor S.S. Tarapore to "lay the road map" to capital account convertibility. In 1997, the committee submitted its report and it indicated few preconditions for allowing Capital Account Convertibility. The five-member committee has recommended a three-year time frame (by 1999-2000) for complete convertibility. The committee recommended that some preparation for the same would be required. Before allowing full convertibility, nation shall ensure that macro-economic conditions are in good shape and the economy achieves certain goal posts as preparatory steps. The goal posts are:

(a) fiscal consolidation—government deficit to be controlled within 3.5%.
(b) a mandated inflation target—inflation to be brought down below 3-5%.
(c) strengthening of the financial sector—banks are to be strengthened by adequate capital and their NPAs to be under 5%, and CRR for the banking system to be at 3%.

In committee's views, when these goal posts are reached, then it will be the right time to allow full convertibility.

Though the steps were initiated by RBI, final decision was delayed. Government and RBI were cautious and did not want the decision to be hurried.

In 2006, the Reserve Bank of India has again set up a committee in consultation with the Government of India to revisit the subject of fuller capital account convertibility in the context of the progress in economic reforms, the stability of the external and financial sectors, accelerated growth, and global integration.

The committee was chaired again by S.S. Tarapore and is known as Tarapore Committee II. It has again made its recommendations for steps to be taken for achieving full convertibility.

The committee has recommended a five-year roadmap to relax regulations on capital account convertibility, to be implemented over three phases to be completed by the year 2011.

According to the committee, following are the main issues to be addressed as preparatory and necessary steps for attaining fuller capital account convertibility:

- reforms in banking sector like encouraging setting up of new banks in private sector, and encouraging foreign banks.
- strengthening of capital ratios for banks and compliance of Basel II accord recommendations.
- all commercial banks should be subject to a single banking legislation and all banks, including public sector banks, should be incorporated under the Companies Act.
- Recommendations on the role of investments by FIIs, non-resident corporate, non-residents. Non-resident corporate should be allowed to invest in the Indian stock markets through SEBI registered entities, including MFs and PMSs.
- Moderation in public sector borrowings.
- The office of public debt should be set up to function independently outside the RBI.

The government is again cautious in its approach to the issue of CAC and though it is committed to achieve fuller capital account convertibility, at the same time it wants adequate preparation for it. Government is moving in this direction. Banks have been strengthened and their NPAs are under control. RBI has allowed foreign investments up to some limit to create confidence in the minds of international players. Foreign funds are allowed to invest in the country on certain terms. Government deficit and inflation are being monitored and are being controlled. Though no time limit is now set, it can be expected that rupee convertibility will happen at an appropriate time in future.

3.5 What is Foreign Currency Reserves, How and Why Foreign Currency Assets are Managed by RBI

Foreign currency assets held by the government through RBI form the foreign currency reserves (also called forex reserves or FX reserves). These assets may be the foreign currency notes, foreign government bonds and securities, bonds and securities issued by foreign companies/organisations, deposits with banks in foreign countries, etc. Gold held by RBI for this purpose is also treated as foreign exchange reserve as gold is acceptable to any country in the world.

Foreign exchange is received in international trade as the proceeds of the exports of goods and services. Foreign exchange is also received when loan is taken by individuals and government from foreign banks or organisations. Non-resident deposits received by Indian banks also is a source for foreign exchange. Investment by foreigners in the country is also a source of foreign exchange.

These foreign exchange received in the country is used for making payments in international trade for imports of goods and services and other payments. It is also used to pay the interest and principal of the loans taken from foreign sources.

Though the foreign trade is between parties, it is the obligation of the government to see that all payments to foreign parties are made in time under General Agreement on Tariffs and Trade established in 1947 (GATT) to facilitate international trade. Now the GATT is replaced by world trade organisation (WTO) established in 1995. Even government is also involved in foreign trade as importer of petroleum crude and many other items. It also has borrowings abroad which has to be repaid. In view of this government has to maintain foreign exchange reserves adequate to make payments to foreign parties as the default in payment even by individual importer due to paucity of foreign exchange reserves of the country will have catastrophic effect and the country will be treated as insolvent. This was the fear the country faced during the BOP crisis in the year 1991.

Reserve Bank on behalf of the government manages foreign exchange reserves. Prior to the year 1992, all foreign exchange received by banks in India were to be handed over to RBI at a RBI determined rate. Hence, RBI maintained all the forex reserves. Now since 1994 banks are not required to surrender foreign exchange to RBI and can use it or dispose it in the market. Now RBI receives only the foreign exchange receipts of the government and it can buy foreign exchange from the market if it desires.

RBI maintains foreign exchange reserves usually in various reserve currencies, mostly the United States dollar, and to some extent the euro, the pound sterling, the Japanese yen, and the Chinese yuan. This reserves are held as foreign banknotes, foreign bank deposits, foreign treasury bills, and short and long-term foreign government securities. RBI also adds gold reserves, special drawing rights (SDRs), and International Monetary Fund (IMF) reserves as the components of foreign currency reserves and publishes the figures.

RBI usually builds up the foreign exchange reserves to the extent to back its liabilities in the country on account of the local currency issued by it, and the various reserves deposited with it by the government or by banks or financial institutions.

After the BOP crisis in the 1991, the forex reserves held by RBI has steadily grown and as on 4th December 2015 the reserves stood at US$ 352 billion shown in the table below. India is now at 9th position in list of countries by foreign exchange reserves. The Economic Survey of India 2014-15 said India could target foreign exchange reserves of US$ 750 billion-US$ 1 trillion.

Foreign Currency Reserves

Item	As on December 4, 2015		As on April 1, 2016		As on June 9, 2017	
	₹ Bn.	US$ Mn.	₹ Bn.	US$ Mn.	₹ Bn.	US$ Mn.
1 Total Reserves	23,415.5	3,52,098.7	23,759.7	359,759.8	24,494.1	381,156.3
1.1 Foreign Currency Assets	21,888.7	3,29,249.9	22,162.9	335,686.6	22,954.2	357,282.0
1.2 Gold	1,172.2	17,543.8	1,334.3	20,115.0	1,297.1	20,095.7
1.3 SDRs	267.8	4,006.2	99.6	1,501.9	94.5	1,470.7
1.4 Reserve Position in the IMF	86.8	1,298.8	162.9	2,456.3	148.3	2,307.9

Source: RBI

3.6 What are Nostro and Vostro Accounts

Nostro Accounts

In order to handle payments and receipts of foreign exchange, authorized dealers (banks and others) maintain accounts at foreign centres with foreign banks through which these transactions are routed on behalf of their customers.

These accounts of Indian banks with foreign banks at foreign centres are called Nostro accounts.

All the banks in the world will require to maintain their foreign currency accounts for any given foreign currency with some bank in the country of that currency. These accounts of the banks with each other is called the Nostro or Vostro accounts. Both Nostro and Vostro accounts are same and the differentiation arises when these accounts are being referred by the banks to each other.

Let us take an example of an Indian bank maintaining a dollar account with a USA bank. This account of the Indian bank is referred by Indian bank as Nostro account (our account with you). The same Indian bank account will be referred by the American bank holding it as Vostro account (your account with us). These accounts are by no way different from the other accounts a bank is having except that the account is held for a bank in foreign country.

Bank maintains Nostro account separately for each currency at the concerned centres. The transactions undertaken by banks on ongoing basis generally results in their having balance in these Nostro accounts. As the currency exchange rates are market determined, bank runs an exchange risk on the foreign currency balances held in Nostro accounts. Generally, banks manage the exchange risk by few methods used internationally. One such option is by spot selling and forward buying, under this the bank sells its foreign currency in the spot market and enters into a forward contract to buy the same at a predetermined price.

3.7 What is Core Banking

Core Banking Solution (CBS) is explained as networking of branches, which enables customers to operate their accounts, and avail banking services from any branch of the bank on CBS network, regardless of where he maintains his account.

The platform where communication technology and information technology are merged to suit core needs of banking is known as core banking solutions. In this, computer software is developed to perform core operations of banking as a single unit.

Under core banking solution the bank establishes a central server and the transactions are processed at this single point. Branches are connected to this central server by networking and in this system the accounting for the entire bank branches are centralized. Hence, branches of the banks are acting as the extending arms of the central server of the bank. As the bank is one combined system, the customer is not restricted to his branch for his transactions and can access any branch of the bank for his banking needs.

Till introduction of core banking solution, the branches of the banks used to work as independent units maintaining books and accounts of their customers.

In India, maximum number of banks moved to core banking solution after the year 2000. This change is a revolutionary change in extending banking services and it enabled banks to start many new delivery channels. The new delivery channels are:

- ATM
- Debit card
- Credit card
- SMS banking
- Mobile banking
- Internet banking

These are all the alternate channels to avail banking services without the need to visit to bank.

Core banking system has enabled electronic payment systems like electronic clearing system (ECS), national electronic fund transfer (NEFT) system, and real time gross settlement (RTGS) system. Card payment systems and transactions at ATMs are also enabled by the core banking solution. Internet banking is made possible due to core banking solution. Mobile banking is also enabled by core banking solution. Thus, core banking solution has brought in paperless payment systems for the customers.

Even in paper payment system (cheque clearing) core banking has enabled cheque truncation system which has now stopped the physical movement of cheques and the collection time for cheques are brought down to two to three days irrespective of the distances involved.

Core banking solution conducts banking transactions in real time instantly which is the biggest advantage for customers.

3.8 Banks Accounting System

Like all business, banks also maintain their books and accounts. The accounting principle followed by banks are based on the double entry bookkeeping principles. Balances in the accounts are shown as either credit balances or debit balances. The general ledger of the bank is thus maintained in self-balancing system of accounting. As per the accounting principles; the credit balance represents either a liability or an income. The debit balances represent an asset or expenditure. Bank also prepares its annual accounts; profit and loss account and the balance sheet to get them audited.

Banks, accounting system and the presentation of accounts are also as per the guidelines of RBI. RBI has introduced prudential norms for banks for accounting purpose from the year 1992. The Institute of Chartered Accountants of India (ICAI) also has prescribed standards for bank financial statements. This standard is known as Indian GAAP (generally accepted accounting principles) standard.

Further, the banks with public shareholding and listed on exchanges also publish their quarterly results on the prescribed formats as per listing agreements with stock exchanges.

Presentation of bank balance sheet is in a prescribed manner. On the liability side, the liabilities are shown in the following order;

- capital and reserves,
- deposits from the public,
- borrowings,
- other liabilities and provisions.

On the asset side, assets are shown in order of their liquidity status as under:

- cash and balance with RBI,
- balance with other banks and money at call and short notice,
- investments,
- loans,
- fixed assets, and
- other assets.

As the footnote to the balance sheet, banks disclose additional information on contingent liabilities and the bills for collection lying with them. These are known as the off-balance sheet items but are very crucial information on the working of the bank. Contingent liabilities are the followings:

- LCs and guarantees issued,
- Forward exchange contracts,
- Acceptances, endorsements and other obligation.

As the countries are following different accounting standards, the world community has evolved a global standard for accounting system. The IFRS Foundation, an independent, not-for-profit private sector organization working in the public interest based in London, U.K., had set up The International Accounting Standards Board (IASB) as the independent standard setting body in 2001. The new IASB has set-up International Accounting Standards which is known as IFRS standards. Most of the countries in the world have accepted it and our country has also accepted it. The Institute of Chartered Accountants of India (ICAI) has adopted it and created IFRS standards for Indian companies known as 'the Ind AS' (the converged IFRS standards). This standard is now being implemented for annual reporting system of the companies. Indian banks may soon migrate to this new standard of reporting the annual accounts.

Bank Disclosures

Banks publish their financial results on yearly basis. Further banks are also required to publish their quarterly results in terms of listing agreements with stock exchanges. There are also reporting requirement to RBI for various purposes.

The important disclosure by banks about their financial health is to the shareholders and the public. Generally, banks disclose the yearly progress in their business which includes growth in deposits, advances, and other business. Banks also disclose their earnings and the status their capital and reserves. These are the basic broad parameters of banking business. These are provided in their balance sheet and profit and loss statements.

Besides the above disclosure, we can find that many important critical information is also provided by banks. Some of them are as per regulatory requirements and some are for the information of investors and financial analysts. Banks also provide some analytical ratios of their working. This information is very important to assess the true strength of the banks. Some of the information are:

1. CASA deposits—CASA deposits are the current and savings deposits.

2. Credit deposit ratio—Credit deposit ratio is the percentage of deposits which are given out as loans.
3. Priority sector advances and ratio—As per regulatory classification of advances.
4. Retail sector loans and ratio—As per regulatory classification of advance.
5. MSME advances and ratio—As per regulatory classification of advances.
6. Gross NPA—Gross NPA are the total non-performing assets as per books of the bank and the amount and its percentage in terms of total (gross) advances is given.
7. Net NPA—Net NPA is gross NPA minus the provisions held for them. This is also given in amount and also as percentage to net advances.
8. Provision Coverage Ratio—PCR is the total provision for NPAs expressed as percentage to total NPA.
9. Cost of deposits and funds—Cost of deposit is the interest cost of the deposits expressed in percentage terms and cost of funds is the interest cost on total funds including deposits expressed in percentage terms.
10. Yield on advances and funds—Yield on advances is the interest earning on advances expressed in percentage terms and yield on funds is the interest earning on total funds (including advances) invested by the bank expressed in percentage terms.
11. Net interest income (NII)—It is the difference between the interest earned by the bank and the interest paid by the bank to creditors. Net Interest Income = Interest Payments on Assets – Interest Payments on Liabilities.
12. Net interest margin (NIM)—NIM is a measure of the difference between the interest income earned by banks and the amount of interest paid out to their creditors (depositors etc. debenture holders). Net Interest Margin = (Interest Received – Interest Paid) / Average Invested Assets. It is expressed in percentage term.

13. Non-interest income—Banks income is divided into two categories; interest income and non-interest income. Non-interest income as the name denotes is the income bank earns as services charges, fees, commission, rent, trading profits including exchange profits, etc. The main source of income for bank is interest income. Now as banks have various other products and services made available to public they earn good income from these services. The present trend in banking is to diversify the business activities and earn as much fee-based income as possible as it will supplement the main income of the bank and improve the bottom-line.
14. Earnings per share (EPS)—It is arrived by dividing the net income by total equity of the bank. It is expressed in rupees as earned per equity share. Earnings per share serves as an indicator of a bank's profitability.
15. Return on equity (ROE)—ROE is the amount of net income calculated as a percentage of shareholders equity. Return on equity measures bank's profitability as how much profit the bank earned with shareholder's money. It is also known as "return on net worth" (RONW).
16. Return on assets (ROA)—It is an indicator of how profitable bank is in terms of its total assets. ROA gives an idea as to how efficiently assets are used to generate earnings. It is calculated by dividing bank's net income by its total assets, ROA is expressed as a percentage. ROA is also referred to as "return on investment".

Some figures of scheduled commercial banks are given in the table below for the purpose of understanding.

	2008-09	2009-10	2010-11	2011-12	2012-13
Non-interest income as% to total income	16.22	16.02	13.97	11.64	11.34
NIM%	2.62	2.54	2.91	2.90	2.79
Cost of fund%	5.99	5.10	4.75	5.90	6.12
ROE%	15.44	14.31	14.96	14.60	13.84
ROA%	1.13	1.05	1.10	1.08	1.03
Net NPA%	1.05	1.12	0.97	1.28	1.68

Source: A Profile of Banks by RBI.

3.9 What are the Capital Standards for Banks—What are Basel Accords

Banks have become very important institutions of the modern economy and the bank failures are the threats to the economy of the country. As banks have grown in size and carry on business at international level, bank failure of a major bank in a country may seriously jeopardise the economic stability of the country. Failure of a major bank may also trigger failure of more banks in the country and may also affect banks in foreign countries who have business relationships with them.

World over bank failures have proved disastrous for the countries concerned and have put the economy in to depression mode. On many occasions, the governments of the countries were forced to bail out the banks in order to save the economy from plunging in to depression. There were many such happening in 1970s and 1980s. The recent example of this calamity is the sub-prime crisis in USA in the year 2008 and failure of Lehman Brothers. US Government had to put in a bailout package for many banks affected by subprime crisis to save them and to save the economy. This subprime crisis also had its impact on many European countries.

In modern times, bank failures cannot be treated as an isolated phenomenon as it affects other banks and also the economy of the country. Governments and the central banks of the countries are concerned with this new threat to the economy and this has led to many discussions to find solution for the malady plaguing the banks.

The important development in this direction is the formation of a committee of central bankers called as the Basel Committee on Banking Supervision formed under the aegis of Bank for International Settlements (BIS). The committee specifically went in to the issue of bank failures and the steps to be taken to avert banking crisis particularly of banks operating at international level. It published its recommendations in the year 1988. The recommendations of the committee were accepted by the governments of participating central banks and came to be known as Basel Accord.

Basel Accord I (1988)

The first accord known as Basel Accord I was reached in the year 1988 and it prescribed minimum capital requirements for the banks participating in international trade. Thus this international accord identified that the capital base of a bank is crucial for withstanding the adverse developments. The Accord prescribed a minimum level of capital in percentage terms at 8% on the bank's assets calculated on risk weightage basis. This prescription of minimum capital took into account the credit risk of the banks on their assets (loans, investments). The accord also included the off-balance sheet exposures of the banks like letters of credit, loan commitments, derivative instruments, and guarantees on the basis of a conversion factor prescribed. This minimum was given as the benchmark to be considered as internationally acceptable level.

The Accord identified two categories of capital: Tier 1 and Tier 2 capital. Tier 1 capital is described as the core capital which has the highest capacity to absorb losses. Tier 2 capital is the supplementary capital made up of hybrid capital or debt instruments of different categories and various types of reserves (Tier 2 capital is further divided in to upper Tier 2 and lower Tier 2 categories depending on its being closer to equity or debt). The Accord has fixed minimum 4% of capital to be the 'core capital' and the balance can be Tier 2 capital.

The 1996 Amendment to the Basel Accord—Introduction of Market Risk

In January 1996, Basel Capital Accord was amended and capital charge for market risk of the banks was included. Market risk for the banks are identified as the risks, banks are exposed due to their open foreign exchange position, trading in debt securities and equities, commodities and services. As the market rates can change anytime due to many factors, banks are exposed to risks which may result in to losses. Banks are required to assess the market risk on ongoing basis and provide capital for this risk in addition to the capital requirement for the credit risk. This amendment also prescribed creation of Tier 3 capital to cover market risks.

Besides the requirement of minimum capital, BIS also advised the central banks to prescribe prudential norms in the working of the banks so that the working of banks becomes more transparent. Prudential norms are defined as the general norms issued by the central bank of the country for the proper and accountable functioning of banks.

The prudential norms and the capital requirement of 8% on risk weighted assets by the banks were immediately implemented by the G-10 countries. Since the year 1993, many other countries have endorsed Basel Accord and started implementing it. Currently, more than hundred countries have adopted the accord.

Prudential Norms and Basel Accord I Implementation in the Country

Narasimham Committee for financial sector reforms in its recommendation for banking sector reforms recommended that Basel capital accord and also the international practices of banking norms be introduced in the country to make the banks stronger and their working transparent. The international practices referred are what are known as the prudential norms.

Basel Accord on banks' capital and introduction of prudential norms for banks' accounting system was introduced together in the country in the aftermath of the BOP crisis in the year 1992.

RBI stipulated capital adequacy ratio of 9% (higher by one per cent than Basel Accord I) to all commercial banks in the country. RBI issued guidelines for risk weightage to be assigned to each type of loan asset from 0% to 100% for the purpose of arriving at the capital requirement. Further, prudential norms were also introduced.

As 9% capital adequacy ratio has been fixed, no Indian banks had adequate capital in 1992-93 and for some banks the gap was huge. Till the year 1992, the capital contributed by GOI in all the nationalized banks (20 banks) was just ₹ 40 billion. In order to comply with Basel norm on bank capital, government made fresh capital contribution aggregating ₹ 164.05 billion from 1993 up to March 1998. Government also diluted its stake in public sector banks and allowed many banks to raise capital from the capital market.

Basel Committee discussions and accords are not one time measures but is an ongoing process in the banking sector of the world. Basel Accord I has prescribed capital norms for the international banks mainly taking into account the credit risk the banks are exposed to. It added the market risk also to the capital requirement by the amendment in 1996. But it became apparent as the world faced many banking crises in 1990s and still later, that banking supervision will have to be further strengthened to safeguard the economies from shocks of bank failures. This has resulted in continued dialogue between the central banks and has resulted in two more accords called as Basel Accord II (2004) and Basel Accord III (2010).

Basel Accord II

In view of inadequacies observed in the Basel Accord I in checking bank failures, Basel Committee on Banking Supervision issued fresh set of guidelines in June 2004. These guidelines are known as Basel Accord II. This was issued in continuation and as further refined and improved guidelines given in Basel Accord I and it replaced Basel I.

Basel II gave more importance to banking supervision and set an international standard for Banking Regulators to create banking regulations in their countries.

Basel II spelt out the approach for bank strengthening as three pillars requirement.

Under the first pillar, it prescribed capital requirement for credit risk, market risk, and operational risk. It added operational risk as a factor for calculating capital requirement in addition to the existing factors of credit and market risk under Basel I. Operational risk is defined as the risk of loss resulting from inadequate or failed internal processes, people and systems or from external events. This includes the frauds which results in to losses.

Under second pillar, supervisory review and internal control of banks are given due recognition. Controllers and management are advised to review the adequacy of systems and control and decide on the level of capital requirement for the bank. Controller can demand higher level of capital for a bank, if considered necessary, based on its review of the bank.

Under the third pillar, enhanced disclosure of more relevant areas/information about the bank and also observance of market discipline was prescribed for the banks. Transparency is considered very essential and banks shall have to follow internationally accepted accounting standards and make the information available to public. This will make the bank management more responsible as they will be open for appraisal and criticism by public and it will act as a check on the banks.

Basel II is the transformation of original Basel I guidelines as Basel I was more of a mathematical formula. But the Basel II is more of supervisory control and improvement in banks internal management. The capital requirement under Basel II remains unchanged at 8% on risk weighted assets. Though under Basel II, three risks: credit risk, market risk and operational risk are specified for capital requirement, the pillar two widens the scope to further capital requirement for many other types of risks depending on the central banks' views on the matter. It enjoins the central banks and the banks to develop risk management capabilities in-house, so that the banks are adequately protected against financial crisis.

Basel II was issued in the year 2004 and all the member countries were to implement the accord and make necessary changes by the year 2008-09. Our country has adopted the Accord immediately and the commercial banks in the country have complied with the requirements of Basel II norms by March 2009.

Basel Accord III

Basel Accords I and II were aimed at removing the threats of major bank failures and the effects of it on the world financial system. Basel II was implemented by all the major countries and was expected to be completed by the year 2009 by all countries who have adopted it. But there was rude shock to the banking sector in early 2008. Subprime crisis in USA erupted and a major investment bank; Lehman Brothers failed and so also few other smaller banks. In the post-mortem of the crisis and in the case of Lehman Brothers, there was an interesting comment on its balance sheet by the auditors which stated—"Whatever was on the left-hand side (liabilities) was not right and whatever was on the right-hand side (assets) was not left."

This crisis and the episode brought out the disturbing fact that despite Basel Accord compliance, the weakness in the asset liability management of concerned banks was not detected or was cleverly hidden. Hence, this exposed the limitations of the Accord guidelines which was a serious matter for the central banks. This has forced the committee to revisit the provisions of the accord and further strengthen it by more stringent norms in the new Basel III Accord.

Basel III has retained the three pillar approach of Basel II and has improved on it. The committee has kept the capital at 8% on risk weighted assets which takes care of credit risk, market risk and the operational risk as in Basel II. But there are certain major changes now prescribed. The important changes are:

- It recommended some changes in the capital structure, i.e. Tier 1 and Tier 2 capital and abolished the Tier 3 capital category. It has now prescribed higher ratio of Tier 1 capital in total capital.
- More importantly, additional capital charge in the form of Capital Conservation Buffer (CCB) of 2.5% has been introduced. It is prescribed that the banks shall build this buffer in good years so that in the years of stress it will provide relief to the banks. The additional capital charge has to come from common equity Tier I capital. This effectively increased the total capital requirement to 10.5% (8% + 2.5%) as against 8% in Basel II.
- Committee has specifically prescribed Liquidity Ratios and Leverage Ratios for the banks (which was though already a subject of second pillar under Basel II).

Basel Committee has now prescribed a global minimum liquidity standard for internationally active banks. It requires banks to maintain the Liquidity Coverage Ratio (LCR) of two types: one is to maintain unencumbered liquid assets to cover an expected net outflows during a 30 days' stress period. This is an important measure to counteract any sudden development putting pressure on bank's liquidity in short-term perspective. Committee has issued detailed guidelines to simulate a 30 days' stress period taking into account all the factors leading to the creation of stress on the banks. This capability once developed by the banks will make them resilient to short-term shocks. The other type of LCR is longer term structural liquidity ratio called the Net Stable Funding Ratio (NSFR) which will have a time horizon of one year. The committee has decided to implement the LCR in stages till the year 2019.

Leverage ratio is relating to all exposure of banks including on-balance sheet and off-balance sheet exposures of the banks like commitments, guarantees, letters of credits. They are also accounted under the market risk in pillar I. It was observed that high gearing in such business (off-balance sheet exposures) can lead a bank to crisis. Basel Committee has now prescribed minimum 3% requirement of leverage ratio with a rider that the central banks may fix higher ratios at their discretion. RBI has fixed it at 4.5% leverage ratio.

Further both Leverage Ratios and the Liquidity Ratios are still under study and testing by the Basel committee which may supplement the guidelines on these in future.

The G-20 leaders have officially endorsed the Basel III framework on 11-12 November 2010. G-20 is the group of 19 major countries of the world and the European Union. India is also a member in this group. The final guidelines have been issued by Reserve Bank of India for implementation of Basel III guidelines on 2 May 2012.

Indian banks were already Basel II complaint in 2009. RBI has issued guidelines in 2012 making it effective from January 1, 2013 for complying Basel III guidelines in a phased manner, to be completed by March 2019.

It is expected that banks will require fresh capital to comply with the new accord. The new accord requires the banks to create additional Capital Conservation Buffer (CCB) of 2.5%.

For Indian banks the total capital requirement will be minimum 11.5% (9% + 2.5%).

Basel Accord is for strengthening the banks' capital base and also for better supervision of banks by the bank itself and by the regulator. The purpose is to ensure that banks remain healthy and provide a stable foundation for the economy and play their crucial role in supporting and developing the economy.

3.10 What are the Prudential Norms for Banks

Prudential Norms Prescribed by RBI

The Basel accord I issued in the year 1988 on bank capital standards advised the central banks to prescribe prudential norms for bank accounting to make it transparent and reliable.

RBI introduced prudential norms for banks accounting standards in April 1992. These are called the Income Recognition and Asset Classification (IRAC) norms. Besides norms for income recognition and asset classification, provisioning norms were also introduced. As these norms are introduced for the first time based on the international standards, RBI allowed some period of transition for the Indian banks to comply with it. Further, many changes in the norms were made by RBI over the years. The norms are detailed and specific to each type of bank assets and gives guidelines to the banks for treatment of each facility type (loans, overdrafts, cash credits, bills, etc.) and also some sector specific guidelines (agriculture, housing, commercial real estate, leasing, restructured accounts, etc.). The present norms applicable as per RBI master circular dated 1 July 2015 are as under:

Income Recognition Norms

Till the introduction of these norms, Indian banks were treating the interest earnings on loans on accrual basis. As per the international practice, the interest income on loans are taken to profit and loss account on actual recovery basis. The income recognition norm now laid down the guideline for treating the interest income as earnings only when it is actually recovered.

Further, the asset classification norms require the bank to identify the non-performing assets, and such assets are treated as not generating income. Hence, bank cannot take the interest chargeable to such loans to profit and loss account.

In a nutshell, banks can book interest charges on good accounts (standard accounts), when recovered, to the profit and loss account of the bank. This guideline serves two purposes. One is that the income of the bank for the year is actual and the other purpose is that the NPA once identified is maintained at the same value without adding any accrued interest to it. If unrecovered interest is added, the asset will be reflecting unrealistic inflated value.

Hence, the income recognition norm on actual recovery basis gives the correct picture on the earnings of the banks.

Asset Classification Norms

Asset classification norms are the central point of prudential norms. Before the introduction of prudential norms, Indian banks were following a health code system prescribed by RBI earlier. This system categorized the loan assets into about eight categories. The last category was the loss asset. Under the prudential norms, bank assets are first categorized in two categories as standard assets (performing assets) and NPAs (non-performing assets). Standard assets are the assets which have no identified weaknesses and considered as good assets.

RBI guideline defined non-performing asset as "An asset, including a leased asset, becomes non-performing when it ceases to generate income for the bank".

The asset is treated as NPA if in case of loan account, the repayment (loan installment) and interest charges are not recovered within 90 days from its becoming due. 90 days' default rule is the general guideline to identify NPA from the accounts under different types of facilities. RBI has issued clear guideline applicable to identify NPA status of the account for each type of facility.

There is one exception from this guideline which is for loans to agriculture. In case of all types of agriculture loans, the default period is not 90 days but it is two crop seasons for short crops and one crop season for the long-term crops. Crop seasons are reckoned as determined by the State Level Bankers' Committee in each State. This is a deviation from the general rule based on the fact that the flow of income for agriculturist is seasonal based on the produce.

NPAs are again classified in to three categories depending on the period of default and some other circumstances. RBI in its guidelines has categorized them as under:

Substandard Assets. With effect from March 31, 2005, a substandard asset would be one, which has remained NPA for a period less than or equal to 12 months. Such an asset will have well defined credit weaknesses that jeopardise the liquidation of the debt and are characterised by the distinct possibility that the banks will sustain some loss, if deficiencies are not corrected.

Doubtful Assets. With effect from March 31, 2005, an asset would be classified as doubtful if it has remained in the substandard category for a period of 12 months. A loan classified as doubtful has all the weaknesses inherent in assets that were classified as substandard, with the added characteristic that the weaknesses make collection or liquidation in full,—on the basis of currently known facts, conditions and values—highly questionable and improbable.

Loss Assets. A loss asset is one where loss has been identified by the bank or internal or external auditors or the RBI inspection but the amount has not been written off wholly. In other words, such an asset is considered uncollectible and of such little value that its continuance as a bankable asset is not warranted, although there may be some salvage or recovery value.

Source: RBI master circular dated July 1, 2015.

Provisioning Norms

After identifying NPA, bank is required to make provisions for its probable loss. The provisions are meant to cushion the banks against the probable loss, in case the loss is to be booked.

Maintaining reserves created out of earnings was an old corporate practice existing even prior to introduction of prudential norms. But earlier it was not based on any systematic calculations or for any specific reason.

Prudential norms makes the provisioning requirement for NPAs as a charge on the profit and loss account for the current year and profit can be declared only after making provisions for NPAs.

Under the provisioning norms prescribed, provision is to be calculated and made for each NPA every year before finalizing the accounts. There are detailed guidelines on the quantum of provision depending on the status of the NPA. The main points of the guidelines are as under:

Loss Assets. Loss assets should be written off, and if loss assets are permitted to remain in the books for any reason, 100 per cent of the outstanding should be provided for.

Doubtful Assets. Provision requirement

(i) 100 per cent of the extent to which the advance is not covered by the realisable value of the security to which the bank has a valid recourse and the realisable value is estimated on a realistic basis.

(ii) In regard to the secured portion, provision shall be made, at 25% (up to one year), 40% (1 to 3 years) and 100% (more than three years) depending upon the period for which the asset has remained doubtful:

Substandard Assets. Provision requirement

(i) A general provision of 15 per cent on total outstanding should be made without making any allowance for ECGC guarantee cover and securities available.

(ii) The 'unsecured exposures' which are identified as 'substandard' would attract additional provision of 10 per cent, i.e. a total of 25 per cent on the outstanding balance.

Source: RBI master circular July 1, 2015.

As per the guidelines the loss assets shall be written off or 100% provision shall be held. For doubtful assets also we can observe from the norms that three-year-old account shall attract 100% provision. For substandard assets 15% or 25% provision is applicable depending on the secured or unsecured exposure.

Besides the provision for NPAs as above, the prudential norms as applicable currently has prescribed some more provisions to be made by banks. These are the norms added over the years. They are:

1. Provisioning for Standard Assets. Currently, banks are also required to make provisions for all their standard assets to create a general provision. This is a measure to build additional reserves, introduced from the year 1999. RBI has prescribed provision for standard assets which are generally between 0.25% to one per cent depending on the category of the loans.

As per guidelines provision for standard asset should not be reckoned for arriving at net NPAs.

2. Prudential Norms on Creation Floating Provisions. Banks are also advised to create additional floating provisions for advances and investments separately. The level of floating provision shall be decided by the bank managements as a policy of the bank.

3. Additional Provisions for NPAs at Higher than Prescribed Rates. RBI has clarified that the regulatory norms for provisions are the minimum requirement and it is for the bank to decide whether they want to create provisions at higher level. Bank can adopt provision rate higher than the regulatory norm as a policy and comply with it on consistent basis. These additional provisions are not to be considered as floating provision mentioned in the paragraph above.

4. Provisioning Coverage Ratio. Provisioning Coverage Ratio (PCR) is the ratio of provisioning to gross non-performing assets. This reflects the buildup of provisions against the loan losses. RBI has prescribed PCR of 70% to be maintained from Sept. 2010 onwards. To arrive at the PCR, bank can reckon the specific and floating provisions made for NPAs discussed earlier.

The income recognition norms, asset classification norms and provisioning norms are aimed at rendering the banks accounts transparent and to reflect the true financial status/ strength of the bank.

3.11 What are Bank Rate, Repo Rate and Reverse Repo Rate

Definition of 'Bank Rate'

Bank rate is defined as the rate of interest at which Reserve Bank of India lends to domestic banks. Generally, these lending are for short duration and banks may borrow from RBI to manage their day-to-day liquidity position. However, these borrowings from RBI is as per the policy of RBI. Bank rate is an important interest rate of the financial system of the country and is treated as one of base rates along with bank deposit rates and government security rates. Generally, we can find that all these rates tend to be very close to each other. Bank rate acts as a signal rate for all other interest rates in the system. RBI announces its bank rate and the same remains in force till the time it makes changes in it. Changes in bank rate will be generally as per the monetary policy of the Reserve Bank and it is made when RBI desires some corrections in the system. By changing the rate, RBI gives signal to the financial system of the country about the intended correction and the desired direction for the financial system to move.

RBI was also using the bank rate as a monetary tool to change the demand for bank loans. RBI can make the changes in bank rate by raising it or by reducing it and this will lead the banks to change their loan interest rates. The change in loan interest rate may affect the demand for bank loans. Higher the interest rate, lower will be the demand for bank loans and vice versa. Thus, RBI can control and reduce credit expansion or allow credit expansion in the banking sector.

Liquid Adjustment Facility (LAF)

Narasimham Committee II report in the year 1998 on banking sector reforms, recommended that RBI may start a new scheme for lending to banks and also use it as a monetary tool to control money supply in the market. Based on this recommendation, RBI in the year 2000 started Liquid Adjustment Facility (LAF) as a new window for banks to access short-term borrowing from RBI for liquidity purposes. The scheme was revised in

March 2004. This system has two legs known as repo and reverse repo. Repo is a process where RBI injects liquidity in to the banking system and reverse repo is the process by which RBI absorbs the liquidity from banking system. Liquidity adjustment facility is also known as Liquidity Corridor. Introduction of LAF has created interest rate stability in the short-term money market.

Repo. Repos are the repurchase agreements between the banks and RBI. Under this banks can borrow from RBI for their short-term liquidity requirements on collateralized basis. The borrowings are for one day. Under its mechanism, bank is selling its securities (government securities) to RBI with a repurchase condition to repurchase at a future date. The interest rate RBI charges for this lending to bank is known as the repo rate. RBI advises its repo rate like its bank rate and the rate can be changed by RBI same as in case of bank rate. Banks can only offer the securities held by them in excess of their SLR holding for borrowing. Maximum borrowing under repo by a bank is as fixed by RBI from time to time. In October 2013, RBI introduced auction of term repo for 14 days and seven days' tenure in addition to the repo on one-day basis.

Effectively, this mechanism is short-term borrowing for the bank to tide over its liquidity crunch by giving securities to RBI. It is a secured loan for RBI. Under this system any bank having securities to provide, can borrow from RBI. This is a better option for the banks as borrowing from RBI under bank rate is an arbitrary system at the discretion of the RBI, even though it can be without security. Under repo, bank is assured of a line of credit available to it from RBI. As the loan is secured one, the repo rate of RBI is generally less than the bank rate. Now banks are generally borrowing from RBI under this scheme. The repo rate is now referred as policy rate of RBI as the banks now generally do not borrow from RBI under its bank rate scheme.

Reverse Repo. Reverse repo is the system where RBI borrows from the banks by lending securities. RBI borrowing has the effect of absorbing liquidity from the market. The tenure of this borrowing is seven working days. This is attractive for the banks as the banks having excess liquidity may prefer to lend it to RBI on secured basis for a reasonable return. RBI announces its reverse repo rate from time to time and generally it is lower than the repo rate. Since the year 2011, RBI has linked the interest rate for reverse repo at one per cent lower than the repo rate and announces both rates together.

At present RBI conducts auctions in repo and reverse repo on daily basis for banks and banks may submit their bids. The minimum size of the bid is ₹ 5 crores and in multiples thereafter. All scheduled commercial banks excluding RRBs can participate in repo and reverse repo auctions.

Marginal Standing Facility. Marginal Standing Facility is a new window created by Reserve Bank of India for banks to borrow from it, in its credit policy released in the first week of May 2011.

Banks can borrow from RBI under marginal standing facility, in emergency situation like when inter-bank liquidity dries up completely and bank has exhausted all sources for raising funds including LAF facility. It is a borrowing of last resort for the bank to tide over its liquidity position. This facility is also a secured facility and banks will require to pledge government securities to avail the limit. Under the scheme, banks can borrow up to one per cent of their net demand and time liabilities (NDTL). However, this limit is subject to change by RBI. The borrowing under the scheme is allowed for one day. The interest rate applicable is one per cent higher than the repo rate and RBI may also increase the rate at its discretion.

This facility is extended by RBI as a liquidity support to the bank which is under difficulties to manage the liquidity position for the day. The purpose is to reduce the volatility in the overnight lending rates in the inter-bank market. RBI allows this facility which is limited to one per cent of NDTL of the bank. RBI also allows the banks to avail this facility even by using the earmarked SLR securities which is not allowed under LAF.

At present as on 8-7-2017 the policy rates are as under:

	as on 8-7-2017
Repo rate	6.25%
Reverse repo rate	6.00%
Marginal Standing Facility Rate	6.50%
Bank Rate	6.50%

3.12 What are CRR and SLR for Banks

As on 8-7-2017

CRR- 4%

SLR- 20%

CRR

Historically, the cash reserve ratio (CRR) is the cash bank needs to keep with itself and with Reserve Bank for liquidity purpose. In a way it is to ensure that the customers can get cash immediately when they need it. The RBI Act 1934 under its Section 42(1) empowers RBI to prescribe the cash reserve ratio for scheduled banks, and banks are required to maintain it. From the year 2007, RBI has the authority to fix this ratio without any floor or ceiling at its discretion. Cash reserve ratio is calculated on the net demand and time liabilities (NDTL) of the bank. Banks shall maintain it either as cash in its vault or maintain balance in current account with RBI.

At present (8th July 2017) CRR is prescribed as 4% of NDTL for scheduled commercial banks and also for scheduled co-op banks. All other types of non-scheduled banking companies (non-scheduled commercial and co-op banks fall under this category) shall also require to maintain CRR on their NDTL in terms of Section 18(1) of the BR Act, 1949. They are also now required to maintain 4% CRR on their NDTL. Banks having no account with RBI are required to maintain balance with other banks as approved by RBI for this purpose.

Earlier RBI was paying some interest to banks for the CRR deposit maintained with it. Now from March 2007 onwards Reserve Bank does not pay any interest on the CRR balances maintained by SCBs.

SLR

Section 24 of Banking Regulation Act 1949 authorises RBI to stipulate statutory liquidity ratio for the banks to maintain in approved assets. SLR is maintained as a safe and liquid investment for banks to ensure that banks do not lend all the resources available but hold some percentage of it as liquid assets with them. As per amendment to banking regulation act in the year 2007, RBI can prescribe SLR up to maximum of 40% of NDTL. All types of banks in the country are covered by the provisions of the Section 24 of Banking Regulation Act.

Banks are required to maintain this SLR in the following approved investments

(a) Cash; or

(b) Gold valued at a price not exceeding the current market price; or

(c) Investment in the following "Statutory Liquidity Ratio (SLR) securities".

- Treasury Bills of the Government of India;
- Dated securities of the Government of India issued from time to time under the market borrowing programme and the Market Stabilization Scheme;
- State Development Loans (SDLs) of the State Governments issued from time to time under the market borrowing programme; and
- Any other instrument as may be notified by the Reserve Bank of India.

SLR securities are the bonds or promissory notes issued by Government of India and State Governments and these securities are backed by government guarantee. They are also called 'gilt-edged securities'.

At present (8th July 2017) banks are required to maintain 20% of their NDTL as SLR investments.

CRR and SLR were also used as tools of monetary control by Reserve Bank. By increasing the ratio, RBI can reduce the lending capacities of the banks and also decrease the money supply in the market. Prior to reforms in banking, these ratios were generally high and at its peak in the year 1991, CRR was 15% and SLR was 38.5% of NDTL. Thus, total 53.5% of banks' resources were impounded leaving little for banks to lend. After the reforms were introduced these rates were gradually brought down to enable banks to lend more. At present (8th July 2017) it is 4% CRR and 20% SLR total of 24%. Now RBI is generally not using these ratios as the monetary tools to control money supply.

3.13 What is LIBOR

LIBOR stands for London interbank offered rate. It is the rate of interest, the leading international banks will charge for short-term loans to each other.

LIBOR is defined as:

> The rate at which an individual Contributor Panel bank could borrow funds, were it to do so by asking for and then accepting inter-bank offers in reasonable market size, just prior to 11.00 London time.

In the international banking LIBOR is an important benchmark rate and a reference rate and practically all other market interest rates are linked to this rate as a base. Generally, the rates are quoted as LIBOR plus so many points (percentage). LIBOR rate is also used as the anchor rate for quoting floating rate interest on loans or deposits.

Publishing of daily LIBOR was started in the year 1986 and it was then administered by British Bankers Association (BBA) and it was called BBA-LIBOR. Later in early 2014, Inter-Continental Exchange (ICE) took over administration of LIBOR from the British Bankers Association. Intercontinental Exchange, Inc. is an American network of exchanges and clearing houses for financial and commodity markets. It owns 11 exchanges and New York Stock Exchange (NYSE) is one of them.

LIBOR rate is announced daily on five major international currencies [U.S. dollar (USD), Euro (EUR), pound sterling (GBP), Japanese yen (JPY) and Swiss franc (CHF)], for seven different maturities (overnight, one week, and 1, 2, 3, 6 and

12 months). This produces 5 × 7 = 35 rates daily. These rates are now administered by the ICE Benchmark Administration (IBA) and is also called as ICE-LIBOR. These rates are worked out on the basis of rate quotes for US dollar collected from 18 major international banks daily in the morning. The rates are published each business day by Thomson Reuters for information of all.

3.14 What are MIBOR and MIBID

MIBOR is the Mumbai interbank offered rate. It is created as a benchmark domestic interest rate on the lines of LIBOR. MIBOR is the interest rate at which banks can borrow funds, in marketable size, from other banks in the Indian interbank market. The Mumbai Interbank Offered Rate (MIBOR) is calculated everyday by the National Stock Exchange of India (NSEIL) as a weighted average of lending rates of a group of banks, on funds lent to first-class borrowers.

Along with MIBOR, NSE also gives another rate known as MIBID. MIBID is the interest rate that a bank participating in the Indian interbank market would be willing to pay to attract a deposit from another participant bank. The MIBID is calculated everyday by the NSE as a weighted average of interest rates of a group of banks, on funds deposited by first-class depositors. MIBID rate is always slightly lower than the MIBOR rate reflecting a margin for banks between deposit rate and loan rate.

The MIBOR/MIBID was launched on June 15, 1998 as an overnight rate. The 14-day MIBOR/MIBID was started in November 1998, and the one month and three month MIBOR/MIBID was started from December 1998. From the year 2008, a three days' MIBOR/MIBID rate specially for Fridays are also introduced (as overnight deals on Friday are repaid on Monday). Now the rates are published for overnight, three days, 14 days, one month and three months.

From the year 2008, Fixed Income Money Market and Derivative Association of India (FIMMDA) also joined NSE for fixing the MIBOR and MIBID benchmark rates and hence now the rates are known as FIMMDA-NSE-MIBOR/MIBID.

MIBOR and MIBID rates are arrived at by polling a few market participants for their rates and summarizing the prices they report. The procedure involves querying bid and offer prices from eight market participants.

MIBOR/MIBID rates are now used as benchmark rates for the for derivatives (Interest Rate Swaps, Forward Rate Agreements), Floating Rate Debentures and Term Deposits and other market deals.

3.15 What is Money Market

Money Market in India

Money market is the pace where money or its equivalents are traded. It is basically lending and borrowing in money for short time maximum up to a year. In contrast, capital market is for long-term lending and borrowing purposes where the instruments dealt in are the equities and debentures.

Money market has both unorganised and organised markets. In the unorganised sector, the players are the indigenous bankers and other private parties. The organised market is the market where the players are commercial and co-op banks, financial institutions, insurance companies, mutual funds, NBFCs, DFHI and UTI, etc. Central and State Governments are involved in the government securities market as borrowers. But their involvement is through RBI or Primary Dealers. The transactions in the money market are generally for large amounts and the turnover is very huge.

Money market has many sub-markets dealing in some particular type of money market instruments. They are the call and short notice money market, government securities (treasury bills) market, CBLO market, commercial paper market, certificate of deposit market, etc.

Transactions in money market takes place as some players may need short-term money for their liquidity purpose and try to borrow it. The other side is that some parties may have surplus money which they may like to lend for short period and earn income. Transactions in money market may be unsecured or secured by securities. Call money market is the unsecured market. Certificate of deposit market and commercial paper markets are also on unsecured basis. Other sub-markets mentioned above are secured markets where the lender is protected as borrowers provide collaterals to secure the amount lent.

The purpose of money market operations is to make available liquidity support in the financial system so that the parties can access it whenever they need short-term funds to manage their liquidity positions. Organised money market is under the control of RBI who prescribes the rules for the conduct of transactions in these markets. The rules also govern the admission of participants to each type of sub-market. RBI also authorises some entity to conduct the transactions and oversee the settlements. RBI itself is the overseer for call money market and government securities market.

The money market instruments dealt in these markets are as under. These instruments are money itself or equivalent to money as the at the conclusions of the transactions money is settled to the credit of the participants accounts.

- Call and notice money
- Government securities/Treasury bills—Repos and reverse repos
- CBLO
- Certificate of deposits
- Commercial papers
- Rupee derivatives (forward rate agreements interest rate swaps).

Call Money Market

Call money or notice money market is most sensitive component of the money market. It provides short-term finance for one day or maximum 14 days. Call money is repayable next day whereas the notice money is repayable on the basis of recall notice. Till the year 2006 the main players were the commercial banks (Indian and foreign, and co-operative banks), Discount and Finance House of India Ltd. (DFHI), Securities Trading Corporation of India (STCI) and they participate as both lenders and borrowers. Life Insurance Corporation of India (LIC), Unit Trust of India (UTI), National Bank for Agriculture and Rural

Development (NABARD) were allowed to participate only as lenders.

Now from the year 2006-07 onwards call money market has been converted as purely interbank market and others are removed from it. Participants in call/notice money market currently include scheduled commercial banks (excluding RRBs), co-operative banks (other than Land Development Banks) and Primary Dealers (PDs), both as borrowers and lenders. RBI has fixed prudential limits which the players must observe both for borrowing and lending in this market. The major call money markets are in Mumbai, Kolkata, Delhi, Chennai and Ahmedabad.

Call money market lending and borrowings are on unsecured basis and banks participate in it to raise liquidity. The rates are determined by the market forces mainly the supply and demand position. The rates can be highly volatile.

There used to be ceilings on the call rate and inter-bank term money rate till the year 1989, and after 1989 the ceiling was removed. Now the rates are market determined.

Government Securities Market

Government securities market has few sub-markets. Governments both Central and States borrow money from the market on long-term basis by issuing bonds. Generally, these are for long duration from 10 to 20 years. This market is not a money market. The issues are handled by RBI or Primary Dealers. The interested parties like banks and other financial institutions buy these securities as they carry government guarantee and are called the gilt-edged securities and also that banks and financial institutions require these securities for SLR purposes. Any investor including individuals can buy these securities. This is the capital issue market and the governments are to repay the money only on maturity and the market is also called the primary market.

The government securities issued as above in the capital market are used in money market for raising short-term loans which is discussed later.

Treasury Bills Market

Central Government also borrows money on short-term basis for maximum of 364 days by issuing promissory notes. These are called the Treasury bills. This issue is managed by RBI on behalf of the government. This is a money market component and the Treasury bills are called the money market instruments. Generally, banks and primary dealers are the buyers of these securities. This is also a primary market. Here also the government is borrower and its liability is only for repaying on the due dates.

Governments do not enter the money market except for borrowing as mentioned above and they also do not participate in secondary market where these securities are traded or in derivative market where these securities are used as the base for transactions.

There is also separate secondary markets for these government securities where the investors may sell their holding or buy from others.

Major players in the government securities market include commercial banks and primary dealers besides institutional investors like insurance companies. Primary Dealers play an important role as market makers in government securities market. Other participants include co-operative banks, regional rural banks, mutual funds, provident and pension funds. Foreign Institutional Investors (FIIs) are allowed to participate in the government securities market within the quantitative limits prescribed from time to time. Corporates also buy/sell the government securities to manage their investment.

There are derivative markets based on government securities which fall under the money market segments. These are:

- Liquid adjustment facility—LAF (repo and reverse repo) and marginal standing facility—MSF, markets operated by RBI
- CBLO market operated by CCIL.

Marginal standing facility, and repos are the liquidity windows provided by RBI for banks in which banks can borrow for short-term from RBI by providing government securities as collateral. Collateralised Borrowing and Lending Obligation (CBLO) is a new money market instrument developed by CCIL and RBI in the year 2002-03. Under this, participants can lend and borrow in secured environment. CBLOs are traded in this market to raise or invest short-term funds.

CBLO can be issued for a maximum tenor of one year. CBLO is a discounted instrument traded on Yield Time Priority. For issuing CBLO the participant has to deposit SLR securities with CCIL. Based on the securities deposited with it, CCIL guarantees the payment of CBLO on maturity. CBLO is useful to banks particularly when their liquidity requirements cannot be managed with borrowing in call money market alone. It acts as an additional window for liquidity purpose.

Reverse repo is a RBI window where RBI borrows short-term funds from banks by providing the collateral of government securities. It is a reverse transaction where RBI absorbs the liquidity from the market. This is not the same as short-term borrowings of the banks for liquidity purpose. When RBI borrows, it is not for its liquidity purpose but it is to provide a short-term investment avenue for banks. RBI may use this to sponge off the excess liquidity in the market.

Certificate of Deposits (CDs) Market

Certificate of deposit was allowed as a money market instrument by RBI in the year 1989. Certificate of deposits are issued by banks as negotiable deposit in the form of a promissory note. They are transferable certificates. All scheduled commercial banks [excluding Regional Rural Banks (RRBs) and Local Area Banks (LABs)] and select All India Financial Institutions permitted by RBI are eligible to issue certificates of deposits. Banks will have to maintain CRR and SLR on this, same as for other deposits.

The period of these deposits are minimum seven days to maximum one year. The FIs can issue CDs for a period not less than one year and not exceeding three years from the date of issue.

Certificate of deposit can be issued in physical form or in demat form. The amount of the deposit shall be minimum ₹ one lac and multiple thereof. All individuals and entities can invest in certificate of deposits.

Certificate of deposits are issued to a discounted value to the face value of the certificate payable at maturity. Banks are free to decide the coupon rate and banks can also issue CDs on floating rate basis. However, Banks cannot give loans against CDs and banks cannot buy back its own CDs from the market.

As the CDs are negotiable the original investor can sell it in the secondary market and transfer the deposit by endorsement and delivery, if the CD is in physical form or transfer through depositories for CDs in demat form. Due to this reason, active trading in secondary market now exists and anyone can buy and sell these CDs according to their liquidity needs.

Commercial Paper Market

Commercial Paper (CP) is an unsecured money market instrument issued by companies in the form of a promissory note. They are transferable like any other capital market securities. It was introduced by RBI in India in the year 1990 to enable highly rated corporate borrowers to diversify their sources of short-term borrowings. Later, primary dealers (PDs) and all-India financial institutions (FIs) were also permitted to issue CP to enable them to meet their short-term funding requirements.

This short-term borrowing by these entities through issue of promissory notes provide an additional instrument to the investors. Individuals, banks, other corporate bodies (registered or incorporated in India) and unincorporated bodies, non-resident Indians and foreign institutional investors (FIIs) are eligible to invest in CP.

As per RBI guidelines the companies with tangible net worth of ₹ 4 crores and above who have sanctioned working capital limits with banks and if their accounts with banks are in standard category, can issue commercial paper. Companies are also required to get the issue rated from SEBI registered rating agencies.

CP can be issued in physical form as a promissory note or in demat form. The minimum amount of CP is ₹ 5 lacs and in multiple thereof. As per guidelines, the CP issuing company is required to appoint an Issuing and Paying Agent (IPA) for the issue and only a scheduled bank can act as an IPA for issuance of CP.

CP is issued at a discount to face value as may be determined by the issuing company and the tenure of CP is for minimum seven days and maximum one year. The issuing company can buy back its CPs before the maturity from the secondary market.

CPs are actively traded in secondary market as a money market instrument.

Some Entities Connected with Financial and Money Market

Primary Dealer (PD). In 1995, the Reserve Bank of India (RBI) introduced the system of PDs in the government securities (g-sec) Market. They are introduced in to the system to strengthen the g-sec market. They can underwrite the security issues and also act like market makers. (Market maker is one who operates in secondary market and gives quotes both for purchase and sale to create an active market for trading in the securities.) Banks or subsidiary companies of banks/financial institutions can become primary dealers in the g-sec market. As on the year 2014, there were 20 primary dealers. 13 of them were banks and seven were the subsidiaries of banks/financial institutions.

Primary dealers can maintain current account and Subsidiary General Ledger (SGL) Account with RBI to enable them to trade in the g-sec market. They can also lend and borrow in the money market. They are also allowed access to the Liquidity Adjustment Facility (LAF) of RBI.

Discount and Finance House of India (DFHI). It was established in 1988 by RBI and is jointly owned by RBI, public sector banks and all India financial institutions which have contributed to its paid up capital. DFHI plays important role in developing an active secondary market in Money Market Instruments. From 1996, it has been assigned status of a Primary Dealer (PD). It deals in treasury bills, commercial bills, CDs, CPs, short-term deposits, call money market and government securities.

Securities Trading Corporation of India Limited (STCI), is a non-deposit taking NBFC. STCI was promoted by Reserve Bank of India in May 1994 with the objective of fostering an active secondary market in Government of India securities and public sector bonds. In 1996, STCI was authorized by RBI as one of the first Primary Dealers in India.

RBI divested its entire shareholding in STCI in stages by the year 2002, to the existing shareholders. Now Bank of India became the largest shareholder in the company. The company created a subsidiary company; STCI Primary Dealer Limited (STCI PD) in 2007 and the activities as primary dealer is now undertaken by this subsidiary.

Securities Trading Corporation of India Limited has changed the name of the company in the year 2011 to STCI Finance Limited and is now become a non deposit taking Non-Banking Financial Company engaged in other activities.

3.16 What is Capital Market and Financial Market

Financial market is the market where finance can be raised by borrowers who need funds for various purposes. Financial market is generally divided in to two main segments. They are the capital market and the money market. The capital market is the market for raising long-term finances generally for over one year. Money market is the place for raising short-term finances generally up to a year.

Capital Market

As the market for raising long-term finances, the capital market is the market for buying and selling equity and debt instruments. These are the two types of securities in this market. Equity or shares of the companies are known as stocks and the debt instruments like the debentures are known as bonds.

Any company or organisation who desires to raise equity or long-term debt offer their equity or bonds in the market. These are taken up by the investors who are looking for long-term investment with assured returns or in case of equity, good dividends and capital appreciation. The market where the initial offers of the companies and organisations for raising long-term funds are made are known as the primary market. The offers are called the initial public offers (IPO) and also referred as the capital issues by the said companies or organisations. In this, the borrowers borrow on the basis of bonds or equity, collect funds and then the offer will be closed. Thereafter, the borrower has only the obligation to repay the money on agreed terms on maturity. In case of equity, it is a perpetual investment and there is no repayment involved. Central and State Governments, government corporations and local bodies also enter the primary market to raise funds through bond issues for their various development programmes. Government securities market is also called g-sec market and it is a capital market.

The participants in capital markets are the individual investors, institutional investors, banks and financial institutions as investors, and local bodies and governments, companies and organizations as the borrowers.

Capital market has a dynamic secondary market which trades in the existing equities and bonds. The secondary market provides liquidity for investors for the long-term securities bought by them in the primary market. These securities are transferable and hence can be sold in the secondary market. The secondary market is also very important as it depicts the market value of the securities concerned. The market value of any security is in fact the price at which it is traded in the secondary market. As the market is free, the prices are the reflection of the demand and supply forces and more importantly the market perception about the worth of the securities in terms of earnings and future prospects. Market rate for any security changes on almost daily basis.

Capital market is very important component of the economy as it is the channel through which the savings of individuals or entities are made available to the users of capital for creating industries, business and infrastructure, etc. The size of a nation's capital markets is directly proportional to the size of its economy. For example, the United States, the world's largest economy, has the largest and deepest capital markets. Indian capital market is also very old and the Native Share & Stock

Brokers Association (forerunner of Bombay Stock Exchange) is the first stock exchange in Asia started in the year 1875.

Government securities market is managed by Public Debt Office under RBI and the other capital markets function through the recognised stock exchanges in the country who provide for both primary market operations and secondary market operations. SEBI is the regulatory authority for the capital market which also functions as watchdog to protect the interest of the investors (see under SEBI and stock exchanges for more details). With the financial sector reforms introduced from the year 1992, the capital market has shown improvements and also has introduced technology enabled platforms for trading.

3.17 What is Dematerialization (Demat) of Securities

India has a vibrant capital market which is more than a century old, and the trading was taking place on the paper-based settlement of trades. To improve the working of capital markets in the country, government enacted the Depositories Act 1996 for transforming the paper based securities to electronic form.

Demat stands for dematerialisation. Dematerialisation is the process of converting physical financial instruments such as share certificates, mutual fund investments, and bonds into electronic form. An investor who wants to hold his securities in demat form needs to open a demat account with depository through a depository participant.

Depository

Depository means a company formed and registered under the Companies Act, 1956 and which has been granted a certificate of registration under sub-section (1A) of Section 12 of the Securities and Exchange Board of India Act, 1992.

Depository holds securities (like shares, debentures, bonds, government securities, units, etc.) of investors in electronic form as a trustee. Depository facilitates holding of securities in the electronic form and enables securities transactions to be processed by book entry by a Depository Participant (DP), who is an agent of the depository.

There are two depositories: National Securities Depository Limited (NSDL) and Central Depository Service (India) Limited (CDSL) in the country.

National Securities Depository Limited (NSDL)

NSDL is the first and largest depository in India, established in August 1996 and was promoted by Industrial Development Bank of India (IDBI), Unit Trust of India (UTI), and National Stock Exchange (NSE) and 11 prominent banks in the country are also its shareholders. It has established an infrastructure of international standards that handles most of the securities held by individual investors in demat account and facilitates trading and settlement in securities.

Central Depository Services (India) Limited

CDSL is another depository established by Bombay Stock Exchange (54.20% share) and few banks in the year 1999 with the objective of providing convenient, dependable and secure depository services to all market participants. Settlement of trades in the demat mode is through BOI Shareholding Limited, the clearing house of BSE.

Depository Participant (DP)

Under demat mechanism, investors are required to maintain their investment account in securities with a Depository Participant (DP) who is authorised by the Depository. Many banks have become depository participants with NSDL and CDSL and maintain demat accounts for customers. Besides banks, brokers, financial institutions, or custodian acting as an agent of the depository are also appointed as DP.

Online trading in securities is now available for Indian investors. This facility requires the investor to have demat account with a DP, trading account with a broker and a running account (SB or current) with a bank. The investor can enter in to trading transactions in securities through Internet and as his DP account, trading account and bank account are interconnected by an arrangement between banks and brokers, the trading and settlement takes place instantly.

While new securities can be issued by the issuer companies in demat form to the credit of demat account of the investor, for old paper securities the investor needs to send the physical certificates through his DP to the issuing company for dematerialisation. The securities thereafter will be held in electronic form and the investor will have his demat account with the DP in which all his securities are shown as book entries.

Demat accounts also help the investors as they receive the dividend and other payments directly to the credit of their link bank account.

Dematerialization of physical scrip is a step to reduce paper work in capital market operations and speed up trading in securities. Today holding shares and securities in physical form is cumbersome as trading in such securities takes very long time.

3.18 Foreign Exchange Business and Market

Foreign exchange business is sale and purchase of any currencies of the world. A traveller going abroad needs his money converted to foreign currency of the place of his visit. An exporter receives his payments in foreign currency and needs to convert it to local currency. An importer needs to pay for imports in foreign currency by converting his local currency. Banks needs this market for handling the business requirements of its customers and also for inter-bank transactions. A foreign investor who wants to invest in our country needs his currency converted to Indian currency. A non-resident who wants to transfer funds to his account in India needs to convert his funds to Indian rupees. The central banks of the countries and the government of countries also need this market to carry out their international financial transactions.

The transactions in forex market are not confined to only few foreign currencies. There are a large number of foreign currencies which are traded in the foreign exchange market.

Foreign Exchange Market

The term foreign exchange is usually abbreviated as "forex" and occasionally as "FX."

The market in which participants are able to buy, sell, exchange and speculate on currencies is called the foreign exchange market. Foreign exchange market is not a single exchange but it is an over the counter market (OTC market). Market is constructed of global network of computers where the participants trade in currencies on one-to-one basis. There is no single authority who controls or monitors this market. Even governments have no control on these markets.

The present foreign exchange market is said to have come into existence from 1970 onwards. After the World War II and prior to 1970, the world's major industrial countries worked with the Bretton Woods system of monetary management, which created a fixed exchange regime for the currencies of the countries. After 1970 the developed countries switched on to floating rate regime. Thereafter, the foreign exchange market gained importance as slowly many developing countries also have shifted to floating rate system for their currencies.

Foreign exchange market is a dynamic market that facilitates international trade and payments. It is said to be the biggest market in world in terms of volume of business transacted with average daily volumes in the trillions of dollars. According to a survey coordinated by Bank for International Settlements (BIS) in April 2010, the average daily turnover was US$3.98 trillion ($1.5 trillion was spot transactions and $2.5 trillion was forwards, swaps and other derivatives).

Location of the Market

As the market is decentralised, there are many important international centres where high volume of business is conducted. London is the biggest centre for forex trade. Other important centres are New York, Tokyo, Hong Kong, Singapore, etc. Market is present in every country generally in all the important commercial centres. Further it is also a continuous market virtually around the clock without break on all working days as the countries in the world enters this market at different times depending on their own time zone.

Players in the Market

The players in the market are the banks, commercial companies, central banks, investment management firms, hedge funds, and retail forex brokers and investors. There are also speculators and arbitragers in the market who seek to profit from trading in the market. They operate in their own interest. Speculators try to make profits by speculating on the movement of exchange rates and arbitragers try to profit from simultaneous exchange rate differences in different markets.

Any type of financial institution (generally banks) that has received authorization from a relevant regulatory authority of the country can act as a dealer for trading in foreign currencies. Only dealers provide quotes both way for purchase and sales. Dealings are entered into with dealers only.

Layers of Forex Market

Forex market is a layered market and in the top layer the players are international banks who buy and sell currencies in very large volumes. It is also called the wholesale market.

The other layer in the market is the retail market where bank customers, investors, forex brokers enter the market to carry out their individual requirements of trade, investment or hedging operations.

Exchange Rates

Interbank quotations are given on two-way basis as "bid" and "ask". A bid is the exchange rate in one currency at which a dealer/bank will buy another currency. "Ask" is the exchange rate at which a dealer/bank will sell the other currency. The difference is the profit margin for the bank.

The actively traded currencies are generally quoted against all major currencies as pairs (like rupee/US dollar, rupee/euro, etc.) and the direct exchange rates are easily available. Sometimes a direct quote may not be available for two currencies intended to be traded (as they are not actively traded against each other). In such cases, a cross rate is worked out. The cross rate is arrived at by calculating their common relationship with a third currency.

The exchange rates of the currencies are market determined and the central bank and the government of the concerned currency country has no control on it. The central banks or the treasuries of governments also enter the market for their commercial requirements. They are also seen sometimes to enter the market in a bid to support their own currency prices in the international market. However, this has little impact on the market as the intervention may last for very short time and cannot change the market trend.

Further though the LIBOR is treated as a benchmark rate, there is no single exchange rate in the markets but a number of different rates depending on the trades at different places.

Segments of Forex Market

Trading in foreign exchange market can be divided into three segments. One segment is called the spot market. In spot market, the selling and buying is made for immediate delivery of the concerned currency and generally the settlement takes place on the third day. This time gap is in view of the time zone differences and to enable the payment through banking system.

Second segment is called the forward market. In this market, the currencies are traded for delivery at a future date but at the rates fixed on the date of the deal. This is an important market for the parties involved as the currency prices are changing daily and cannot be predicted. Any party who has a commitment to make payment in a particular currency at a future date (like for import on credit, loan repayment) can enter in to this forward market and fix the exchange rate immediately and hedge himself against the risk of fluctuations in the rates of the currency. However, the forward rates are generally higher than the spot rates.

The third segment of the forex market is called as the swap market. In a swap deal, it is two contracts involving the same currencies for the same amounts. For example, one contract is for spot buying of the currency and the other contract is for forward selling the same currency at an agreed rate and agreed future date. Both the contracts are for the same amount. The other kind of swap is spot selling linked with forward buying.

In a way, it is two-way agreement for buying or selling both on spot and forward basis and the second leg of swap reverses the original trade. Counter parties are reverted back to their original status. This deal is entered into by parties who either wants to dispose the current surplus balance of a currency held by them but they will require the same at a near future date, or buy it in case they are short of it but expecting to receive the currency at the near future. This deal is also used as a hedge to minimise the risk due to fluctuations in currency rates.

CCIL Operated System for Forex Business in the Country

In our country, Clearing Corporation of India Ltd. (CCIL) provides a guaranteed settlement system for its members for forex trade between them for inter-bank USD/INR spot and forward trades. This scheme was started in the year 2002. This scheme is applicable only for USD/INR spot and forward trades between banks based in India who are the members of CCIL. The rupee leg is settled through the member's current accounts with RBI and the USD leg through CCIL's account with the Settlement Bank at New York.

3.19 Who are the Authorised Dealers in Foreign Exchange in India

Authorised Money Changers

Foreign Exchange Management Act (FEMA) 1999 stipulates that all foreign exchange transactions are required to be routed only through the entities that are licensed by the Reserve Bank to undertake such transactions. Such entities are defined as authorized persons in Section 10 of the Act.

RBI issues different types of authorization for handling foreign exchange business to different categories of entities. At present (from 2006) the following types of authorizations are issued.

1. Authorized Dealer Category I. These are generally issued to commercial banks (excluding RRBs) and very few state co-op banks and urban co-op banks. At present there are 102 banks under this category. They are authorized to do all permissible current and capital account transactions. Major players under authorized dealer category-I are the foreign banks, public sector banks and the new private sector banks. These banks can maintain Nostro accounts in foreign currencies abroad through which they can handle all the permissible forex transactions. These banks are authorized freely to undertake import and export transactions and other permitted transactions for the parties.

2. Authorized Dealer Category II. These licenses are issued to eligible urban co-op banks, RRBs, financial companies in forex business and few others who are involved in forex business. Some existing FFMCs are also upgraded in to this category.

Authorized dealer category II are allowed to buy and sell currencies with some restrictions for undertaking certain types of foreign exchange business. They generally have authority to release foreign exchange for large number of purposes for non-trade current account transactions (like travel, medical treatment, studies abroad Registration/Subscription/Membership fees to International Organizations visa fees and many others). They are also permitted to issue forex pre-paid cards to residents travelling on private/business visits abroad. Authorised dealers category II are also permitted to maintain Nostro accounts with banks in foreign centers.

3. Authorized Dealers Category III. These are the few financial institutions who by their nature of activities require to undertake foreign exchange business. CCIL, Exim bank, SIDBI, and few factoring companies are authorized under this category and they are permitted to deal in foreign exchange to the extent and as per requirement of their particular business.

4. Full-fledged Money Changers (FFMC). They are entities authorized by RBI who can undertake sale/purchase of foreign exchange for private and business visits abroad. FFMC has to be a company registered under the Companies Act, 1956 with minimum Net Owned Funds (NOF) of ₹ 25 lakh for single branch FFMC and ₹ 50 lakh for multiple branch FFMC.

AD category I, AD category II and FFMCs are also called as authorized money changers (AMC). These three categories of money changers are also allowed to enter into franchisee agreements and appoint franchisees for the purpose of carrying on Restricted Money Changing business, i.e. accepting and conversion of foreign currency notes, coins or travellers' cheques into rupees. Franchisees cannot sell foreign currency and the foreign currency that they receive shall be surrendered to their AMC. Generally, hotels and other business establishments who receive foreigners and extend services to them are allowed to become franchisees. A franchisee can be any entity which has a place of business and a minimum Net Owned Funds of ₹ 10 lakhs.

3.20 Who are Business Facilitators (BFs) and Business Correspondents (BCs)

In the year 2006, RBI permitted commercial banks to use the services of business facilitators and business correspondents for the purpose of achieving greater Financial inclusion so that banks can reach out to places where there are no bank branches. In the year 2010, RBI permitted, on selective basis, urban co-op banks also to appoint BCs and BFs. These BFs and BCs are to be appointed by the banks as their agents and bank will be responsible for their conducts. Banks also require to take permission from RBI for appointing BCs, as BCs are given the financial powers in their duties. Business facilitators have no financial powers with them and banks are free to appoint them.

Business Facilitator

Under the "Business Facilitator" model, banks may appoint intermediaries, such as, NGOs/farmers' clubs, cooperatives, community-based organisations, IT-enabled rural outlets of corporate entities, Post Offices, insurance agents, Panchayats, Village Knowledge Centres, Agri Clinics/Agri Business Centers, Krishi Vigyan Kendras and KVIC/KVIB units, etc. for providing facilitation services. From the year 2008 banks are allowed to engage any individuals also as Business Facilitators (BFs).

BFs can perform following functions for the banks:

(i) identification of borrowers and fitment of activities;

(ii) collection and preliminary processing of loan applications including verification and submission of applications to banks;

(iii) educating about banking services and creating awareness;

(iv) promotion and nurturing Self Help Groups/Joint Liability Groups;

(v) post-sanction monitoring;

(vi) follow-up for recovery.

Business Correspondent

Under the "Business Correspondent" model, NGOs/MFIs, societies, Section 25 companies, registered NBFCs not accepting public deposits, and Post Offices may be appointed as Business Correspondents. In 2008, RBI has decided to permit banks to engage retired bank employees, ex-servicemen and retired government employees and many other individuals as Business Correspondents (BCs), in addition to the above-mentioned entities.

As per guidelines, while engaging such intermediaries as Business Correspondents, banks should ensure that the individuals or entities are well established, enjoying good reputation and having the confidence of the local people.

BCs can function as business facilitators and in addition to it, they are also given financial powers to transact on behalf of the bank. These financial powers are as under:

(i) disbursal of small value credit,

(ii) recovery of principal/collection of interest,

(iii) collection of small value deposits,

(iv) sale of micro insurance/mutual fund products/ pension products/other third party products, and

(v) receipt and delivery of small value remittances/other payment instruments.

These financial transactions conducted by the BCs outside the bank must be recorded in banks books on the same day or next day. Every BC will be attached to and will be under the oversight of a specific bank branch. Banks are now experimenting with technology solutions to link BCs with the banks.

Most of the commercial banks have appointed BCs and BFs. Major banks are SBI, ICICI bank and HDFC bank.

Business correspondent scheme is in fact a new channel for delivering banking services to people.

3.21 What is a Non-Banking Financial Company (NBFC)

A Non-Banking Financial Company (NBFC) is a company registered under the Companies Act, 1956 engaged in the business of loans and advances, accepting deposits, acquisition of shares/stocks/bonds/debentures/securities issued by government or local authority or other marketable securities of like nature, leasing, hire-purchase, insurance business, chit business, etc.

NBFCs are under the supervisory authority of RBI from the year 1964 by an RBI Amendment Act of 1963 which amended Reserve Bank of India Act, 1934. NBFCs now require to be registered under Section 45-IA of the RBI Act, 1934, for starting business operations. RBI has statutory authority to control and monitor their operations. RBI also prescribes prudential norms for the accounting system of NBFCs. NBFCs are required to submit many returns to RBI for the purpose of supervision.

Housing finance companies, merchant banking companies, Stock exchanges, Companies engaged in the business of stock broking/sub-broking, venture capital fund companies, Nidhi Companies, Insurance companies and Chit Fund Companies are also NBFCs but they have been exempted from the requirement of registration under Section 45-IA of the RBI Act, 1934 subject to certain conditions. This is because these companies are regulated by some other statutory authorities. For example, for housing finance companies National Housing Bank is the regulatory authority, for capital market SEBI is the regulatory authority and for insurance business, insurance regulatory and Development Authority is the regulatory authority. Generally, these companies do not come under the purview of RBI's authority.

NBFCs are engaged in business similar to a bank like accepting deposits, giving loans, investing in securities. But the main differences between a bank and NBFC are as under:

- NBFC cannot open demand deposit accounts (current and savings) for customers and use cheque books for withdrawals.
- NBFC cannot participate in any payment settlement system in the country.
- Deposits with NBFC is not insured under the insurance scheme of DICGC.
- They cannot use the word 'bank' in their name.

NBFCs are categorised mainly in to two categories, deposit accepting NBFC and non-deposit accepting NBFCs. Deposit accepting NBFCs have to comply with the statutory liquidity requirements prescribed by RBI.

Within this broad categorisation some sub-categories of NBFCs are as under:

- Asset Finance Company (AFC)
- Investment Company (IC)
- Loan Company (LC)
- Infrastructure Finance Company (IFC)
- Non-Banking Financial Company—Micro Finance Institution (NBFC-MFI)
- Residuary Non-Banking Companies (RNBCs)

NBFCs whose asset size is of ₹ 500 crores more as per last audited balance sheet are considered as systemically important NBFCs. These NBFCs are considered important as they will have a bearing on the financial stability of the overall economy.

3.22 What is Cheque Clearing, How it Takes Place

Cheque Clearing Houses—System

The usage of cheques as payment instruments and the provision for crossing the cheque made it necessary for banks to be involved in the collection of crossed cheques. As the bank customers deposit the cheques received by them with the bank, the bank has to present the cheques to banks on whom they are drawn and collect payment from them. As the volumes of cheques increased, this became a major and tedious job for all the banks. As a solution to this problem, banks started clearing houses as voluntary organisations for all banks to meet at a place at fixed time and exchange cheques and also make or receive payments from other banks.

Origin of clearing system is traced to England. It is informed that the daily cheque clearings began around the year 1770 in England when the bank clerks met at the Five Bells, a tavern in Lombard Street in the City of London, to exchange all their cheques and settle the balances in cash. This was an informal arrangement.

This informal arrangement then led to starting the first organization for clearing cheques—the "Bankers' Clearing House" in London in the early 19th century. It was founded by Lubbock's Bank on Lombard Street in a single room where clerks of London banks met each day to exchange cheques and settle accounts.

In our country, the first clearing house was established at Calcutta followed by Bombay and Madras in 19th century and were managed by presidency banks and the final settlement between member banks was effected by means of cheques drawn upon the Presidency Banks. The three presidency banks acted as the managers of clearing houses. Later Imperial Bank of India which was formed by merger of three presidential banks, took over these functions. After RBI was formed in the year 1935, RBI started managing clearing houses at centres it had offices and at other centres, the Imperial Bank of India continued managing. SBI then took over from Imperial Bank of India.

Though this is the tradition, any other bank also can manage the clearing house since it is a local arrangement with mutual consent of local banks. Bankers clearing houses are now functioning in all the big centres where there are many banks present. In the year 2010, there were about 1139 local clearing houses in the country. They are all functioning now also except for the changes mentioned little later about the clearing system.

Though the clearing houses are voluntary associations of banks, in view of its importance in payment settlement for the trade and commerce, RBI has prescribed uniform rules for the conduct of clearing houses.

How Clearing House Works

Under the clearing house system daily clearing is held at a fixed time when all the banks will attend the house. They will exchange the cheques (deposited by their customers drawn on other banks) with each other. At the end, banks will arrive at a net position for each bank by netting the money they have to collect from other banks and the money they owe to other banks on the cheques exchanged in the house. The manager of the clearing house will have the accounts of all participating banks with it and the net position of each bank arrived for the days clearing will be credited or debited to these accounts. With this all the cheques presented in the clearing house stands paid.

But this payment is conditional payment as the cheques received at clearing house will have to be taken to the respective bank branches for payment. If there are no funds available in any customers account or for any other valid reason the cheque can be returned by the bank on whom it is drawn. Hence, the clearing house will conduct another session daily for the return of the unpaid cheques. Once the session for unpaid cheques are held and settled, the clearing (payment) of all other cheques presented are to be presumed and the clearing settlements are treated as final. Time taken from the first presentation of cheques in the clearing house till the conclusion of returning the unpaid cheques is known as the clearing cycle.

As the clearing of cheques are conducted in batches, there will be no individual payment confirmation for the cheques. Payment shall be presumed if the cheque is not returned unpaid within the clearing cycle. Banks allow the customers to withdraw the money of the cheques deposited after the clearing cycle is over.

High Value Clearing—In order to help the business community with fast settlement mechanism for high value cheques RBI introduced separate clearing daily in clearing houses for high value cheques of ₹ one lac and above in all the major cities of the country. It was first started in the year 1989 in Chennai and then introduced at other major cities. Under this, the high value cheques are cleared on the same day. This system was later withdrawn as electronic fund transfer systems of NEFT and RTGS are introduced which offered much faster payment systems for the business.

Introduction of MICR (Magnetic Ink Character Reading) Technology

With the increase in trade and commerce, the usage of cheques as payment instruments increased tremendously. The volume of cheques handled at clearing houses in metro cities became phenomenal. This increase in workload till recently was handled manually by bank staff. However, due to enormous increase in the number of cheques, the clearing process was slowing down. In order to improve the cheque clearing system and to make it faster, MICR technology was introduced.

MICR technology was developed in the Western world in 1950s. In USA, American Bankers Association adopted it for speeding up the cheque clearing process and American banks started printing the cheques with MICR codes in 1958. By 1960s many countries in Europe adopted MICR technology.

RBI introduced MICR technology first in Bombay in the year 1984 and then added more centres. By the year 2010, 66 major centres in the country were under MICR clearing. MICR technology has greatly improved the cheque clearing process.

MICR technology requires cheques to have a magnetic band at the bottom of the cheque which contains the relevant pre-printed coded information like the drawee bank branch, cheque no., account no., type of instrument, etc.

Once the cheque is deposited by the customer for collection, the bank collecting it will have to print the amount of the cheque on the magnetic band with the help of an Encoding Machine. After encoding the amount, the cheque can be lodged for MICR processing at the clearing house/MICR centre.

These cheques are mechanically processed by a Reader Sorter Machine at the clearing house which records all the vital information and also sorts the cheques bank-wise and branch-wise. Reader sorter machine is computer supported and it takes care of the accounting and settlement functions. The sorted cheques are then handed over to the banks on whom they are drawn along with a summary statement. This technology replaced human intervention in this process and made the process accurate and much faster.

Introduction of Speed Clearing

After the year 2000 Indian banks started shifting to Core Banking Solution (CBS). By 2005 most of the major banks were on CBS platform. Core banking has changed the traditional banking which required customer to approach his branch for his financial transactions. Under core banking, Any Branch Banking became a reality and customer can avail banking services at any of the branches of the bank.

This 'any branch banking' feature enabled to stop the physical movement of cheques to the drawee branch of the bank as the cheque can be now paid at any branch of the bank through the core banking system. Keeping this new progress in mind, RBI introduced Speed Clearing in June 2008.

Speed clearing means collection of outstation cheques in the local clearing itself. Speed clearing is leveraged on the core banking system of banks. Under this, outstation cheques are no longer sent to drawee bank-branch for payment. Instead the outstation cheque is presented in local clearing to the concerned bank. Once the cheque drawn on upcountry branch of the bank is presented to the local branch of the same bank, the local branch of the bank is required to make payment of it, using bank's core banking capabilities to access the account of the customer with upcountry branch. Thus, the time required for the physical movement of the cheque is eliminated and even the upcountry cheque is paid in same manner as the local cheque.

This development is a major change in cheque clearing system for outstation cheques. The time for collection is reduced to be same as for local cheques. However, this is applicable to banks who are on core banking platform. Further, this is possible only when the drawee bank has a branch in local clearing area. In case the drawee bank has no branch in the local clearing area then the cheque will have to be sent for collection same as before.

The speed clearing concept developed leveraging the core banking platforms of the banks is later used in cheque truncation system also.

3.23 What is Cheque Truncation

Introduction of Cheque Truncation Technology

Cheque truncation is a revolutionary change in the cheque clearing system. It has been made possible by the technologies supported by computers and communication systems/networks. Actually, it is an invention to solve the tedious process of handling cheques for the purpose of settling the payments.

In the mid-1990s cheque truncation technology was developed in Western world as a solution to do away with the physical movement of the cheques in the clearing system and instead an electronic image of the cheque was moved through the clearing process.

As this technology has many advantages and reduces the time taken for cheque clearing process, RBI introduced this system in our country. This technology is in further improvement over speed clearing system started earlier and also replaced the MICR technology in use.

RBI has explained cheque truncation system as under:

> Truncation is the process of stopping the flow of the physical cheque issued by a drawer at some point by the presenting bank en-route to the paying bank branch. In its place an electronic image of the cheque is transmitted to the paying branch through the clearing house, along with relevant information like data on the MICR band, date of presentation, presenting bank, etc. Cheque truncation thus obviates the need to move the physical instruments across bank branches, other than in exceptional circumstances for clearing purposes. This effectively eliminates the associated cost of movement of

the physical cheques, reduces the time required for their collection and brings elegance to the entire activity of cheque processing.

This technology aims at stopping the physical movement of the cheques and to reduce the time taken for clearing process of cheques.

As per existing practice, cheque is issued by a person to a beneficiary for payment. Beneficiary deposits the cheque with his bank. His bank sends the cheque to the drawee bank through the mechanism of clearing house. Then the cheque is sent to the drawee bank-branch for payment. In case the cheque is unpaid then the cheque travels back from drawee bank to collecting bank through clearing house. The collecting bank returns the cheque to the beneficiary.

Cheque truncation system stops the physical movement of cheque from collecting bank onwards. At the point of collecting bank an electronic image of the cheque is created and sent to drawee bank through the Clearing House. The drawee bank shall make the payment on the basis of the electronic image of the cheque after verifying it for details. The electronic image is the replica of the original cheque and enables the drawee bank to process the cheque and also verify the signature on the cheque. Thus lot of time and logistic involved in physically moving cheques is avoided. The process of stopping the physical movement of the cheque by creating an electronic image of the same is called Cheque Truncation. The electronic image of the cheque forwarded to the drawee bank is called the Truncated Cheque.

But in order to adopt cheque truncation technology some legal changes were needed. Under the existing banking laws cheque shall have to be paid by drawee bank-branch on physical presentation of it. There is no provision to make payment in the absence of original cheque, or on the basis of an image of the cheque.

Introduction of cheque truncation technology was facilitated by amendments to the existing laws in the year 2002. The amendments made were mainly in The Negotiable Instruments

Act of 1881, The Bankers Book Evidence Act of 1891 and The Information Technology Act of 2000. These amendments permitted payment of cheque on the basis of the image of the cheque.

RBI introduced Cheque Truncation in the year 2008 at Delhi. Then it was started in Chennai in the year 2011 and at Mumbai in the year 2013. At these centres, the cheque truncation system, replaced the existing MICR clearing system. Under this system cheques are truncated at the level of presenting banks and thereafter only the image of the cheque travelled to the paying bank through the clearing house. Thus, physical movements of cheques are stopped, saving the time and the logistics involved in moving the cheques during the clearing process.

National Cheque Truncation Grids

Cheque truncation technology has now changed the face of cheque clearing system of the country and in place of number of independent bankers clearing houses functioning in different locations/cities, it has forged it as a single national system for cheque clearing.

In the year 2013, RBI has created three national cheque truncation grids centred at Delhi, Chennai and Mumbai integrating all the existing 66 MICR processing centres of the country. The entire geographical area of the country is divided in to three grid areas. They are named as southern grid (Chennai) western grid (Mumbai) and northern grid (Delhi).

Each grid covers a geographical area covered by the MICR clearing houses existing there earlier and RBI has the authority to make additions to the grid jurisdiction. Grid jurisdiction is also based on the geographical area of the states under the grid. Any other clearing houses functioning in the grid area may voluntarily join the CTS grid.

By November 2014, these three grids have taken over the clearing functions of individual MICR clearing houses and integrated it to a common system. The 66 MICR cheque processing centres are discontinued.

Banks are now issuing only CTS 2010 standard cheque books to their customers at all the branches in the country.

At present the cheques drawn on any bank anywhere in the country received at the erstwhile 66 MICR centres are truncated and presented to the respective banks for payment like local cheques. However, the banks in remaining centres having their local clearing houses cannot present cheques received by them in CTS system as they are not currently linked to cheque truncation grids. But they can opt for inclusion into the grid by adopting the required technology to participate in CTS cleating. RBI is now planning for inclusion of all remaining local clearing houses in the country.

CTS grid system has changed the earlier system of collecting the payments of the cheques through number of independent clearing houses at different centres, to a single national system.

Technically speaking, now the entire country has one single clearing house in which cheques drawn on any bank branch anywhere in the country can be presented by means of a truncated cheque and it will be paid as a local cheque. The physical movement of the cheques are totally eliminated and there is no difference in time norms for payment of cheques irrespective of the locations of the bank branches.

RBI has mandated National Payments Corporation of India (NPCI) to manage the CTC Clearing House. Under this mandate, NPCI is acting as a Clearing House/Cheque Processing Centre (CPC) and the Management of Clearing House is with the President of Clearing House as per already existing system (with RBI or any other bank identified by RBI as President). Settlement of clearing is undertaken by Reserve Bank of India on the basis of session-wise settlement files submitted by NPCI.

With the grid-based CTS system, the distance barrier has been finally broken and each grid area (comprising nearly 1/3rd area of the country) has become a local area for the purpose of clearing, taking the same time for payment of cheques irrespective of the geographical locations of the bank branches. There are no charges for collection of cheques payable in the same grid area. The cheques from the other grid areas are treated as outstation area and some collection charges are levied. But the time taken for clearing the inter-grid cheques are also same as the local area cheques.

The national grids of CTS clearing in the year 2015 accounted for 82-84% in terms of value of the entire clearing of the country under single system and the physical movement of the cheques have stopped. In the year 2015, clearing of cheques worth 16-18% in value, remain outside the CTS grid as they are still processed by nearly 1000 small local clearing houses across the country. They are yet to be mechanized. RBI is now planning to shift all these clearing houses to magnetic media based clearing system.

The business volume of cheque clearing operations in the country can be understood from the following figures:

Cheque clearing data for the month March 2015					
		Volume in million	Value in billion	% volume	% value
1	Total for all clearing houses in the country	102.80	8,027.11	100	100
1.1	Clearing handled by CTS grids	88.54	6,666.52	86.1	83.05
1.2	Clearing handled at other centers	14.25	1,360.59	13.9	16.95

Source: RBI

The national grids of CTS clearing has enhanced the relevance and usefulness of cheque payment system as a modern payment system.

3.24 What are the Payment Systems

Payment systems are the modes through which one can make payment to third parties for various purposes.

Before the banking system was evolved, the payments were made in cash/money only. Once the banks came on the scene, they enabled customers to use cheques. Slowly, the cheques became an instrument of payment used in trade and commerce. Once the cheques are regularly used as payment instruments, banks started local clearing houses to facilitate the payment of large number of cheques issued by bank customers. Thus, cheque payment system was established and it received legal recognition. Cheque payment systems are managed by bankers clearing houses. For long time, till the advent of computers and communication technology in banking, cheque payment was the only payment system existing. Besides cheque payment system, banks were offering fund transfer facility by mail transfer, telegraphic transfers and by issuing bank drafts. Bank drafts are similar to cheques for the purpose of payments and are collected through clearing houses.

Computerisation and communication technology has created additional payment systems known as the electronic payment systems. These systems provide an alternate for either use of cash or cheque to make payments. These new payment modes available to the citizen are as under:

- Debit, credit and prepaid cards
- Internet banking
- Mobile banking
- Electronic remittance facilities of banks.

It may be noted that ATMs are only cash disbursing machines and cannot be used for making payments to third parties. It only facilitates the bank customer to draw cash from it instead of going to bank and using a cheque for withdrawing the cash.

All others offer third party payments to be made for different purposes and all payments are conducted electronically without using any paper instrument for payment.

Debit, credit and prepaid cards can be used at POS for making payments for purchases and they can also be used at service providers for the payments of services availed.

Internet banking can be used to make many payments like payments for utilities, payments for travel tickets and payment to third parties for any other purpose.

Mobile banking also enables small third party payments for various purposes by using the mobile.

Electronic remittance facilities of banks are of three types: electronic clearing services (ECS), National Electronic Fund Transfers (NEFT) and the Real Time Gross Settlement (RTGS) systems. These are basically remittance facilities through which payment to third parties for any purpose can be effected. RBI operates these payment systems.

All these payment systems are linked to the bank accounts of the customer. Payment system involves transfer of money from customer's account with his bank to the credit of third party's account with any bank. Unless both are having accounts with the same bank, the payment system has to make settlement between two banks.

As the number of transactions are very high in each category of payment modes, the settlement takes place at fixed time intervals and on net basis. Netting means bunching up all transactions and arriving at a net figure for each bank (as either payable or receivable) and settling it. All the settlements of payment systems are on net basis except payment settlement under RTGS which is on transaction to transaction basis (gross basis).

For each of the payment systems, there is different kind of mechanism that makes the settlement between the parties. The agency that provides this mechanism and makes settlement between parties is called the system provider.

Under the Payment and Settlement Systems Act, 2007 (PSS Act, 2007), government has authorised RBI as the controller of all payment systems in the country and only RBI or RBI authorised agency can conduct any payment settlement system in the country. This law and rules under it are for the purpose of protecting all parties involved in payment systems so that the settlement takes place smoothly without default.

RBI is the only system provider for payment settlements in cheque clearing system and electronic clearing systems like ECS, NEFT and RTGS.

For other payment systems like the card payment system RBI has authorised few agencies like Visa International, MasterCard, American Express Bank, National Payment Corporation of India (NPCI), etc., who provide the system and conduct settlements. NPCI is also authorised to provide and conduct mobile banking payment systems.

Besides the above payment systems, payment settlement system is also required for ATM sharing business between banks and money market transactions of banks. RBI has authorised few system providers for ATM sharing business including NPCI for ATM sharing by banks under NFS. For financial and money market operations, RBI has approved only one agency, Clearing Corporation of India Ltd (CCIL) to conduct payment settlements. CCIL provides payment settlement systems for banks and others for trading in g-sec market, trading in CBLO, trading in foreign exchange market and trading in rupee derivative market.

There are few more payment systems like 'cross border money transfer', 'prepaid cards' payment system, etc. and RBI has authorised few agencies to conduct these payment systems.

3.25 What are NEFT and RTGS

National electronic fund transfer (NEFT) is the payment system or gateway provided by RBI in the year 2005 to banks for electronic fund transfer between bank accounts across the country. NEFT is a component of electronic clearing system.

This is RBI operated and managed system and the payment settlements between the banks are effected by RBI to the credit/debit to individual banks accounts. NEFT is conducted in batch mode in several batches in the day and hence it takes couple of hours for conclusion. There is no restriction as to the minimum and maximum amount per transaction in NEFT. Customer has to approach his bank for availing this service or he can avail it through Internet banking also.

RTGS is the payment system or gateway provided by RBI in the year 2004. The system is a straight through process where each transaction is processed separately on real time basis and the transaction is concluded instantly on one-to-one basis. Both debit and credit to banks involved in the transaction takes place simultaneously and the risk of payment is removed. For RTGS the minimum amount per transaction is ₹ two lacs and there is no maximum ceiling. As RTGS is introduced as the fastest mode for fund transfer from bank to bank, RBI has discontinued the high value clearing of cheques.

For facilitating interbank transfer of funds under NEFT or RTGS scheme, RBI has allotted Indian financial system code (IFSC) numbers to all the bank branches to identify the bank branches correctly. Customer can approach the bank branch for making electronic fund transfer under NEFT or RTGS scheme by providing the beneficiary's name, his account number, name of the beneficiary's bank branch with its IFS code. Bank customer can also effect fund transfer under these schemes through Internet banking.

These systems are available only on bank working days.

Besides the customer-related interbank transactions mentioned above, RTGS system is also used for final settlements of other payment systems. RTGS system is used by banks for interbank financial transactions. The CCIL, operated settlements for money market transactions in g-sec, CBLO and foreign exchange trading are finally settled between the banks through RTGS system. However, only the net figures as advised by CCIL is effected through RTGS.

RBI is encouraging all the 'Systemically important payment systems' (SIPS) of the economy to be settled through RTGS mechanism for the final net figures. This is because the failure in settlement of any major payment systems of the country can endanger the economy. RTGS is the straight through payment process which makes the payments immediate, final, irrevocable and risk free for the participants. Final settlement (on net basis) through RTGS system eliminates the risk of delay or failure of the settlements.

3.26 What is Electronic Clearing System

Cheque clearing system was the only payment system till the electronic age developed. Computers and the networking communication system developed by the modern technology has now provided alternate payment systems to the bank customers. Instead of cheque payment, now electronic payment modes are increasingly used for making payment.

But there are large number of electronic payments similar to cheque clearing system and there is the need for separate payment settlement systems. Settlement takes place in batches as each payment cannot be handled individually by banks. The payments are bunched for the day or shorter duration (like few hours) and the settlement takes place for the net figures payable or receivable by each bank. Such bunched payment settlements are called the clearing by netting the transactions, or settlements of net position. The clearing system is called the electronic clearing system.

Electronic clearing is paper-less clearing of payments and settled through electronic medium. Presently, there are following types of electronic clearing systems in operation

- Electronic Clearing Service (ECS) credit and debit
- National Electronic Fund Transfer (NEFT) (details are given earlier)
- Immediate Payment Service (IMPS) (details are given under mobile banking).

Electronic Clearing Service (ECS)

Electronic clearing services is an electronic mode of payments or receipts operated by RBI that are required by the parties to make payment or receive payment periodically. It is suitable for companies or entities for payments like the dividend, interest, salaries pensions, etc. and also to utility companies who receive bulk number of payments from subscribers.

Under this system there are two categories ECS credit and ECS debit:

Under ECS credit, the companies can make periodical large number of payments like dividend, interest, salary, pension, etc. to large number of individuals or entities.

ECS debit can be used by companies who receive periodical payments from large number of parties like the consumers of utility companies of electricity, telephone, water, gas supplies, etc.

Under this system, the large number of payments/receipts are pooled and a single credit or debit is made in the account of the company. Individual accounts will be credited under ECS credit and individual accounts are debited under ECS debit service. The individuals whose account will be debited periodically to make the payment to utility/service provider or for repayment of loan instalments will have to issue authority to the bank for such debits.

ECS is operated by RBI and under the system there are three types of ECS arrangements: local ECS, regional ECS and national ECS. Local ECS is suitable for local companies who operate within the small geographical area. Regional ECS offers a much larger area of operation covering states. National ECS allows the operation in national level.

National Automated Clearing House (NACH)

NACH is scheme started by NPCI in the year 2013. This service is an improvement over ECS (electronic clearing service) started by RBI earlier. NACH has combined both credit ECS and debit ECS under one system. It is a central system for the country which eliminates the multiple ECS systems and is an alternate to RBI operated system. It serves the same purpose as ECS credit and debit system of RBI for making high volume, low value debit/credit transactions that are recurring in nature. NACH is slowly taking over the ECS clearing under its scheme.

3.27 What is Money Laundering

Criminal activities such as drug trafficking, smuggling, human trafficking, corruption and others, generate large amounts of ill-gotten money for the individuals or groups carrying on these criminal activities. Tax evasion also leads to creation of black money, though the origin of the money is through legal means, by avoiding taxes the money becomes ill-gotten. As the amount involved is large, the criminals and tax evaders run the risk of drawing the attention of the authorities to the underlying criminal/illegal activity and exposing themselves to criminal prosecution. The ill-gotten money cannot be openly used due to this reason. In order to benefit freely from the proceeds of their crime, they require to conceal the illicit origin of these funds and show it as if earned by legal means. This is the basis and the reason for money laundering activities.

Money laundering is the process by which illegal funds and assets are attempted to be converted into legitimate funds and assets. Once the money is put in a bank account and then used, the source of the money gets camouflaged to some extent, and then onwards it appears as good money not differentiable from other good money.

Generally, the modus operandi for money laundering is observed as below:

1. **Placement:** Illegal funds or assets are first brought into the financial system.
2. **Layering:** This is done by indulging in a series of transfer of funds using multiple accounts, banks, intermediaries, corporations, trusts, countries so as to disguise the origin. A maze of transaction chain is created to make it difficult for anyone to trace the origin of funds.
3. **Integration:** Laundered funds are made available as legitimate funds and invested.

All money laundering transactions may not go through layering process and the same may be skipped and the funds are sometimes directly invested.

Though the use of banking services by criminals and tax evaders is not new to banking as it existed in the past also, its menace came into sharp focus once the world started experiencing rise in terrorist activities from 1970s.

Financial Action Task Force (FATF), an international body of nations, made certain recommendations in the year 1990 to control the menace of money laundering and terrorist financing by better control on banking operations and by legal provisions to bring the culprits to books. It was felt that there is a nexus between money laundering and terrorist activities.

The United Nations Security Council issued guidelines to the governments to arm themselves with suitable legal provisions to control money laundering and terrorist activities immediately after the 9/11 terrorist strikes on USA in 2001.

In view of the above developments, GOI enacted Prevention of Money Laundering Act, 2002 (PMLA, 2002), a new legislation to fight against money laundering and created FIU-IND (Financial Intelligence Unit of India), a statutory body under Ministry of Finance to implement the provisions of PMLA.

PML Act, 2002 defines money laundering offense as under:

> Offence of money-laundering: Whosoever directly or indirectly attempts to indulge or knowingly assists or knowingly is a party or is actually involved in any process or activity connected with the proceeds of crime and projecting it as untainted property shall be guilty of offence of money laundering.

The act empowers FIU-IND to collect information on banking/financial transactions from banks and others. The information collected is decimated by it and in case it is felt that the transactions shall have to be looked in to, then FIU-IND passes on the information to respective enforcement agencies for investigation.

Under the Act and the rules, banks and others are duty bound to report certain transactions to FIU-IND on regular basis. Section 12 of the Act prescribes maintenance of records of transactions and reporting requirement. Further, banks/FIs are prohibited from informing the customers about the disclosure of information on their accounts as it may hamper the investigation process, if desired by authorities. Hence, submission of information to FIU-IND is strictly confidential.

At present (as of July 2015) under the rules issued by FIU-IND, banks are obliged to submit reports as under:

1. Cash transaction report (CTR)—for cash transactions of ₹ 10 lacs and above either single or number of transactions integrally connected.
2. Counterfeit Currency Report (CCR)—All cash transactions where forged or counterfeit currency notes or bank notes have been used as genuine or where any forgery of a valuable security or a document has taken place facilitating the transactions.
3. Suspicious Transaction Report (STR)—Suspicions transaction means a transaction whether or not made in cash which, to a person acting in good faith—gives rise to a reasonable ground of suspicion that it may involve the proceeds of crime; or appears to be made in circumstances of unusual or unjustified complexity;

or appears to have no economic rationale or bona fide purpose.

4. Report on Non-Profit Organisation—The report of all transactions involving receipts by non-profit organizations of value more than rupees ten lakh or its equivalent in foreign currency.
5. Cross-border Wire Transfer Report (CWTR) is required to be filed for all cross border wire transfers of the value of more than five lakh rupees or its equivalent in foreign currency where either the origin or destination of fund is in India.

Thus, in order to check and identify instances of money laundering, the PML Act requires the banks and FIs to provide information to FIU-IND as will be desired by it. Further banks are also duty bound to scrutinise the transactions undertaken by it for the purpose of identifying and reporting transactions of suspicious nature. This responsibility of banks combined with the KYC regime for identifying the customers is the legal framework created for controlling the money laundering activities.

The rules under the PML Act requires banks and others to nominate a senior officer and coordinator and compliance officer under the act. The Section 13(2) of PML act was amended in the year 2012 and banks are now advised to nominate a Director on their Boards as "designated Director" to ensure compliance with the obligations under the act.

3.28 What is Capital Adequacy Ratio (CAR) and Capital to Risk (Weighted) Assets Ratio (CRAR) for Banks

CAR and CRAR are the same ratio which is expressed in terms of percentage, the capital of a bank bears to its risk-weighted assets. This is now an important barometer to judge the financial strength of a bank as prescribed by the regulator (RBI) under the capital norms based on Basel Accords.

As we have seen earlier under capital standards for banks, Basel Accord has prescribed minimum 8% capital requirement and RBI has stipulated 9% capital requirements for Indian banks. This percentage is calculated by dividing the total capital of the bank by the risk adjusted assets of the bank. Assets are not taken on their notional value but their values are adjusted according to the risk weightage system applicable to each type of asset. Risk weight is given from zero to 100% for different kinds of assets. Thus, the asset carrying zero risk or marginal risk up to 10 to 20% requires less capital charge and the assets carrying higher risk will attract higher capital charge.

Hence, any bank which has less than the minimum CRR is considered as the weak bank financially. This status of weak bank has serious ramifications now as the other banks particularly the international banks may not enter into business relationship with them.

Further, under Basel III norms the requirement of capital has been increased by 2.5% as Capital Conservation Buffer (CCB) as discussed earlier. For Indian banks RBI has prescribed the minimum capital requirement at 11.5% inclusive of this new additional requirement. Basel III norms are made applicable for Indian banks from the year 2012 and by the year 2019 banks will have to comply with the capital level minimum at 11.5%.

Banks in India are mainly in public sector and due to government ownership the capital size of the banks were not considered important earlier. Banks capital was not looked into as important. But after the banking sector reforms were introduced, it became obligatory to fall in line with the international standard for the capital size of the banks. This has led to infusion of fresh capital by the government and government also decided to dilute its stake in banks and allowed public sector banks to raise capital from the capital market.

Till the year 1992, the capital contributed by GOI in all the nationalized banks (20 banks) was ₹ 40 billion. Government contributed total fresh capital to nationalized banks aggregating ₹ 164.05 billion from 1993 up to March 1998. After the year 1994, many public sector banks raised capital from capital market. Again during the years 2010 to 2015, GOI infused additional capital of ₹ 656.24 billion to public sector banks.

In July 2015, the Finance Minister announced a ₹ 70000 crores capital infusion package to public sector banks in the next four years to enable the banks to comply with Basel III norms by March 2019.

By the year 2009, Indian banks as a group have complied with the capital norms under Basel II guidelines which was fixed at 9% by RBI. Maximum number of banks in the country have achieved the standard. But under Basel III norms which is adopted in the year 2012 banks will require more capital.

The following table shows the capital adequacy ratios of Indian banks as groups.

The CRAR of Indian banks group wise at present is as under:

Average CRAR (Capital to Risk Weighted Assets Ratio) for All Banks—March 2009 to March 2013

Sl.No.	Group	2009	2010	2011	2012	2013
	All SCBs	13.97	14.54	14.19	14.24	13.88
1	SBI & Subsidiaries	13.96	13.46	12.25	13.70	12.67
2	Nationalized banks	13.24	13.18	13.47	13.03	12.26
3	Old private sector banks	14.74	14.85	14.55	14.12	13.73
4	New private sector banks	15.33	18.03	16.87	16.66	17.52
5	Foreign banks	14.32	17.26	16.97	16.75	17.88

Source: From A Profile of Banks, 2012-13 by RBI.

CRAR of all Indian banks in the year 2013 was 13.88% and RBI has reported that the same was 13% as at March 2014. Though it appears that banks have complied with minimum requirement of 11.5% under Basel III, in reality banks will require more capital—they will have to maintain additional capital of 2 to 3% above the minimum. This is because the capital requirement will go up every year with increase in business and banks shall have to make adequate provision for growth of business. If the capital is not increased as an ongoing measure continuously, then it can restrain the bank from expanding the business.

3.29 What is Asset Liability Management (ALM) for Banks

Basel Accord for bank capital standards has identified many risks banks face in their business. They are mainly the credit risk, market risk, and operational risk. It is advised that banks shall develop risk management capabilities to identify these risks, quantify them, manage them and take corrective actions and also to provide capital to absorb these risks.

Risk management for banks has been identified as an integral function along with the business growth. Risks for bank is in its portfolio of assets and liabilities as these are exposed to various types of risks which may result in loss of value. Hence, risk management is also called the Asset Liability Management (ALM).

Credit risk has been separately identified as the risks in loans and investments and the accord has recommended risk weightage for the assets and provision of minimum capital to take care of credit risk.

Market risk is another risk bank is exposed to and it is a major factor affecting the financial performance of banks. Under the market risk, following risk categories have been identified:

1. Liquidity Risk,
2. Interest Rate Risk,
3. Foreign Exchange Rate (Forex) Risk,
4. Commodity Price Risk, and
5. Equity Price Risk.

Banks accept deposits from public on running accounts and as term deposits. Banks in our country are required to maintain CRR and SLR as prescribed by RBI as safe and liquidity measures. The remaining funds are used to give loans or invest in interest bearing securities. Loaning functions of banks are crucial for banks to earn returns so that it can earn profit after meeting interest cost on deposits and other overhead expenses. However, loaning and investment make the funds blocked in these assets. But banks will have to keep in mind that the depositors can demand their money any time and bank has to make it available to them on demand. Hence, maintaining liquidity is of utmost importance to the bank.

Banks were using their own judgement for the liquidity requirements. Though CRR and SLR are liquid, they are not available to banks in the normal course of business. Banks will have to maintain some amount of liquidity with them to meet the day-to-day demands of their customers. How much liquidity is required for the bank is important to know.

We can observe that all the current account and savings account deposits are payable on demand and there can be demand by customers anytime. Savings and current deposits are called CASA deposits. For Indian banks, this category of deposits forms a sizeable chunk in their total deposits. It is now in the range of 22 to 45 per cent for different banks in India. Technically speaking, this entire deposit can be withdrawn and banks need to provide for it. Similarly, banks accept term deposits for different period with maximum period of ten years. These deposits are maturing at different dates and on maturity the term deposit can be withdrawn. Banks by tradition also allow premature payment of term deposits and hence all term deposits are subject to withdrawal any time.

Banks will have to presume some percentage of deposits as withdrawable any time and provide liquidity for it. How bank calculate this probable percentage of expected demand and how bank will meet this demand is an important question.

As we know banks are giving loans and also investing in securities. These funds are illiquid as they are repayable after some time. Bank gives term loans to various purposes the repayment period is spread generally up to seven years and in case of loans to housing sector and infrastructure sector it can be up to 20 years. The term loans are blocked funds and bank can expect only the repayment instalments fixed to be available to it every year. Working capital loans are generally given for one year and is generally renewed. Hence, repayment in this category of loan is not expected. The investments are also generally for long-terms 10-15 years and till then the funds are blocked. The only comfort is in case of marketable investment is that it can be disposed in the secondary market and cash can be generated.

Asset liability management for bank is based on these features of bank's business and it aims to managing the liquidity on some realistic basis so that the bank is prepared to face the demand from customers both in the normal circumstances and also in case of seasonal or unexpected and sudden demands from customers.

In modern time, this predicament of banks for maintaining adequate liquidity to take care of demands from customers has engaged the attention of banking regulators. It is experienced that even a strong bank with adequate good assets, more than its liabilities, can run into trouble and be forced to close down due to its default to meet the demands of customers in short-term on day-to-day basis. This can happen when the bank's liquidity is fully stretched to the limit and again there is some unexpected demand on it due to any reason. Hence, when bank is short of liquidity, it can fail despite it having sufficient good assets.

This has given rise to working out some standards for liquidity position the bank need to maintain to be safe from adverse developments in short-term perspective. This standard shall have to take into account the very nature of bank's business and work out some logical and scientific basis to find out the liquidity requirement for a bank. This can be worked out only by studying the profile of a bank's assets and liabilities. It is on individual basis and no generalisations across banks is useful as the composition of assets and liabilities of each bank is specific to it.

Asset liability management system introduced for banks tries to create a system of managing the assets and liabilities to ensure preparedness against liquidity crisis and also against interest rate risks.

RBI issued guidelines for Asset Liability Management system (ALM) and made it operative from the year 1999. These guidelines were again fine-tuned in the year 2007.

The scope of ALM function is described as follows:

- Liquidity risk management
- Management of market risks
- Trading risk management
- Funding and capital planning
- Profit planning and growth projection

The basic function of ALM is the study of structural liquidity of assets and liabilities and all other functions are based on this study.

Assessing/Measuring Liquidity Risk

As measuring and managing liquidity needs are vital for commercial banks, RBI has prescribed a model for assessing liquidity position and maturity pattern of both assets and liabilities. This model requires segregation of assets and liabilities in to definite time buckets starting from one day to over five-year duration based on their residual maturity.

Under this exercise, bank looks at all its assets and liabilities to find out a maturity pattern discernible from them. It is a systematic study to find out the maturity pattern of assets and liabilities based on actual and known status and also on the basis of behavioural pattern for assets and liabilities which have no definite maturity dates.

All term deposits will have fixed maturity dates. All term loans/fixed loans have fixed duration and only yearly instalments are expected from them. All investments other than investments in equities have a fixed due date.

CASA deposits are payable on demand but it is unlikely that all the deposits will be withdrawn at a time. All working capital loans are revolving in nature with no fixed maturity. Similarly, there are some other assets and liabilities with no maturity dates. Hence, a behavioural pattern based on historical data is identified in all these cases. It is translated to a formula developed and advised by RBI under which all the assets and liabilities that have no fixed maturity dates are also identified as maturing at some future dates. Sometimes a particular asset or liability is split into many parts and placed in different time buckets.

After identifying the maturity of pattern as above all the assets and liabilities are placed in a table segregating them into definite time buckets. Wherever the assets and liabilities have a definite contractual due date the same are placed in the particular time bucket based on their residual maturity period.

Assets and liabilities that have no fixed maturity dates are placed in different time buckets based on the formula adopted. After this, totals of each time bucket are drawn.

1	2	3	4	5	6	7	8	9	10	11	12
	Residual maturity										
Outflows	1 day	2-7 days	8-14 days	15-28 days	29 days and upto 3 months	Over 3 months and upto 6 months	Over 6 months and upto 1 year	Over 1 year and upto 3 years	Over 3 years and upto 5 years	Over 5 years	Total
Liabilities 1. A 2. B 3. C 4. D 5.											
A. total outflows											
B. cumulative outflows											
Assets 1. A 2. B 3. C 4. D 5.											
C. total inflows											
D. mismatch (C-A)											
E. mismatch as % to outflows (D as % to A)											
F. cumulative mismatch											
G. cumulative mismatch as a % to cumulative outflows (F as a % to B)											

RBI has prescribed a format on which the liquidity study shall be made and submitted to it for supervision. To understand the exercise, the following table is created as an abridged version of the statement prescribed to show how the exercise is done.

The statement of both assets and liabilities so worked out is known as the Statement of Structural Liquidity. It reflects the inflow and outflow of cash over the time horizon. A maturing liability is a cash outflow while a maturing asset is a cash inflow.

The Statement of Structural Liquidity will show all the future cash inflows and outflows in the maturity ladder according to the expected timing of cash flows. With this exercise, bank is now able to see whether it has assets in each time bucket matching or more than the similar time bucket of liability. Bank can also know the time horizon in which it has gaps and this is a potential danger signal for the management. Bank can take remedial measures and plan in advance for the necessary corrective steps.

This study also enables the bank management to monitor and control growth of asset or liability in a particular time bucket and take management decisions for immediate actions. For example, if bank finds that the term loans are disproportionately increasing which has the impact on assets being pushed to medium- and long-term buckets, serious mismatch can be visualized and management can take decision to curb sanction of term loans for longer duration and shift to working capital loans or bill advances. Management will also know the period of deposits (whether short-term or long-term) to be encouraged either by increasing rate or by adding benefits in order to remove the mismatch in the particular time bucket.

Further there are detailed guidelines issued by RBI for banks to follow depending on the findings of this study.

Interest Rate Risk (IRR)

Another important ALM function for the bank is analysing interest rate risks. It is part of market risk.

Interest rate risk for the banks arises due to changes in interest rates. Earlier RBI prescribed interest rates for both deposits and advances and banks enjoyed a protected Net Interest Margin (NIM) in their favour. This allowed banks to earn profits and they were not unduly worried about the interest rates, or its movement either way. Once the interest rates are deregulated in phased manner and banks are asked to fix the rates themselves, banks are no longer having a protected NIM. Banks cannot have protected NIM now as the interest rates for deposits and advances are not interlinked and both are independently determined by the market forces. Market conditions are difficult to predict. This has exposed banks to interest rate risk on both sides of their balance sheet.

If the interest rates on deposit goes up bank's cost on deposits will go up. But there is no link or guarantee that loan interest rates will also go up. If loan interest rates do not change, then banks profitability will come down. Increase in deposit interest will not change the rates for existing deposits as they are contractual. But the fresh deposits or the renewal of deposits will cost more. Hence, impact of interest rate increase for deposits is felt gradually.

Similarly, if the loan interest rates come down, banks' earnings are immediately impacted as maximum loans are with floating rates and the changes are immediate for all floating rate interest loans. Here also banks' profit will come down as bank cannot reduce the deposit interest cost.

On the other hand, if the deposit interest rates come down or the loan interest rates go up, banks will be benefitted and profit will go up.

Hence, the changes in interest rates on assets and liabilities pose risk for banks as their profitability is affected.

But how to know or predict the impact of interest rate changes on bank's profitability? For example, if the interest rate on deposits go up by one per cent then by how much bank's profit will come down presuming other things remaining same? Or how much bank will be losing if the interest on loans come down by one percentage?

To find answers to these questions, the risk management techniques have been developed and this technique uses a model and attempts to study the impact of interest rate movements on bank's profitability. It involves analysing the assets and liabilities as to their interest rate sensitivity and then conduct a simulation study presuming the future interest rate movement in percentage terms. This study attempts to measure the interest rate risk.

To measure this risk, it is necessary to understand the impact of interest movement on each type of asset and liability of the banks. Interest rate changes may have different impact on assets and liabilities. Some assets/liabilities may be interest rate non-sensitive. Examples are capital and current account deposits on liability side and cash and fixed assets on asset side.

Other assets and liabilities are interest rate sensitive to varying degrees. For example, a term deposit is non-sensitive till its maturity but becomes sensitive after maturity as it will be repriced. Loans carrying fixed rate of interest is non-sensitive whereas the loan with floating interest rate is sensitive as the interest changes immediately. In view of this, banks are required to segregate rate sensitive assets (RSA) and rate sensitive liabilities (RSL) according to the maturity of their becoming rate sensitive. This means that the rate sensitive assets and liabilities remain non-sensitive until due dates or maturity and thereafter shall be repriced (become sensitive) as per market movements of rates.

All the rate sensitive assets and liabilities are to be segregated and placed in the time buckets based on their residual maturity or due dates (as they shall be repriced thereafter). It is similar to the exercise carried out for liquidity risk measurement discussed earlier.

RBI made some changes in the year 2010 in the maturity buckets and presently for gap analysis banks are using time buckets as under. The table shown below is only for the purpose of understanding and it is not same as the prescribed format.

The model introduced by RBI in the year 1999 (and modified in 2010) is called as the Traditional Gap Analysis (TGA) as a suitable method to measure the Interest Rate Risk for banks.

Gap is the difference between Rate Sensitive Assets (RSA) and Rate Sensitive Liabilities (RSL) in each time bucket. The positive gap indicates that it has more RSAs than RSLs whereas the negative gap indicates that it has more RSLs.

Sl.No.	Time bucket (based on residual maturity)	Assets	Liabilities	Gap
i	1-28 days			
ii	29 days and upto 3 months			
iii	Over 3 months and upto 6 months			
iv	Over 6 months and upto 1 year			
v	Over 1 year and up to 3 years			
vi	Over 3 years and up to 5 years			
vii	Over 5 years and upto 7 years			
viii	Over 7 years and upto 10 years			
ix	Over 10 years and upto 15 years			
x	Over 15 years			
xi	Non-sensitive			

Under this model the gap is used as a measure of interest rate sensitivity. The Positive or Negative Gap is multiplied by the assumed interest rate changes to derive the Earnings at Risk (EaR). The EaR method facilitates to estimate how much the earnings might be impacted by an adverse movement in interest rates.

Now based on this it is possible to simulate interest rate changes and study the impact on the earnings of the bank. For example, bank can have simulation study to find out the impact of say one per cent increase in deposit rates and see how much the bank is losing in its earnings. Likewise, bank can also study the impact of decline in interest rates on deposits and similarly increase or decline in interest rates on advances. Bank can also know whether positive gap (RSA > RSL) or negative gap (RSL > RSA) in the time buckets is working in their favour or against them, in the scenario of interest rates increasing or declining. The gap can therefore be used as a measure of interest rate sensitivity. The simulation study with changed interest rate can also measure the likely changes in the Net Interest Income (NII) or Net Interest Margin (NIM).

This model enables banks to predict the impact of interest rate changes on their profitability.

Market Value of Equity (MVE). The changes in market interests have two implications for banks. One is its impact on the earnings of the bank as discussed above. The other perspective is its impact on the market value of bank's equity. The Market Value of Equity (MVE) changes with the change in interest rates as the underlying assets and liabilities of the banks undergo economic revaluation by the market. This revaluation is finally reflected in the equity price of the bank.

Though the change in MVE of the bank is an external factor and does not affect the balance sheet of the bank, it is very important for the banks as MVE depicts market sentiments about the bank and its financial status. One reason for change in MVE due to change in interest rate is because the earning per share (EPS) changes and EPS has a role in determining the share price.

As Indian banks have now computerised which is enabling them to have reliable Management Information System (MIS), RBI has in the year 2010 advised banks to evaluate the risk in MVE by using a technique known as Duration Gap Analysis (DGA). Some changes were made in the time buckets (as already shown above) and RBI has prescribed a model and a format for working out DGA which is in addition to TGA for interest rate risk.

Interest risk measurement for finding out impact on the earnings of the banks and also the MVE of bank is a new area and models used to calculate the same are also undergoing changes with improvements in MIS data and experience of the banks with such analysis. More models called as the Modified Duration Gap, Simulation, and Value at Risk (VaR) are now developed internationally and international banks are using them as management tools. Each model has its own utility and also limitations. These may be introduced for Indian banks in future.

Another important risk under ALM functions for Indian banks is the foreign exchange risk they run on their foreign currency assets and liabilities.

Asset Liability Committee (ALCO). The RBI guidelines advised banks to form Asset Liability Committee (ALCO) to look after the ALM functions as an executive committee headed by CEO or Executive Director, responsible for evaluating the risk profile of the bank on various parameters, take decisions to correct the situation and then oversee the implementation of its directives to ensure that changes are happening in the desired directions.

Banks have formed Asset Liability Committee and the role of ALCO is as a decision-making unit responsible for balance sheet planning from risk-return perspective including the strategic management of interest rate and liquidity risks. In this role, ALCO is monitoring the liquidity position of the bank on regular almost daily basis. ALCO is looking into the business issues and considers, product pricing for deposits and advances, decides on the desired maturity profile of the incremental assets and liabilities, and then monitor the risk levels of the bank on continuous basis.

Basel Accord has prescribed the capital requirement standards for credit risk, market risk and operational risk to which banks are exposed. ALCO is the body in the bank to look into these areas of risks and develop strategies to counter act these risks. ALCO is responsible for capital planning and to decide the type of capital and source of capital to be procured. ALCO is also responsible for business growth planning and profit planning. All these functions of ALCO are interrelated and hence called as risk management functions.

4

Banking Important Organisations

4.1 International Monetary Fund (IMF)

After the World War II, all the countries in the West were in economic difficulties and the international trade was seriously affected. In order to find a solution to the economic woes, the representatives of 45 governments met at the Bretton Woods Conference in the Mount Washington Hotel (in Bretton Woods, New Hampshire, USA) to discuss a framework for post-war international economic cooperation and how to rebuild the economies of the countries.

World Bank and IMF were the outcome of this conference and the countries participating signed agreements for creation of these two world financial bodies.

IMF came into existence in 1945 with 29 member countries and as per the financial mechanism agreed by the member countries, countries will contribute, through a quota system, funds to a pool and this funds can be lent to countries experiencing balance of payments difficulties. IMF basically is meant for providing short-term loans to countries facing balance of payment difficulties. Besides this function, IMF also work for the global monetary cooperation to facilitate international trade. IMF's Headquarters is located in Washington, D.C. and at present 188 countries are the members of IMF.

From 1952 IMF introduced the system of conditionality for borrowing from it. Under this, the country borrowing has to accept certain conditions and suggestions of IMF with regard to international trade practices adopted by the country. This was introduced to point out the deficiencies in the country's policies which are hampering growth in international trade and creating balance of payment problems for the country. The purpose is to guide the member country towards better management of its economy and to align it with the global environment.

IMF gives loans to low-income countries on concessional terms, and the following line of credits are extended to them.

- Extended Credit Facility (ECF)
- Standby Credit Facility (SCF)—is generally with conditionality
- Rapid Credit Facility (RCF).

For others IMF gives non-concessional loans, under following lines of credit:

- Standby Arrangements (SBA)
- the Flexible Credit Line (FCL)
- the Precautionary and Liquidity Line (PLL), and
- the Extended Fund Facility (EFF).

IMF provides emergency assistance for members facing balance-of-payments problems via the Rapid Financing Instrument (RFI). There is a ceiling on borrowing by a country from IMF and it is known as access limit, generally it is a multiple of country's contribution to the IMF fund.

4.2 World Bank (IBRD)

World Bank is an international financial institution created in 1944 by Bretton Woods Conference along with IMF. It comprises two institutions: the International Bank for Reconstruction and Development (IBRD), and the International Development Association (IDA). The World Bank is a component of the World Bank Group (consisting of total five organisations), and World Bank Group is part of the United Nations system.

World Bank is located in Washington DC and by tradition the president of World Bank group is an American.

The World Bank's official goal is the reduction of poverty in the world. The bank's mission is to achieve the twin goals of ending extreme poverty and building shared prosperity.

The capital of the bank is contributed by 188 member countries. USA is the biggest contributor followed by Japan and China. World Bank also raises funds by issuing international bonds every year to fund its lending operations. According to World Bank's statement, it issues bonds of approximately USD 40-50 billion per year.

World Bank gives loans to developing countries for capital programs. The International Bank for Reconstruction and Development (IBRD) lends to governments of developing and low-income countries. The International Development Association (IDA) provides interest-free loans called credits and grants to governments of the poorest countries for investment in areas such as education, health, public administration, infrastructure, financial and private sector development, agriculture, and environmental and natural resource management.

World Bank and the IMF work in close association with each other. Member countries of both these organizations are common. While World Bank extends long-term loans to the governments to remove poverty, the IMF provides short-term loans mainly for the purpose of assisting the balance of payment position of the countries.

4.3 Bank for International Settlements (BIS)

The Bank for International Settlements (BIS) is the banker to the central banks of the countries. It is considered as the oldest international financial organisation in the world established in the year 1930.

The head office of the bank is in Basel, Switzerland. It has 60 member central banks representing the countries. Reserve Bank of India is also a member of this bank.

The mission pursued by BIS is as under:

- fostering discussion and facilitating collaboration among central banks;

- supporting dialogue with other authorities that are responsible for promoting financial stability;
- carrying out research and policy analysis on issues of relevance for monetary and financial stability;
- acting as a prime counterparty for central banks in their financial transactions; and
- serving as an agent or trustee in connection with international financial operations.

As a bank, the BIS does not accept deposits from, or provide financial services to, private individuals or corporate entities. BIS extends banking facility to only central banks and international organisations for their international payments and transactions.

BIS provides forum for central banks to interact on issues relating to promote international stability in trade and payment systems. It hosts international committees and standard-setting bodies. Basel committee on banking supervision has evolved the Basel committee reports I, II and III to strengthen the banks and to improve regulatory control of central banks to provide stability in international financial sector.

4.4 Reserve Bank of India—RBI

The Reserve Bank of India Act was enacted in the year 1934. RBI came in to existence at Calcutta in the year 1935. It was created as a joint stock company with government holding some shares. In the year 1937, RBI was permanently moved to Mumbai. RBI was nationalized in the year 1949, and was made an autonomous authority as the central bank of the country. Now the RBI is fully owned by the Government of India.

RBI derives its authority mainly from the Reserve Bank of India Act, 1934 and the Banking Regulation Act, 1949. Both these acts have been amended many times to widen the authority of RBI.

The Preamble of the Reserve Bank of India describes the basic functions of the Reserve Bank as "to regulate the issue of bank notes, to keep reserves with a view to securing monetary stability in India and generally to operate the currency and credit system in the best interests of the country".

Main functions of RBI are:

- RBI is the monetary authority of the country, which formulates, implements and monitors the monetary policy (interest rates, credit policies, money supply) with the objective for maintaining price stability and ensuring adequate flow of credit to productive sectors.
- Regulator and supervisor of the banking system and other financial system.
- RBI is the manager of foreign exchange reserves of the government and regulator of foreign exchange business in country.
- RBI is the issuer of currency notes and coins.
- Banker to the central and the state governments.
- RBI manages public debt office (Central and State Government borrowings).
- Banker to banks maintains banking accounts of all scheduled banks and the banker of last resort who lends to banks.
- Provides settlement platform for cheque clearing, NEFT, RTGS and ECS.
- Under the Payment and Settlement Systems Act, 2007, RBI is the authority to operate or authorise others to operate payment settlement systems.
- RBI provides deposit insurance to bank depositors through its wholly-owned subsidiary DICGC.

RBI is managed by a central board of directors all nominated by GOI and is headed by Governor. RBI has four Deputy Governors.

RBI is the monetary authority of the country which decides the monetary policy including credit policy for banks. Monetary policy decides on money supply, interest rate movements and bank credit. Monetary policy is aiming to have stability in the economy and control on inflation. Whereas GOI is the fiscal authority of the country which decides the fiscal policy for the country like the taxation and other matters.

4.5 Export Credit Guarantee Corporation of India Ltd. (ECGC)

After independence, government was keen to promote exports and based on recommendations of Kapur Committee, government set up the Export Risk Insurance Corporation (ERIC) on 30 July 1957 in Mumbai as a state-owned Private Ltd. Company. It provided insurance cover to exporters against the payment risks. In 1962, it started issuing guarantee cover to banks for their loans for exports. The name of the company was changed to Export Credit & Guarantee Corporation Ltd. in 1964. Again in 1983, the name was changed to Export Credit Guarantee Corporation of India Ltd. to give it the national character.

Export Credit Guarantee Corporation of India Ltd. (ECGC) is a Government of India enterprise which functions under the administrative control of Ministry of Commerce & Industry, and is managed by a nominated Board of Directors.

ECGC has evolved various export credit risk insurance products to suit the requirements of Indian exporters and commercial banks. At present its authorised capital is ₹ 5000 crores with paid capital at ₹ 1200 crores.

The Corporation helps exporters and banks in the country by providing following services:

1. It provides information on worthiness of the buyers, bankers and the countries to Indian exporters to assist them in taking decision to export.
2. It provides insurance policy/cover to exporters/banks to protect the Indian exporters against unforeseen losses due to non-payment for any reason (like failure of the buyer or bank or problems faced due to government policies at buyer's country, etc.).
3. It also issues surety insurance covers for bankers to facilitate banks to sanction adequate bank finance to the Indian exporters.

4.6 Export-Import Bank of India (Exim Bank)

Export-Import Bank of India is an export finance institution established in the year 1982 under the Export-Import Bank of India Act, 1981. Its objective is to provide financial assistance to exporters and importers with a view to promote international trade.

Exim Bank is wholly owned by Government of India and as on March 31, 2015, the paid up capital stood at ₹ 5,059 crores and the net worth stood at ₹ 9,902 crores.

The Exim Bank has at present various schemes for financing as under:

- Overseas Investment Finance
- Project Finance
- Line of Credit
- Corporate Banking
- Buyer's Credit Under NEIA

Exim Bank extends finance for export of manufactured goods, project exports, exports of technology, services and export of computer software. It finances exporters to set up projects abroad and also finances import of project/technology to be set up in the country. The bank facilitates two-way technology transfer by financing Indian company's investment abroad for setting up joint ventures, subsidiaries or undertaking overseas acquisitions and also for import of technology into India.

Exim Bank extends Lines of Credit (LOCs) to overseas financial institutions, regional development banks, sovereign governments and other entities overseas to enable buyers in those countries to import developmental and infrastructure projects, equipment, goods and services from India, on deferred credit terms.

Exim bank provides refinance facilities to commercial banks and also re-discounting facility for export bills.

4.7 Deposit Insurance and Credit Guarantee Corporation (DICGC)

Before 1960, there were many bank failures in the country and depositors had lost their money. In the year 1960, two fairly big banks: Palai Central Bank Ltd., and the Laxmi Bank Ltd. failed which prompted government and RBI to start deposit insurance scheme to protect bank depositors. Deposit Insurance Act, 1961 was enacted and deposit insurance corporation was created in 1962. DICGC is wholly owned by RBI.

Initially, only the commercial banks were covered under the deposit insurance scheme and in the year 1968 co-op banks were also included under the scheme.

Reserve Bank of India introduced a Credit Guarantee Scheme in July 1960 for guaranteeing the advances granted by banks and other credit institutions to small scale industries. The Reserve Bank of India operated the scheme up to March 31, 1981.

In the year 1971, the Credit Guarantee Corporation of India Ltd. (CGCI) was promoted by Reserve Bank of India for providing guarantee cover for the loans and advances granted by the credit institutions to small and needy borrowers covered under the priority sector.

Then in the year 1978, Deposit Insurance Corporation (DIC) and the Credit Guarantee Corporation of India Ltd. (CGCI) were merged to form Deposit Insurance and Credit Guarantee Corporation (DICGC). In the year 1981, the credit guarantee scheme for SSI units operated by RBI was also shifted to DICGC. Hence, DICGC became the corporation extending both deposit insurance and credit guarantees.

Deposit insurance is made compulsory for all banks (commercial and co-op banks) and the cost of the insurance shall be borne by the banks, banks cannot recover the cost from the depositors. Under the provisions of deposit insurance rules, insurance cover per individual is fixed and it applies to per individual depositor for all his accounts held in “same right and in the same capacity” in all the branches of the bank taken together.

Under the provisions of Section 16(1) of the DICGC Act, the insurance cover was originally limited to ₹ 1500 only per depositor for deposits held by him in "the same capacity and in the same right" at all the branches of a bank taken together.

The Act also empowers the Corporation to raise this limit with the prior approval of the Central Government. Accordingly, the insurance limit was enhanced from time to time as follows:

Effective from	Insurance Limit ₹
1962	1500
January 1, 1968	5000
April 1, 1970	10,000
January 1, 1976	20,000
July 1, 1980	30,000
May 1, 1993	1,00,000

From the year 1993, the deposit insurance cover per individual is ₹ one lac payable in case the bank fails and closes down. DICGC claim settlement is immediate and without waiting for the winding up or liquidation of the failed bank. Under the provisions of the law, DICGC will join the liquidation process with its claim for the amount paid by it and try to recover the amount from the liquidator.

As on March 31, 2016 the number of registered insured banks was 2127 banks comprising 93 commercial banks, 56 regional rural banks (RRBs), 4 local area banks (LABs) and 1974 co-operative banks.

Since inception of deposit insurance scheme till March 2016, DICGC has settled claims in respect of 27 commercial banks (₹ 2,959 million) and 332 co-op banks. (₹ 46,801.28 million) that have failed.

While the deposit insurance cover is compulsory for banks, banks were given the option to withdraw from the credit guarantee schemes for priority sector lending. Slowly, banks opted out of credit guarantee scheme as it was not helping them and at present no bank is covered under credit guarantee schemes. DICGC has now become solely a deposit insurance corporation.

4.8 Securities and Exchange Board of India (SEBI)

SEBI is established in the year 1988 as a non-statutory body. SEBI was made a statutory body in 1992 by the Securities and Exchange Board of India Act. This was done on the basis of recommendations of the committee on financial sector reforms. SEBI is now the regulator for the securities market in India.

The office of the Controller of Capital Issues was the regulatory authority for the securities market earlier and SEBI replaced it and the office of the Controller of Capital Issues was abolished.

The Preamble of the Securities and Exchange Board of India Act describes the basic functions of the Securities and Exchange Board of India as "...to protect the interests of investors in securities and to promote the development of, and to regulate the securities market and for matters connected therewith or incidental thereto".

The securities market is constituted by following three groups:

- The issuers of securities (companies)
- The investors
- The market intermediaries (stock exchanges, brokers and others).

SEBI has regulatory authority to frame rules and guidelines for issue of securities by companies and for others involved in the securities market which is as under:

1. To approve by-laws of stock exchanges. To inspect the books of accounts and call for periodical returns from recognized stock exchanges.
2. To approve the issues of securities by companies and make rules for issue and listing of securities.
3. To register and regulate the working of stock brokers, sub-brokers, share transfer agents, trustees, merchant bankers and all those who are associated with stock exchange in any manner.
4. To register and regulate the working of the depositories, depository participants, custodians of securities, foreign

institutional investors, credit rating agencies and such other intermediaries.

5. To register and regulate the working of mutual funds, etc.
6. To regulate takeover of the companies.

SEBI is the regulator of capital market in much similar way as the RBI is the regulator of banking and the money market.

SEBI is the watchdog for the securities market and prohibits fraudulent and unfair trade practices relating to securities markets to ensure that all the participants in the market conduct themselves in ethical manner and observe the norms fixed by it. In order to protect the interest of the investors, SEBI particularly checks on;

- Price rigging in any issue
- Any insider trading happening
- Any fraudulent and unfair practices used by issuing companies and also that companies do not make any misleading statements to the investors.

SEBI is empowered to investigate cases relating to the above matters and take action against the offenders. SEBI is empowered to take any of the following measures, either pending investigation or inquiry or on completion of such investigation or inquiry:

- suspend the trading of any security in a recognised stock exchange.
- restrain persons from accessing the securities market and prohibit any person associated with securities market to buy, sell or deal in securities.
- suspend any office-bearer of any stock exchange or self-regulatory organisation from holding such position.
- impound and retain the proceeds or securities in respect of any transaction which is under investigation.
- attach, on approval by the Judicial Magistrate of the first class having jurisdiction, for a period not exceeding one month, one or more bank account or accounts of any

intermediary or any person associated with the securities market involved in violation of any of the provisions of the Act, or the rules or the regulations.

- direct any intermediary or any person associated with the securities market in any manner not to dispose of or alienate an asset forming part of any transaction which is under investigation.

SEBI has development role also and it has taken many initiatives for the development of market by introducing improvements in the system.

4.9 Stock Exchanges—BSE and NSE

Stock exchanges are the trading places for securities and the securities are defined in the Securities Contracts (Regulation) Act, 1956 as shares, scrips, stocks, bonds, debentures, debenture stock or other marketable securities of a like nature in or of any incorporated company or other body corporate. Stock exchanges provide for primary issues of securities by companies and also the secondary market to trade in these securities. For secondary market trading, stock exchange provides and facilitates payment settlement system. Besides securities, stock exchanges also provide trading in derivatives related to and based on securities or currencies.

The companies who want to raise capital or long-term funds from the market and also want the secondary market for trading in their securities are required to enter into a listing agreement with the stock exchanges after which their securities will be allowed to be traded in the stock exchanges.

Stock exchanges shall be recognised by the GOI under the provisions of the Securities Contracts (Regulation) Act, 1956 for commencing trading in securities. SEBI is the regulatory authority for stock exchanges.

Bombay Stock Exchange (BSE)

BSE is the oldest stock exchange in India which came into existence in the year 1875. It is functioning for last 140 years and it is also the oldest stock exchange in Asia. BSE is the first stock exchange to receive permanent authorization in the year 1957, by Government of India under the provisions of the Securities Contracts (Regulation) Act, 1956.

Bombay Stock Exchange was initially Incorporated in the 1875 and was known then as "The Native Share & Stock Brokers Association." In 1980, the exchange moved to the Phiroze Jeejeebhoy Towers at Dalal Street, Fort, Mumbai. In August 2005, BSE converted itself as a corporate entity under company's act and is named as BSE Ltd. It is now the 11th largest stock exchange in the world. More than 5500 companies, highest for any stock exchange, are publicly listed on the BSE.

BSE has been a trend setter and market leader in trading of securities. BSE introduced the first equity index known as S&P BSE SENSEX in the year 1986. Sensex index reflects the shares of 30 leading companies listed on the BSE, that represent about 45% of the market capitalization of all the listed companies with BSE. Sensex is the barometer now which reflects the market trend whether the share prices in general are moving up or down.

Historically, BSE was an open outcry floor trading exchange, and it switched to an electronic trading system in 1995. This automated, screen-based trading platform is called BSE On-Line Trading (BOLT). The BSE has also introduced a centralized exchange-based Internet trading system, which enable investors anywhere in the world to trade on the BSE platform. In March 1999, BSE promoted Central Depository Services Limited (CDSL) as a depository for demat securities for enabling trading in demat securities.

National Stock Exchange India Ltd. (NSE)

The National Stock Exchange (NSE) is largest stock exchange of the country. It came in to existence as a company in the year 1992 and was recognised by the government as a stock exchange in the year 1993. NSE is started as automated screen-based online trading exchange covering large number of cities in the country, creating a national reach for trading in securities. By the year 1995, it became the largest stock exchange of the country. NSE's headquarters is in Bandra-Kurla Complex in Mumbai.

NSE is owned by a set of leading financial institutions, banks, insurance companies and other financial intermediaries and is managed by professionals. It is a demutualised stock exchange where the owners do not directly or indirectly trade on the exchange.

It is a modern stock exchange and has pioneered many innovations in the trading of securities. It introduced a new stock index CNX Nifty. Nifty index is based on 50 shares of the leading companies listed with NSE. In Feb. 2000, NSE commenced Internet trading for investors. It launched mobile trading for all investors in November 2010.

NSE provides the trading and payment settlements in equities, derivatives and debt instruments similar to BSE. Almost all the big companies of India are listed on both BSE and NSE exchanges. NSE has a dominant share in spot trading, and near monopoly in derivatives trading.

About 1696 companies are listed with NSE. NSE was instrumental in creating the National Securities Depository Limited (NSDL), a depository for demat securities which allows investors to securely hold and transfer their shares and bonds electronically.

4.10 The Small Industries Development Bank of India (SIDBI)

Industrial Development Bank of India (IDBI) was established in the year 1964 as development financial institution for promoting industry. The government policy then identified industry under three categories: large, medium and small sectors. IDBI was looking after the development needs of all these segments of industries.

Later, Small Industries Development Bank of India (SIDBI) was established on April 2, 1990 by enactment of The Small Industries Development Bank of India Act, 1989. The act envisaged SIDBI to be "the principal financial institution for the promotion, financing and development of industry in the small-scale sector and to co-ordinate the functions of the institutions engaged in the promotion and financing or developing industry in the small-scale sector and for matters connected therewith or incidental thereto.

SIDBI took over these functions which were hitherto performed by IDBI. The head office of the bank is situated in Lucknow. When SIDBI was established, it was a fully-owned subsidiary of IDBI. Later, IDBI divested its share to large extent and now remains as the single biggest shareholder. More than 80% shares are now held by other public sector companies like banks insurance companies, etc. There are about 33 shareholders at present.

GOI subsequently authorized SIDBI and widened its scope to work for the development of micro, small and medium enterprises, in addition to SSI units. At present, SIDBI is the premier financial institution extending support to Micro, Small and Medium Enterprises [MSME] sector.

SIDBI is also authorised by RBI to accepts fixed (term) deposits from public for one to five years' term.

SIDBI has evolved a range of products and services to the Micro, Small and Medium Enterprises [MSME] sector. SIDBI is providing refinance to State Level Finance Corporations/ State Industrial Development Corporations/banks, etc., against their loans granted to small-scale units. SIDBI is also directly financing MSME projects. SIDBI is also assisting transport, health care, and tourism sectors and the professional and self-employed persons.

In the year 2000 SIDBI and the Ministry of Micro, Small and Medium Enterprises, Government of India established Credit Guarantee Fund Trust for Micro and Small Enterprises (CGTMSE) to start the Credit Guarantee Scheme (CGS). This scheme provides guarantee cover to banks and FIs up to ₹ 100 lacs per borrower for loans sanctioned to MSME sector without third party guarantee and collaterals.

4.11 National Bank for Agriculture and Rural Development (NABARD)

National Bank for Agriculture and Rural Development was set up in the year 1982, by the National Bank for Agriculture and Rural Development Act, 1981 as a development financial institution. It took over the functions of Agricultural Refinance and Development Corporation (established under the Agricultural Refinance and Development Corporation Act, 1963) and also some functions from RBI relating to rural development.

NABARD has its headquarters in Mumbai, Maharashtra. NABARD is owned by GOI and RBI. The paid up capital as on 31 March 2017, was ₹ 5000 crores with Government of India holding ₹ 4,980 crores (99.60%) and Reserve Bank of India holding ₹ 20 crores (0.40%).

NABARD is an apex development bank of the country with a mandate for facilitating credit flow for promotion and development of agriculture, small-scale industries, cottage and village industries, handicrafts and other rural crafts. It also has the mandate to support all other allied economic activities in rural areas, promote integrated and sustainable rural development, and secure prosperity of rural areas.

The main functions of NABARD are in under noted areas:

1. Providing refinance to lending institutions for lending in rural areas.
2. Bringing about or promoting institutional development.
3. Regulating, monitoring and inspecting the co-op banks (other than urban co-op banks) and Regional Rural Banks.

NABARD is the regulator and controller for regional rural banks and co-op banks (except urban co-op banks) and prescribes regulations and supervises them in line with the RBI regulations on banks and coordinates with RBI.

NABARD provides refinances to state co-operative agriculture and rural development banks (SCARDBs), state co-op banks and RRBs, and commercial banks for their short-term loans and long-term loans to eligible borrowers.

Besides extending refinance, NABARD is also directly lending to many segments in the economy. It gives loans to producers' organizations and for infrastructure development projects of state-owned institutions/corporations.

NABARD is also promoting financial support to Self-Help Groups. Its Self-Help Group-Bank Linkage Programme (SHG-BLP) encourages banks to lend to self-help groups (SHGs). The national bank provides 100 per cent refinance assistance to banks for financing SHGs.

4.12 National Payments Corporation of India (NPCI)

After the Payment and Settlement Systems Act, 2007 was enacted and RBI was made the authority to control the payment systems in the country, RBI promoted National Payments Corporation of India (NPCI) as a payment settlement provider in retail payments systems.

National Payments Corporation of India (NPCI) was incorporated in December 2008 and was promoted by RBI and 10 other core promoter banks (State Bank of India, Punjab National Bank, Canara Bank, Bank of Baroda, Union Bank of India, Bank of India, ICICI Bank, HDFC Bank, Citibank and HSBC). It is positioned as an umbrella organization for retail payment settlement systems.

It took over the NFS (national financial switch) from the arm of RBI and is at present acting as payment settlement agency for ATM sharing by banks. In addition to this, NPCI has evolved new payment systems as under:

1. Immediate Payment System (IMPS) of mobile banking services.
2. Affiliation of RuPay Cards (debit cards/prepaid cards) issued by banks and co-branded credit cards issued by non-banking financial companies (NBFCs) or any other entity approved by the RBI. RuPay Cards are started in 2012.
3. National Automatic Clearing House (NACH) started in 2013.
4. Aadhar Enabled Payments System (AEPS)—new product to be started.

NPCI is acting as payment settlement provider for the above segments of retail financial services.

Now it is also managing the cheque truncation system started by RBI and submitting settlement statements to RBI.

4.13 Clearing Corporation of India Ltd. (CCIL)

The Clearing Corporation of India Ltd. (CCIL) is promoted by RBI as an exclusive settlement provider for money market, g-sec market and foreign exchange market.

CCIL was set up in April 2001 and is owned by banks (62.50% share), financial institutions (21.50% share) and primary dealers (16.00% share). CCIL provides exclusive clearing and settlement system for transactions in money market, g-sec market and foreign exchange market. These are the wholesale financial markets where the participants are the banks, financial institutions and the primary dealers.

CCIL at present operates payment system for following business of banks and FIs.

(i) Securities segment covering government securities;

(ii) Collateralised Borrowing and Lending obligations (CBLO);

(iii) Forex Settlement Segment comprising sub-segments

- USD-INR segment;
- CLS segment—Continuous Linked Settlement (Settlement of Cross Currency Deals);
- Forex Forward segment;

(iv) Rupee Derivatives Segment—Rupee-denominated trades in IRS (interest rate swaps) and FRA (forward rate agreements).

Collaterised Borrowing and Lending Obligation (CBLO) is a new money market instrument developed by CCIL and RBI in the year 2002-03. Under this, participants can lend and borrow in secured environment and CCIL holds the government securities provided by the borrowers to cover the transaction and it provides guarantee to the lenders.

The role of CCIL is unique as it provides guaranteed settlement in the government securities, USD-INR forex exchange (both spot and forward segments) and Collaterised

Borrowing and Lending Obligation (CBLO) markets. CCIL has created a risk-free settlement system for the participants. This process by which the counter-party risk is eliminated is known as 'Novation'. Under this, CCIL plays the role of a central counterparty whereby, the contract between buyer and seller gets replaced by two new contracts—between CCIL and each of the two parties. CCIL assumes the risk and guarantees payment, thereby eliminating the credit risk between the buyer and seller.

4.14 National Housing Bank (NHB)

NHB was set up on July 9, 1988 under the National Housing Bank Act, 1987. NHB is wholly owned by Reserve Bank of India, which contributed the entire paid-up capital. The management is with a board of directors. The head office of NHB is at New Delhi.

The Preamble of the National Housing Bank Act, 1987 describes the basic functions of the NHB as:

> to operate as a principal agency to promote housing finance institutions both at local and regional levels and to provide financial and other support to such institutions and for matters connected therewith or incidental thereto....

NHB is also a regulatory authority over housing finance companies in the country. National Housing Bank is empowered to determine the policy on housing loans and give directions to the housing finance institutions and also to their auditors. Housing finance companies are required to be registered with it. The purpose of regulatory function of NHB is to protect the interests of the house buyers.

NHB supports housing finance sector by extending refinance to different primary lenders (banks and housing finance companies) for housing loans to individuals and for project loans to various house building agencies.

NHB also lends directly in respect of projects undertaken by public housing agencies for housing construction and development of housing-related infrastructure.

4.15 State Bank of India (SBI)

State Bank of India is the India's largest bank and occupies a unique position in banking industry. In terms of network of branches and the reach, it has no competitors and other banks are far behind it. It has a unique history and place in Indian banking.

The roots of the State Bank of India are traced to the three Presidency banks: Bank of Bengal (1806), Bank of Madras (1843) and Bank of Bombay (1840) incorporated as joint stock companies by the Royal Charters during British rule of the country. In the year 1861, government gave these three banks the exclusive right to issue paper currency notes on behalf of government. This right was held by these banks and then by Imperial Bank of India until the formation of the Reserve Bank of India.

The Presidency Banks Act came into operation on 1 May 1876, and brought the three presidency banks under a common statute. These presidency banks dominated banking scene in 19th century and acted as government bank, central bank and as Commercial banks. All the three presidency banks were merged to form Imperial Bank of India in the year 1921.

State Bank of India Act was passed by Parliament in May 1955 and the State Bank of India was constituted on 1 July 1955. It took over Imperial Bank of India. Imperial Bank at the time had 480 offices comprising branches, sub offices and three local head offices. In terms of business, more than 25% of the resources of the Indian banking system was under the direct control of the State Bank of India at that time.

Later, the State Bank of India (Subsidiary Banks) Act was passed in 1959, and the State Bank of India took over eight former state-associated banks as its subsidiaries (later named Associates). Two of these banks: State Bank of Bikaner and State Bank of Jaipur were merged together in 1963, to form State Bank of Bikaner and Jaipur. Later, two subsidiary banks were merged with SBI (State Bank of Saurashtra was merged with SBI in 2008, and State Bank of Indore was merged with it in 2010).

SBI had following five subsidiary banks in its group that continued to function till 31-3-2017.

1. State Bank of Mysore
2. State Bank of Hyderabad
3. State Bank of Patiala
4. State Bank of Travancore
5. State Bank of Bikaner and Jaipur

These five banks were also now merged with SBI w.e.f. 1-4-2017.

After formation of RBI, State Bank of India is now acting as agent to RBI for conducting government business. It also manages clearing houses in many places, wherever RBI does not have its offices.

At the time of formation, State Bank of India was owned by the government through RBI, which held more than 95% of the share capital. Then in the year 1994, SBI issued fresh shares to public and the RBI holding came down to nearly 60%. In 2008, the Government of India took over the stake held by the Reserve Bank of India. At present, government holding is 58.60% of the total capital of the bank.

Immediately after its formation in the year 1955, SBI was asked by the government to expand its branch network and open 400 new branches in order to provide banking support to government for its development plans. Thereafter, SBI started branch expansion in massive scale. From a mere 480 offices at the time of its formation, SBI after merger of five subsidiaries and also Bharatiya Mahila Bank on 1-4-2017 now has 24017 branches and 59263 ATMs. Total assets of SBI are now reported to be over ₹ 33000 billion (as per annual report of SBI for March 2017).

The assets of SBI and its associate banks with no. of branches and ATMs as at March 2015 are given in the table below:

SBI Group Banks—as at March 2015

	Assets ₹ billion	No. of branches	No. of ATMs
SBI	20480.80	16333	42454
Five Associate banks	5585.78	6554	8561
Total SBI group banks	26066.58	22887	51015

Source: SBI.

SBI is the largest bank in the country with assets of ₹ 20480.80 billion as at March 2015. Besides banking subsidiaries (associate banks), SBI has many non-banking subsidiary companies also.

SBI is the only bank from India which appears in the list of top hundred banks of the world. As per the list of 100 biggest banks in the world released by SNL Financial, based on assets as at March 2015, State Bank of India ranks 58 (assets valued at US$ 432.57 billion) in the ranking.

4.16 Bharatiya Mahila Bank Ltd.

In the year 2013, GOI decided to open Bharatiya Mahila Bank Ltd., the first of its kind in the banking industry in India, with a vision of economic empowerment for women.

It is aiming at the financial inclusion of economically neglected, deprived, discriminated, underbanked, unbanked, rural and urban women and also to develop new products and services to suit the needs of women of all segments including self-help groups, women entrepreneurs, salaried women, high net worth individuals and corporates.

It is opened as a public sector bank fully owned by GOI. It received banking license from RBI on 25 September 2013 and was launched immediately in the same year with its corporate office at New Delhi. The bank has a capital of ₹ 1000 crores fully subscribed by GOI.

However government decided to merge this bank with SBI. According government view the SBI group already has 126 exclusive all-women branches across the country. Hence it was felt that the merger of this bank with SBI will ensure greater banking outreach to women. This bank was merged with SBI on 1-4-2017. At the time of merger the bank had 103 branches in 29 states with business figure of about ₹ 1600 crores.

Bharatiya Mahila Bank was Savings Bank interest of 5% for ₹ one lakh and above and, the interest rate of 4.5% for amount less than ₹ one lakh. Probably, the only second bank in India to offer more than 4% interest on savings bank after Yes Bank.

4.17 Post-Office Savings Bank (POSB)

Origin of post office banking in the country can be traced to the time of British rule of the country. Savings bank business in India was conducted by government right from the time of the East India Company. Separate government savings banks were established in the three Presidency towns between 1833 and 1835 and later at selected district Treasuries in 1870. These banks played some role in mobilising savings from the public by developing the banking habit.

Post offices started opening savings bank accounts in 1882 and 1883, throughout the country and took over the business of the district savings banks in 1886 and of Presidency savings banks in 1896.

India Post is a department of Government of India. The Department of Posts comes under the Ministry of Communications and Information Technology. It also works as bank apart from its primary function of postal work. Post offices across the country acts like bank and maintain savings bank accounts for individuals just like a bank. It offers cheque book facility to its savings customers. It also participates in cheque clearing system. This is the only exception in our country where an entity other than bank is offering banking services to the public.

Besides savings accounts, post offices also accept term deposits from the public just like banks. It also offers recurring deposit accounts and monthly income deposit scheme to public. These are the four deposit products similar to banks.

Post offices also manage many other investment schemes on behalf of Government of India. They are national savings schemes where deposit is accepted for 4-6 years and national savings certificates (NSC) are issued. It also manages Indira Vikas Patra (IVP) scheme and Kisan Vikas Patra (KVP) schemes similar to NSC scheme on behalf of government. It also manages public provident fund (PPF), an investment scheme for public. Many of the schemes carry tax benefits for the public.

Post office savings bank is under the direct control of GOI which generally consults RBI for fixing interest rates on its different deposit schemes for the public.

Currently, there is a move to spin-off this Post Office Savings Bank as a separate bank.

On 28 February 2015, during the presentation of the Budget, government announced that India Post will use its large network to run a Payments Bank. Recently (on August 19, 2015) RBI issued license to post-office to start Payments Bank under its new guidelines to start Payments Banks.

POSB has technologically upgraded its banking activities and from December 2014 started opening its ATMs and started issuing ATM-cum-debit cards to its customers.

As per the licence issued by RBI, the Department of Post (GOI) promoted India Post Payments Bank which is incorporated as public sector bank with 100% GOI equity. India Post Payments Bank has started functioning from 31-1-2017 with two branches at Ranchi and Raipur. According to India Post the bank will have about 650 branches in this year 2017.

4.18 Industrial Credit and Investment Corporation of India (ICICI) (now ICICI Bank)

ICICI Ltd. was formed at the initiative of the World Bank, the Government of India and representatives of Indian industry in the year 1955.

The principal objective was to providing medium-term and long-term project financing to Indian businesses. ICICI was a development financial institution and in 1990s it diversified its activities and entered into various types of financial services through its new subsidiaries.

After the banking sector reforms were introduced, ICICI promoted ICICI Bank in 1996 as wholly-owned subsidiary. Later after the public issue of ICICI Bank in the year 1998, the stake of ICICI in ICICI Bank came down to 46%. Again later in 2002 ICICI merged with ICICI Bank. ICICI Bank is now a universal bank in private sector.

Three fairly big old private sector banks were merged with ICICI Bank as under:

- Bank of Madura (started in 1943 it had about 280 branches) in 2001.
- Sangli Bank (started in 1916 it had 198 branches) in 2006.
- Bank of Rajasthan (started in 1943 it had 463 branches) in 2010.

It is the third largest bank of the country based on asset size in the year March 2017. ICICI Bank currently has a network of 4850 branches and 13882 ATMs across India.

4.19 Industrial Development Bank of India (IDBI) (Now IDBI Bank)

IDBI was constituted as a statutory company under the Industrial Development Bank of India Act, 1964 as a Development Financial Institution (DFI). It was wholly-owned subsidiary of RBI. The ownership of the bank was transferred from RBI to GOI in the year 1976. In the year 1995, IDBI made a public issue and after the public issue government stake came down to about 75%.

IDBI is the premier-term lending institution for industrial units including small-scale units. Subsequently, SIDBI was formed which took up financing small-scale units.

After banking sector reforms were introduced, IDBI promoted IDBI bank in the year 1994. In the year 2004, IDBI became a Company under Companies Act and was named IDBI Ltd. Later IDBI Ltd. merged with IDBI Bank in 2005. With all these changes now Government of India has 73.98% (as at 31-3-2017) in IDBI Bank.

United Western Bank an old private sector bank (started in 1937 it had about 230 branches) was merged with IDBI bank in the year 2006.

IDBI bank is now a universal bank in public sector. In the year March 2017, IDBI bank is the 10th largest bank of the country on the basis of asset size with assets of ₹ 3617.67 billion. It has 1922 branches and 3537 ATMs across the country.

4.20 Indian Banks' Association (IBA)

The Indian Banks' Association (IBA) was formed in the year 1946 as an association of banks with 22 members. Banks carrying business in India and who are governed by the Banking Regulation Act, 1949 are eligible to become members of the association. The local offices of the foreign banks are also eligible as members. Urban coop banks can also become members of the association.

IBA has two classes of membership known as ordinary member and associate member. The banks or eligible institutions which do not fulfil the criteria for ordinary membership are given the associate membership. Membership is open to public sector banks, private sector banks, foreign banks having offices in India, co-operative banks, regional rural banks and all India financial institutions.

As on December 28, 2015 the total membership of the association is 237 with 139 ordinary and 98 associate members.

The main objectives and functions of IBA are as under:

- IBA is the representative body of bank managements and plays a crucial role to represent banking sector in any official forum or with RBI and Government of India.
- To promote and develop sound and progressive banking principles, practices and conventions and to contribute to the developments of creative banking.
- To render assistance and to provide various common services to members and to the banking industry.
- To develop and implement new ideas and innovations in banking services, operations and procedures.
- To promote education and knowledge of the law and practice of banking.
- To conduct talks, discussions, and negotiations with the representatives of bank employees, and to arrive at settlements for the whole banking industry in the country. It also provides assistance and guidance to members in interpretation and implementation of awards, settlements, etc.

IBA has taken many initiatives in the areas of customer service in general and relating to deceased accounts and complaints handling. It also brought out the model citizens' charter in the year 2000 and evolved 'Bankers' Fair Practice code' in the year 2004 followed by "Fair practice code for credit card operations" and "Model Code for Collection of Dues and Repossession of Security", much before the BCSBI came into existence and took over these functions.

IBA has developed a scheme for recommending names of road transport operators to banks for the purpose of accepting transport receipts as security for advances against bills.

IBA played an important role along with Central Board of Direct Taxes (CBDT) and RBI in conceiving and implementing On-Line Tax Accounting System (OLTAS) from the year 2005. OLTAS is an innovative system that facilitate on-line transmission of details regarding tax collection/refund, etc. between banks and offices of Income Tax Department and also RBI for settlement of funds.

4.21 Foreign Exchange Dealers' Association of India (FEDAI)

FEDAI is an association of foreign exchange authorised dealers (banks) started in the year 1958 as a self-regulatory body and is incorporated under Section 25 of The Companies Act, 1956. At present the total members of the association are 102 (as of December 2017).

During British rule of the country, foreign exchange business was handled by a class of banks known as exchange banks and mostly they were the foreign banks operating in India. These exchange banks had their association known as Exchange Banks Association. Later RBI started authorising Indian commercial banks to undertake foreign exchange business by issuing authorised dealers license to them. After the Indian commercial banks became authorised dealers, the existing Exchange Banks Association, was changed to form the Foreign Exchange Dealers Association of India in the year 1958.

FEDAI's role is as an advisor to member banks and it regulates the rules governing foreign exchange business by the member banks to create a uniform practice. Its main functions are:

- Issuing guidelines and rules for forex business.
- Training of bank personnel in the areas of foreign exchange business.
- Accreditation of forex brokers.
- Advising/assisting member banks in settling issues/ matters in their dealings.
- Representing member banks before the government/ Reserve Bank of India/other bodies.
- Announcement of daily and periodical rates to member banks.

The rules and guidelines of FEDAI have undergone many changes after the deregulations were introduced from the year 1991. Presently, banks have discretions on many matters pertaining to foreign exchange business keeping in line with the liberalised policy of RBI/Government. However, FEDAI plays an important role in framing the rules to bring uniformity in interbank dealings and dealings with customers in the interest of member banks and customers. It also coordinates with other official bodies representing other financial and money markets in working out the guidelines as suitable under the liberalised regime.

Supplementary Index

Supplementary Index—where to find the following: